Alison Carpenter Davis
@LettersStanford

Letters Home
❧ from ❧
Stanford

125 Years of Correspondence from
Students of Stanford University

REEDY PRESS

Library of Congress Control Number: 2016940393

ISBN: 9781681060484

Cover images: Courtesy of Laine Bruzek, Class of 2016, (Quad) and the Stanford University Archives (letter).

Printed in the United States of America

17 18 19 20 21   5 4 3 2 1

"This summer has passed faster than any I ever knew. Just think, in about four weeks this rightest and greatest (yet to be) University in the world will have its wheels set in motion, to grind on so long as civilization lasts."

—Francis J. Batchelder, in a letter to his family, August 30, 1891

To my grandmother
Allie Meek Lesnett,
who saved all of my mom's letters home from Stanford

And to my mom,
Mary Lesnett Carpenter, Class of 1948,
who saved all of mine

Table of Contents

Preface

When my mom first left for Stanford with hat, gloves, and trunk aboard the Coast Daylight train in July 1944, she also had in hand her first graduation requirement: write home twice a week or tuition would be pulled. And when my grandmother issued an edict, there was no fussing. More than seventy years later, those letters remain, arranged carefully and chronologically in four notebooks.

When I started at Stanford in September 1975, there was more angst in the air, fewer edicts issued, and more phone use. Nonetheless, like her mother before her, my mom saved those letters I did write, now arranged carefully and chronologically in one notebook.

Dipping into the two sets of correspondence on and off over the years, a few impressions started to take root.

First, taken as a whole, each group of letters told a story, and my mom's in particular read like a book. But why should her correspondence home—or anyone's—matter? Because the words we send home, whether penned or typed, stand as pieces of personal history, as well as Stanford's, and pieces of history itself. As Stanford history professor Jack Rakove observes, "Personal letters are often our best primary sources because, unlike memoirs, they are often written as close to the event as possible, making them the best record of what people originally felt and experienced." If a single Stanford student actually were to write a letter today, tomorrow claims it as history. Ditto for emails, texts, and the ever-evolving ways students communicate with home.

Second, when I read my mom's and my own letters as a younger alum, what I had perceived as an expansive gulf between our college experiences narrowed. We both wrote about questioning our academic abilities, getting crushed in a Big Game throng, and walking reflectively under Quad arches, wondering how to span the here-and-now to the out-there-and-beyond. Was I reading about my mom, or myself?

The same holds for the correspondence of generations of Stanford alumni and their counterparts who walk the Quad today. Our collected correspondence speaks to the common human experience of breaking out and trying to find our way as we observe the world around us and look over a shoulder toward home. From first letters home freshman year to questions about laundry and questions about self, universal themes thread through the decades.

Consider what Lucy Allabach wrote her mother on March 22, 1894: "Don't kiss [me] and talk out loud in the library when you come."

Sound familiar? For no other reason than we are human, and regardless of an eighteen- or twenty-year-old's blind presumption or dogged insistence otherwise, some things don't change.

But many do. Between the era of letter writers and texters, Stanford, like the world beyond the Quad, has changed. There has been movement toward the diverse and inclusive student body of today. And our correspondence over time reflects this.

When I first approached the Stanford University Archives staff, they already had a number of letters in hand. Together, we set out on a search-and-rescue mission to increase the size and scope of our collected letters home. I am honored to have been part of the conveyor belt of correspondence that then moved from attics, shoe boxes, and cell phones to the archives, onto my computer screen, and into your field of vision here.

As I read through the letters, emails, and texts of our history, more themes emerged. For starters, we know students don't tell their parents everything that happens in college, no matter how much parents may want to believe otherwise. But the reverse also occasionally proves true. Students sometimes write the adults in their lives about situations and thoughts not shared with their friends—or anyone. In so doing, these students allow us a view into an interior Stanford. Take Fred, who wrote his mother that he was ashamed to bring his friends home, or M.C., who didn't tell one person on campus she felt like "a failure." But she did tell her parents—in a letter.

Second, reading all types of correspondence also pointed to the tremendous changes in the format and delivery of student-to-home communiqués. For many years, by the time a parent received a letter, mulled over its contents, responded by letter, mailed it, and the student received and read it, a problem the student may have written home about was often a problem solved. Contrast that to the play-by-play parents sometimes engage in today with college students via text. What is optimum?

And finally, the correspondence profoundly reminded me of the power of words to inform, move, challenge, and inspire. The letters that struck me and stuck with me more than any were those of Joe Jacobs, Class of 1965. Joe was killed in Vietnam less than two years after he wrote this to his parents on March 1, 1965: "That way we can get together to celebrate Carl's and my birthday a couple of days late—which I think

would be nice. God only knows when it will happen again."
Knowing fate's course for Joe, who reads that without pause?

Among other things, Joe was a writer; in fact, he wrote for the *Stanford Daily.*[2] Joe cared about the telling of stories, he cared about words. He seemed to appreciate their meaning, value their presentation, and understand their push to transmit and transcend.

I tried my very best to treat the words of our collected past with respect and due diligence.

Alumni, current students, and/or their family members submitted correspondence to the Stanford University Archives, except in a few isolated cases, when they submitted it directly to me.

As this project grew in scope and substance, so did the definition of home. At some point it seemed silly to regard home only as the structure in which a person grew up and the people at the dinner table therein. Home is where someone considers it to be, shared dinner table or not.

In the interests of privacy, writers or their designated family members sometimes opted to change or delete names mentioned in correspondence, which reflects only the views of the writers and the facts as they put them forth. Writers or their descendants gave permission for correspondence to be included in this volume, which I in turn edited for clarity and space.

I aimed for ease of reading, not perfect prose. Obvious misspellings have been silently corrected, though some spellings unique to a particular era or person have been left per original, as has most punctuation and grammar. Students often feel rushed or distracted when writing home, and I wanted to capture the informal nature of their correspondence.

The notes at the back of the book have been written to provide context for a multigenerational Stanford audience, as well as for those unfamiliar with the Farm.[1] For example, some readers may not have heard of Jolly-Ups, while SLE may be an unknown acronym to others.

The book, along with the notes, is organized in such a way that you don't need to read it from beginning to end, or all in one sitting. I hope you crack the cover, turn to a chapter you respond to, and dive in. Correspondence does need to be read in light of the era and historical context in which a student wrote home.

As hard as I tried, I could not control what topics were covered in correspondence collected. There are historic events and social upheavals that remain unrepresented, and I hope they will be covered in correspondence submitted to the archives in the days and years to come. I chose to use this book as a means to request future submissions (lettershomefromstanford.com).

In particular, I invite submissions of handwritten, typed, or electronic correspondence from anyone who for whatever reason fell silent, or felt silenced, during their years as a student. If you couldn't talk about it, maybe you wrote home about it? Either way, I also direct you to the fantastic Stanford Historical Society Oral History Project, as well as the Stanford Alumni Legacy Project, which collects all kinds of alumni memorabilia.

Letters Home from Stanford is my own, and not supported by the university financially in any way. I researched and edited this as a freelancer, and this project hangs on my coat rack alone.

As I connected with current students and alumni, their families and friends, responses varied:

"We just threw my grandfather's letters away last month."

"Thank you. I have saved my grandmother's letters all these years. I didn't want to throw them away, but I had no idea what to do with them."

"My mom recently passed away, and I was going through her things. She'd kept all my letters from freshman year. I had no idea. . . ."

That mom saved them, as did my mom, the mother before her, and countless others. I have felt this enormous need to continue their legacy of letters by finding an alternative to the wastebasket, DELETE, and history lost. And I have.

Long after Stanford students leave the Quad, their words live. Through words written, let's continue to tell our story—together.

Al

All Aboard: Mary Allie Lesnett, July 1944

Courtesy of the Lesnett Family

Acknowledgments

To Nicole Sunahara Scandlyn: Thank you for embracing this idea, helping me launch, and being a touchpoint throughout. This would not have happened without you.

And you, university archivist Daniel Hartwig, who started the Green Library[3] wheels turning. You picked up the phone at 4:45 p.m. on a Friday, possibly with "No Caller ID" flashing, and listened when I said, "I have this idea." I wonder how many conversations on campus start with those four words, or thereabouts, on any given day? You embody the Stanford spirit. Thank you.

And thank you to assistant university archivist Josh Schneider for your positivity, for answering my emails, and for working shoulder to shoulder. To the entire Special Collections Department: management & processing archivist Jenny Johnson, for organizing and organizing; administrative officer Charlotte Kwok Glasser, for your input and support; and Nan Mehan, Tim Noakes, and Larry Scott, thank you for all your help—almost every darn day for a while. I appreciate you so.

To the Stanford Alumni Association's Lauren Black, Judy Heller, Adam Miller, Jake Wellington, and Greg Yee, and to Marcia Hansen and the Parents' Club of Stanford University, thank you for letting alumni, parents, and current students know about *Letters Home from Stanford*. And to Howard Wolf, SAA head, thank you for shepherding a group of people who still can connect and grow.

Thank you to the Stanford Historical Society, the Stanford Department of Athletics, and all those around the Quad who gave an assist: Greg Boardman, Kate Chesley, Richard W. Cottle, Stephanie Denton, David Evans, Alan George, Dick Gould, John Hennessy, Joy Leighton, Olga Malinowska, Andrew Mather, Jack Rakove, Richard H. Shaw, Troy Steinmetz, Stephanie Stewart, Rob Urstein, Tobias Wolff, Maile Yee, and Kevin Zhang.

To the offices and student centers whose administrators and staff met with me and/or helped get the word out about submissions. In particular, thank you to Jeremy Ragent at Hillel. And thanks to Teri Adams, Virginia Bock, Vanessa Gomez Brake, Joseph Brown, Kathleen Campbell, Mona Damluji, Alana Dong, Rabbi Serena Eisenberg, Bob Hamrdla, Marta Hanson, Linda Hubbard, Ken Hsu, Adina Glickman, Irene Kennedy, Natalie Marine-Street, Dustin Noll, Brent Obleton, John Pearson, Carole Pertofsky, Elvira Prieto, Peggy Propp, Annie Vleck, and the LGBT Community Resources Center staff.

To Laine Bruzek, Class of 2016, thanks for punching out designs with flair, for being a reference on current student life, and for not fitting in any particular box. Wasn't I supposed to be the mentor? To the *Letters Home from Stanford* interns—Ben Diego, Kady Richardson, Kathryn Rydberg, Emilia Schrier, and Jason Seter—thanks for being flexible, being current, and being you. And thank you to students Andie Grossman, Julia Howell, Selby Sturzenegger, and Samantha Wong.

Thank you to everyone who submitted correspondence. I only wish I could have used it all. Published or not, your words matter. Thank you to alumni letter writers Anne Peters Battle,

Vanessa Hua, Chrissie Huneke Kremer, Lanny Levin, and Natasha Pratap for additional support, and thank you to Carl Jacobs for sharing the letters of your twin brother, Joe. And to Joe and your ultimate price paid, I never knew you, but now I know of you, and I am grateful.

Thank you to my '79 classmates who participated in some way: M.C., Erik Hill, and Jenny Smith, as well as Vickie Bennett, Beppie Weintz Cerf, Steve Grossman, Carlos Hernandez, David Henry Hwang, Lex Passaris, John Sargent, and Rebecca Trounson. And thanks to Dean Fred for throwing us together in the first place. To all my classmates: You are the best gifts Stanford ever gave me. You stretch me still.

Thank you to those in the broader Stanford community: Jill Baldauf, Russell Barajas, Claude Baudoin, Susan Christiansen, Austen Creger, Christopher Carlsmith, Lauren Dunbar, Jan Ellison, John-Lancaster Finley, Mason Funk, Allan Harris, Terry and Sue Johnson, Patricia Klindienst, Erika Soto Lamb, Linda Long, Christopher Lowman, Joan Little Ragno, Stacy Robinson, Jim Rutter, and Tom. And thank you to those in the community beyond Stanford: Hannah Brown, Linda and Megan Buiocchi, Karen and John Sandifer, the Palo Alto Historical Association, the Vi at Palo Alto Continuing Care Retirement Community, Ken Wilson, and Craig Wright.

Thank you to the *Stanford* magazine staff—Kevin Cool, who has seen fit to print two of my essays; Mike Antonucci, my first contact at the magazine; and Jennifer Worrell, an amazing editor who goes deep with words and their matter. You all weren't involved in this project, but you welcomed me back when I returned to the Farm.[1]

Thank you to my publisher Josh Stevens for your patience and understanding. You know when and how to guide—and when to allocate space. And to production director Barbara Northcott, who makes me LOL—thanks for your humor and belief. We'll make it work.

Most importantly, thank you to my family. Thank you to Cork, who stays in the game even when my body is standing in the kitchen but my head is writing words. That's not always easy for a person of practicality. And thanks to Stanford's ResEd office for not changing my dorm assignment freshman year—over my protests. Because of you, I missed the dorm of my dreams but found a life partner.

To my own emerged adults, you make me proud. Thank you to Jax for your tech help, Em for consistently asking how it's going, and Els for reading a draft with no notice. With you as indication, there's hope.

Al

Chapter 1

First Letters Home

"Nobody wears [rubber boots] except the freshmen whose 'mamas' have them take them when they leave home. I do enough freshman tricks unconsciously without doing those that I know I will be made fun of for."

—Julia Hamilton Conkling, Oct. 9, 1911

Letter from Lucy Allabach to her mother

Roble Hall[4]
September 30, 1891
[The day before the opening of Stanford University]

Dear Mama:

We are here safe and sound and well and not disappointed as yet, though Roble Hall is in a rather confused state. They are working very hard and soon all will be in order and it is a very nice hall indeed. Our room is a corner one at least twenty-foot square with three large windows, stationary washstand, two iron bedsteads, oak dresser, light wood wardrobe, large table, two straight-backed chairs, two rockers, rugs, and what else we can't tell till we are in order. We are being fed at the boys' hall [Encina[5]] for a day or two. Theirs is larger and rather finer than ours but this is very pretty indeed. The parlor has rough walls, as have all the rooms, painted in delicate shades. Ours is light blue and ecru. The parlor is pale blue and pink. A large long room. At either end is a pretty mantle and by each a pink as well as a blue chair with large ribbon bows. There are two very large moquet rugs, in deep electric blue and rose, two pretty tables, a grand piano, lace curtains with China silk draperies, plush table covers, rose bowls, vases, fine pictures etc. I am too tired to write very well and there is so much to tell.

The studies marked on the schedule [are the ones] I am taking, or at least it is so for the present. You see it only makes three recitations a day, and I guess it won't be too much. If it is I will get permission to change. Things are fully as nice as we expected if anyone asks. . . .

Your loving Lucy

Letter from J. B. (Jesse Brundage) Sears to his father

[Undated]

Dear Father,

I am well pleased with the outlook and believe that I shall like my work fine when I get into it. I shall be under at least three of the greatest men here. They are Dr. Jordan,[6] Pres. of [the] University, in Bionomics; Cubberley, in Education; and Angell in Psychology. . . .

I will have 16 hours of work per week, which will be all I can carry. I have: history of education in Europe, public education in America, sources in the history of education, and educational journal club, which makes 8 hours in education. Then I have chemistry 4 hours, psychology 3 hours, and bionomics, or biological evolution, 1 hr.

The profs have treated me fine. The committee on entrance allowed me to enter without ceremony for which I am duly obliged I tell you. I told Dr. Elliott, the registrar, that I would try not to make them sorry of their action. They did it because of my experience in teaching. . . .

Sincerely,

J. B.

Letters from Julia Hamilton Conkling to her mother

Wed. Aug. 30 [19]'11

Dear mother,

At last I will sit down and write. I did not feel like writing when my trunk hadn't come, but now that it is here and mostly unpacked I will. . . . My roommate . . . lives at Los Gatos, Cal. Her father & mother are both practicing physicians and she (Gladys) has a whole shelf filled with various medicines. . . . I like her very much, the only objection is she is always having some ache or pain and is taking this or that kind of pill or powder or liquid or using the hot water bag or something but she probably will get over that. She is almost 20. . . .

. . . I suppose father . . . also told you about my trunks not coming and about my registering at the hygiene department & about having to write all the diseases I have had during & since childhood, the time and consequences, where my father was born & if dead what he died of and so forth & so on, what his business is etc. Then I had to present my vaccination scar which I did not have, so I told her I had none. . . . She (Doctor Mosher), a Johns Hopkins woman who wears rubber heels & no corset peered, then, over her glasses and . . . proceeded to lecture me before about fifty girls on "Vaccination." I was terribly embarrassed. "No intelligent person walks around without a successful vaccination every five years. If your vaccination does not take, keep on being vaccinated until it does. I wish I could vaccinate you. I could make it take alright. Well we will have a council about your case, and if you do not have to be vaccinated now you will a year from now. My dear, there is no such thing as being immune." Then she told me to meet her at 2:30 Sat. at Roble Gym. There I will have to strip. The girls have told me about it. You have to take off everything but your stockings & if there is a single wrinkle on you from your corset you get a terrible lecture. She measures you & your corset & if there's a half-inch difference. Goodness!

Well—I guess father told you when he left I was bawling so I will go on from there. It seemed as though I could not stand to see him go and leave me alone without my trunks yet I did not want him to stay as I knew he had to be back and then when I saw the train pull out with him on it I nearly died. I was so tired, I could not see straight but I was bawling so I felt cheap to get on the car so I walked back to Roble bawling all the way & up to my room I went, and there I bawled & bawled. Never before did I know what homesickness was. After a while Gladys came and she tried to comfort me and told me she would lend me everything I needed & then the supper bell rang but I felt cheap to go down with red eyes so I bawled some more, till I had bawled it all out, when I got up & washed my face & combed my hair & went downstairs. There I met a lot of girls, and since then I have been too busy to get homesick again. That night my! how my legs ached, those four flights of stairs. The minute I hit the bed I was asleep. . . .

Wed. evening
[Aug. 30, 1911]
The eating here at Roble is pretty good. Tell Joe[7] I have found a job for him when he gets here waiting on tables at Roble. Did father tell you how the first thing I got called down for [was] taking men upstairs without permission? I took him, I never thought you know. Every time an expressman comes upstairs a maid has to precede him to keep the girls out of the halls half-dressed. . . .

The fees here are terrible. There is a fee for everything. I am keeping track of all the money I spend. I hope father will send me more right away. My chemistry fee was $25, registration $15, gym suit $7.50, Y.W.C.A. $1, hospital $2.00, Roble club, $2.00, and I have not yet to pay my board & for my school books and things for my room. I have to get a fountain pen tomorrow. . . .

. . . Sat. at 4:00 o'clock p.m. is the Sophomore-Freshman Rush. You know they (both classes) try to catch each other and tie and pen them up. That is just for the boys but of course the girls go to cheer for their boys. . . . The freshman boys wear little grey caps with a red button on top, the sophomores red hats, the juniors carderoes (?), and the seniors sombreros.[8] The freshman boys have already painted big red 15's all over everything. Hazing in every form, manner, & shape has been prohibited in both Encina and Roble. Here in Roble the freshmen have to answer the telephone during meals and every night after supper, the girls dance in the hall and the freshmen have to take up the rugs and put them down when they are through. They have to do it. Then when the big receptions come, next week, the freshmen have to serve. I mean the receptions that Roble gives. . . .

The lights all go off at 10:30 except on Fri., Sat., and Sun., when they go off at 11:00. The rising bell rings at 6:45 and the breakfast bell at 7:30 and classes begin at 8:15. . . .

Wed. morning. [Oct. 11, 1911]

. . . Am going home with Gladys Frid. night & stay till Mon. morning. I am sorry I won't be here Friday night to put flour in the soph's beds & bureau drawers. Maybe we can go Sat. morning. Fri. night is the Sophomore Jolly-Up[9] you see & they will all be at that. . . .

. . . This a.m. one of the girls was sick & not able to go down to breakfast so the rest of us girls, to have some fun, each swiped one, two, or three pieces of toast from the table & one by one went in & told her we had brought her some breakfast, till finally she had 31 pieces of toast and she was so sick at [sic] her stomach anyhow she couldn't see straight.

Then Sun. afternoon after the breakfast at the creek we took all the buns & wieners that were left over & strung them on a long string & lowered them from a 4th-floor window down to the front porch where all the dignified seniors & juniors were queening their young men and tacked the 4 strings of them so they hung just above their heads. But the strings broke & the wieners & buns fell & immediately Mrs. Rolker appeared upstairs all out of breath, after climbing 4 flights of stairs, poor woman, to make us go down in a hurry to pick them up. She was so afraid some visitors would come & see them. She kind of likes us though because we treat her nicer than the older girls so she didn't say much but my the Queeners were mad! . . .

Julia

Letter from Hope Snedden to her father

Stanford Univ., Calif.
October 24, 1918

Dear Dad,
. . . I have met one very nice girl. She is from Hawaii & talks about how she likes to climb coconut trees. And the strange thing is that both her father & mother went to Stanford. It must have been about your time. . . .

Now for Mother's questions:
1. We don't get any supervision here, we are a quiet bunch & get more time to study than at Roble, where they dance, have marshmallow roasts etc.

2. Other people here are elderly,[10] both men & women. We never see them except at meals.
3. My room faces north,—very nice.
4. No roommate, but [there's] a girl next me who comes in & tells me all her troubles by the hour. I don't give a hang whether she marries Arthur or Dick.
5. I purchased besides sheets & pillowcases 1 pr. gray cotton blankets, but am cold so think I'll get an Army blanket, wool, $5.85. (?) . . .

Much love,
From, Hope

Letter from Alice Louise Clark to her family

Oct. 17, 1935

Dear Family:
. . . The reason I haven't typed any of my letters home is because I like the relaxation of sitting down in a soft chair, and scrawling out an occasional something in longhand.

Enclosed you will find a clipping from the Stanford Daily[2] which tells about one of my profs. Dr. Stuart's class in American diplomacy is quite interesting—first he talked at great length upon neutrality. The only trouble with Am. neutrality is that it has been very successful up to the point where it ceased because the U.S. had gone into the war. Such opinions sound quite debatable to me, but take it all in all international law is rather a disappointing institution. We have also taken up such matters as international rivers and bays, immigration, and are now talking about Pan Americanism. (Next installment soon.). . .

For your benefit, Mother, I am still wearing a bandage on my vaccination. . . .

Miss Bert just paid me $7.50 for phone duty up to Oct. 15. Besides this I have earned $3.00 for the month of Sept. and $1 for some extra typing I did. I'll have $15 coming on the N.Y.A.,[11] another $7.50 for the rest of the month, and about $3 or $4 for commission . . . [at] the store. Makes a grand total of $37 or $38, which is the greatest part of my board-and-room bill. Maybe I can do even better next month. . . .

Lots of love to my family.
Alice Louise

Letter from (Mary) Carol Stearns to her mother

Box 1743
Stanford University
Calif.
10/8/43—8:10 p.m.

Dear Mom—

. . . 10:25 p.m.
Oh, man—guess where I've been! When I started this letter, I was garbed in my classy striped pajamas—&—my buzzer rang twice (meaning a caller).[12] I thought—Ye Gods what'll I do. So I slammed into a brown skirt & powder blue sweater in 2 sec. flat & scarcely combed my hair. I presumed & hoped it would be Jim—maybe. But when I glided (?) into the lobby I saw—at quite a distance—a rather unfamiliar boy, all dressed up—stand when I came in. . . . And it was Don Landale. . . . Was I

pleased. . . . Anyway he sort [of] assumed—in some smooth manner—that I'd just love to go to Paly & get something to eat. Anyhow, we did. Now I can say I had a date my first night on campus. He's a dealer, too—head (coordinating head) of Pre-reg Day. Gee, did I feel big time—We went & got a milkshake at the "Bowl"—& came home & talked. . . .[13]

About the trip . . . It was wonderful driving. We just took it easy—complying on occasion to the speed laws. . . . We had to eat in a drive-in because he [Jim] couldn't lock the door of the car. When we finally arrived at Paly about 8:30 p.m.,—we got lost. Finally when we got to Stanford we spent a long time trying to find Roble. When we did find it—I went in alone—dressed as I was when I left home—only minus the dirty socks (just no socks)—my bandana still intact. I walked in, looking as green as any new freshman just out from the sticks. There were about a dozen girls & boys (upperclassmen) sitting around. If you'll remember, there is no obvious desk or receptionist. No one said anything—but just sort of shut up. Well—I wandered down one aisle—& saw nothing that looked hopeful then back the other way—right in front of the kids. There was a woman, very nice & middle aged, sitting at the switchboard. She said it would not be possible for me to leave my baggage there for the night. . . . About then I was most rattled—mad, wanted to cry, & go home—I'll continue in the a.m.—cause it's late & I'm dead. . . .

6:10 AM—10/9/43
. . . There are five Carols in our corridor. I've never been any place where I've known so many. That happens to be our sponsor's name, too. There are several—or I should say—a lot of cute girls in this corridor. Also a few drippy ones—You . . . all

said that Stanford girls look not too good. My first opinion does not agree. . . .

Gee, it sure does stay dark a long time in these parts. It's 6:30 & still black outside.

Better call it quits, I guess,—need to study my English. What if I flunk?

Love, Carol
P.S. . . . I'm on the 3rd floor center—# 337.

Letters from Mary Allie Lesnett to her parents

July 4, 1944 [Summer Quarter]

Dear Mother and Daddy,
Although I literally live in a daze up here, I have not been doing too awfully in my school work. I got a B in my French test, a B- in my geology test, I am doing above the class average work in English, but in history, that is a different story. We've had two tests, on both of which I got a C, and we're having a very important one on Wednesday. For once in my life I am really petrified over a history test. . . .

The electric cycle[14] here is 50, but I would like for you to see about getting me one, for this one loses about half an hour every night, which is very inconvenient in the morning. The bike has not arrived, but it usually takes about two weeks to get it delivered to Roble. Please don't forget I need the formals by the 19th and that I need some more sheets. . . .

July 22, 1944

I have just come back from a three-hour geology lab. It consisted of hiking all over the hills and breaking rocks to see what kind they were. . . .

. . . I also know now why the girls said that you didn't very often go out with the soldiers here. I was talking to some of them the other night and they didn't want to be tied down to the Stanford honor system.[15] Of course all the regular Stanford students have to abide by it, but the Army can vote whether they want it or not. It just made me boil when they said they were going to vote down the honor system, because if they can't be officers without cheating, they certainly have no business being officers. . . .

August 30, 1944

I have had a very nice week, that is until tonight. I have finally caught up with all my back homework, only I still have to work real hard because we are having a test in Western Civ.[16] on Friday, and also in French, which means that I have to review my whole play. My Saturday morning lab has been changed to Thursday night and that is pretty bad since that means I can't study from seven until ten tomorrow night. Today though I wrote two compositions for English and I felt that that was an accomplishment for one day.

Every night this week I've had a "coke date too." They are dates at the "Cellar"[17] from about 9:30 until 10:30. Sometimes they are pretty good to have since you try and arrange your work so that it's all finished by the time you have to go, then you always go to bed right when you get home. Therefore, you don't fool around after dinner about getting your homework started. Monday and Tuesday night I had them with Tom

Harris who is a big soldier about campus. I was supposed to have another one with him tonight, but things didn't turn out quite that way. Rob Haines came by to see me too, he'd come several times before so I couldn't show him out the door, especially since he's the nicest anyway. So we went and picked [up] Betty Smith (the med. student she goes with was with Rob), at the library and then proceeded to the "Cellar." Of course we sat down in a booth right across from Tom and I asked him how he was. I don't think he appreciated it very much, especially since I'd said that I didn't know whether I could meet him or not because of my studying. I certainly never thought that I'd have trouble like that, but now I know.

You needn't worry about my going into San Francisco anymore. About six of us are going to stay with one of the girls who is going to that party and who lives in San Francisco. . . .

Love,
Mary

Letters from Nancy Christine Smith to her mother

Lorie's office
Monday, Sept 23, [1946], Evening—

Dear Mother,
What a day! And I thought registration day at Tufts was bad! I've been standing in line almost continuously since 8 this morning. They're really having their troubles here with 7,000[18] students instead of the normal 4,500. I can't imagine what it must have been like at the University of California at Berkeley with 22,000!

Here the lines went for miles. I was in one line with more than 2,000 ahead of me. Stayed there (I hate to admit this—but Bill will say it's only to be expected of me) for more than 3 hours before I finally found out that graduate students didn't need to! . . . Finished registering at about 6 . . .

. . . I shall have to stay for four quarters instead of three (which is really what I expected) so will not be able to get home until the end of August. I shall really have to ask Uncle Frank for money because they tack onto the tuition about $40 worth of infirmary fees, etc., to total $166.65 a quarter. So I have left after paying this one—$450.34 (the Houghton Mifflin check did come as you see), and will need to use all of that plus another $50 for tuition alone—unless I can get a fellowship—for which I shall naturally work. Besides that comes books and board. This living with the Tarshis' really is a money-saver for me. Of course I shall work as much as possible, and that will be some income, but not enough of course. If I can get a fellowship my problems will be solved, but that remains to be seen—. But I don't want you to borrow any money on your bond, Mother. Since Uncle Frank has offered to help I think it better to ask him. . . . Please do not try to raise the money yourself!

. . . At 5:30 this morning there were already 500 or more in line to register, and the office didn't open until 8:00. I arrived shortly before 8, and it took me until about 10 to get up to the window! But they were all friendly and joking—some singing, others playing cards, doing crossword puzzles or other games, others just talking—And even by 6:00 they were still in good spirits—less talkative, but naturally so. Thought my own back would break, myself. But even after realizing my mistake—actually it wasn't so stupid a mistake, because there was absolutely no indication as to a distinction between graduate students and underclassmen. . . .

The campus is huge, and quite strange. A great long quadrangle is the center, and that's where most of the classes are held. You can imagine me, Bill, trying to get oriented when each corner was the same as the one before, and all the alcoves and courtyards more or less alike! But I didn't hesitate to ask, and people were very helpful. I probably did walk 4 or 5 unnecessary miles, but I'll chalk it up to experience. It will be rather embarrassing, though, if by the end of the year I'm still asking—don't you think?

While I was walking along trying to figure out the map (which was really not much help because even if I knew where I was—which was not often I admit—I never knew which direction to follow on the map until I'd walked some distance to another point on it), someone said, "How long have you been here?" Of course I knew no one so I didn't look up until someone grabbed my arm, and there was a boy who'd been in the U-12 at Tufts and who had been on a round-table discussion with me in the economics club! What a thrill to see a familiar face! . . .

. . . I'm taking three courses, two of which meet every day—advanced theory at 11:00 with Haley, the head of the department who is extremely nice—he helped me a lot to figure out what I'd need—and statistics at 3:15, which is a course not to be counted toward my graduate work, but one which I really need, and one which will go to make up 5 of the 15 credits of undergraduate work I must have. The third course meets 3 times a week at 10—theory of prices with a new man to Stanford, a Hungarian named Scitovsky. I shall try to look as Hungarian as possible when I talk with him, and shall no doubt try to impress him with my family background. They sound like good courses, and I've been warned by Haley that there's plenty of work to be done in them. . . .

Well, I've rambled on enough. Do write as often as you can—your letters are so good—but don't attempt to do so when you're too tired. And don't work too hard! . . .

Nicer than New England: The people, and the weather, Nancy Christine Smith, 1946

Courtesy of the Stanford University Archives

Friday evening, Sept. 27, [1946]

Dear Mother,

I mailed your birthday present today. It might not reach you by Wednesday, but I hope it does. . . .

Stanford's really wonderful. It's really a scream the way I've conditioned myself to the surroundings. . . . I expect people to be friendly, and consequently I myself am terrifically friendly. Heavens, I think nothing of sitting down at lunch with some boys I've never seen before, and we have a nice chat as though we were old friends! But I'm sure I go around with a beaming countenance all the time and thus practically force people to be nice to me— who knows—but anyway the atmosphere is about the nicest I've ever seen. The sales girls and men in the shops all around the vicinity are so nice—waitresses, too. They're all so friendly and helpful. Really something compared to New England.

My courses are really going to be tough. They've already assigned loads of books to read—And I'm still in the process of settling down. Find I'm just reading words instead of getting any sense out of my reading. I'm hoping that will soon pass once I get into the swing of things. . . .

Love to all, Nancy

Postcards from Johnny (John) Murray Huneke to his mother

[Oct. 6, 1947]

Postcards Home: John (Johnny) Murray Huneke, Oct. 6, 1947
Courtesy of the Stanford University Archives

Letter from Jim to his mother

[1948]

Dear Mom:

We were having a bull session the other day at Encina, and we worked around to the subject of "What one thing here at Stanford has impressed us the most?" Of the four other fellows with whom I was talking, three of them deliberated for only a moment before they decided either the spiritual life or the church. That came from several fellows who, like me, ordinarily went to church just at Christmas and at Easter. Now as I think over the activities of the first week at Stanford, there is one event that clearly sticks in my memory—Freshman Sunday. We all attended church on that first Sunday—our first time as a class. The men were on one side and the women on the other, clear to the doors. More of us joined together for that service than for any other pre-reg. activity, I believe. There were frosh representing nearly every church. Some knelt for the prayers and others bowed their heads. Some said "debtors" and others said "trespassers" during the Lord's Prayer. No one worried about it. It was not like most non-denominational services— formal, stiff, and conventional. It had a welcome naturalness. When one of the speakers gave a short welcoming message, he emphasized the history of the Memorial Church[19] saying, "Mrs. Stanford meant this to be both the physical and spiritual center of the campus. We want you to make it the center of your lives." Before, when I attended church services, I always felt a kind of disinterest in the scripture readings. They seemed to be a kind of time-filler which the minister used to lengthen his service. But when students read the lessons, they present thoughts which often apply directly to college life. The setting of Stanford's church itself is so conducive to worship that it is a pleasure to spend a Sunday morning there. The acoustics favor the well-trained choir voices which float overhead from the rear balcony and echo throughout the long cathedral-styled chapel. The sun shining through the stained-glass windows on the hand-painted mosaics adorning the walls makes the faces look different from time to time. I heard one fellow say, "I've been

here for two years and have never noticed that angel before."
From the outside the church can be seen all the way down
University Avenue as it rises in the center of Inner Quad. It is
around this building that is built a fine tradition of the Stanford
Family.

—*Jim*
Letter courtesy of the *Stanford Daily*

Letters from Carol Hodge to her family

24 September 1953

Dear Mom, Dad, and Grandma,

Today I began my life at Stanford University!
. . . Jean has the corner room to the right of mine; Barbara has
the one on my left. Both girls have to come through my room
to get to theirs, while I will have to use the sink in one of their
rooms.[4] At the moment I don't think any of us is too crazy
about the setup, but we will learn to like it, I guess. . . .

When you left for home, I suddenly realized I am really on my
own now. There was a bit of a lump in my throat as you drove off,
but, with so much to do, that empty feeling soon disappeared. . . .

At the freshman assembly in Frost Amphitheater, we were
officially welcomed by the President of the University,
Dr. Wallace Sterling,[20] and by the student body president. The
University Chaplain said a few words, as did Rixford K. Snyder,
the Director of Admissions. He said we are the biggest class
ever to enter Stanford, but he also warned that as many as ⅓ of
us may not end up graduating from Stanford. Sitting in the

beautiful amphitheater with our whole class really made me feel very lucky to be a part of it all, and I don't intend to be part of that unfortunate ⅓. . . .

. . . We had our first corridor meeting where we were told some of the rules and regulations of Stanford, plus some of the old traditions. The talk included rather a lecture about the exchanges we are to have with the boys' dorms. We are to MINGLE, not stand around looking awkward and shy. Hmmm? All of the girls in the corridor seem friendly. We have what is called the "open-door policy"; none of us lock or even close our doors unless sleeping or wanting quiet study. It is supposed to develop trustworthiness and help create a more friendly atmosphere.

25 September 1953

. . . Breakfast was at 7:15 after which I went directly to the English Placement Test at 8 o'clock. It wasn't too bad. In fact, I feel I may have done pretty well on it. However, the French test that I took this afternoon was horrible. The vocabulary part wasn't too difficult, but the comprehension was. Heaven only knows how I did!

I got my post office box today, #1457. In getting it, though, I was late to the assembly they had to introduce us to the dean of students. In fact, I missed most of it, but at least now I can receive some mail. The assembly was held in Memorial Auditorium,[21] better known as Mem Aud (it seems everything here is abbreviated!) . . .

I cashed my first check today, too, buying a history book at the bookstore for $6.54. We register for our classes on Monday, and I'm kind of dreading it. I hear it is quite confusing, and the rest of the student body will be here by then . . .

This evening, the boys from Encina came over here for an exchange dinner outdoors. I had my first fresh pineapple—messy but good. It was kind of fun with singing on the front lawn after dinner. There was a campus movie, called flicks,[22] after the sing. . . .

26 September 1953
. . . Tonight was the Jolly-Up. . . . It was a tangle of people, not too well organized, but, I must admit, kind of fun. It was held out at the Village[23] in the auditorium, and it was so crowded that one could hardly move, let alone dance. I spent time talking with Jim, but he got lost in the crowd when George cut in. The rest of the guys I danced with aren't worth mentioning, nor do I remember their names. There was entertainment of some kind, but it couldn't be heard above the noise.

5 October 1953
. . . The English class was somewhat better today. Perhaps the teacher isn't as bad as I thought, or maybe I am just getting used to him. On the first essay which we wrote in class last week, he gave no A's, only 3 B's, a few C's, some D's, and mostly F's. I was one of the "fortunate" D+ students with plenty of room for improvement. I guess you would say this grade was a blow to my ego after all the A's and B's in high school. The main thing criticized was probably my style, not my grammar. He said I lack originality, and I probably do. . . .

19 October 1953
I got my third English composition back today with a C+. I can't understand that man. He told the class that mine was the only original theme handed in, yet still I got a C.

Things aren't much better in Civ. I wish I could think of something to contribute to the discussions. I think I'm afraid I'll make a fool of myself, but guess I'll have to swallow that fear if I want a decent grade! Jean is in that discussion group with me, and she doesn't seem to be having any trouble participating. Most of the rest of the class is male.

Love,
Carol

Letters from Elaine Lavis to her family

September 21, 1960

Dear Family,
. . . Freshman Convocation[24] was quite impressive. The program is enclosed, if you're interested. Sterling gave some statistics which were interesting, also. . . . There are 425 women and about 850 men in our class—73 less total enrollment than the last freshman class. We come from 43 states, and about 10 foreign countries. Just a little over 50% of our class is from California. About 11% of the class have sisters and brothers at Stanford, and a larger percentage (about one-fifth of the class, I think) had parents who went to Stanford. Thus ends today's vital statistics report. . . .

September 24, 1960
Well, another couple days of Pre-Registration, and hectic busyness have passed. Soon they will be over, and I imagine that no one will be too sorry to see them go. By this point almost everyone is tired of smiling incessantly at everyone else, and

making inane comments, just to keep conversation going. Meeting people can be interesting, but not when you have to do it for five or six days straight, all day long. In fact, this whole thing is a big campus joke, and the humor magazine even puts out a regular manual for us, telling us how to practice smiling in front of our mirrors, and shaking hands with doorknobs, just to get in shape. . . .

. . . On Friday afternoon, we heard the dean of students, Dean Winbigler, speak to us. . . . After hearing him, we broke up into groups of about fifteen freshmen each, and went to faculty teas. These are teas planned by the Faculty Wives Association,[25] and given in the homes of the professors. The main point of the whole thing is to prove that teachers are also people. . . .

This afternoon was a Stanford game—we lost, per usual. Today has been extremely hot, and the game was no exception. Everyone came back sunburned, and wringing wet. Oh well, the joys of watching Stanford lose.

Tonight was the Frosh picnic, and then Jolly-Up, both of which were extremely jolly. These events were held in Wilbur Hall,[26] right across the street, which couldn't be much more convenient for us. . . .

October 9, 1960
. . . We had a football game on Saturday afternoon. (It was on television, and we lost by another close score of about 29–10— need I say more?) I only stayed through the first half of the game—I couldn't take anymore, and felt that I could be doing many better things—anything would be better. We had had a football rally Friday night after dinner, but even that didn't seem to help. . . .

This afternoon I went to the Western Civ.[27] library to study. This is a special library on campus, with all the readings required and recommended for the course. You have to read them there, as you can check them out for two-hour periods only. I am finding the entire course fascinating—it covers so much—from political and economic history, to art, literature, religion, and philosophy. This quarter, we will study the period from the descent of man through about 800 A.D. This will cover the ancient civilizations, i.e., Stone Age, Egyptian, Mesopotamian, Hebrew, Greek, Roman, Hellenistic, Islamic, and the rise of Christianity. Our readings are drawn from one main text, a text on the history of art, a supplementary reading text, and then other books. A week's reading may include such varied things as an epic poem, selections from the Bible, Greek philosophy, or a tragedy. The assignments are made on a two-day basis; in other words, one assignment is due each time the history quiz-section meets. . . . In addition to our thrice-weekly quiz sections, there is a lecture for the entire class (all 1,200 of us) every Monday morning in the auditorium. There is a different lecturer each time—this way we get to hear from many different professors, each speaking on his own speciality. . . .

Well, I guess I better go to bed now. It's fairly late, as you can probably tell by the quality of the typewriting. And, don't bother writing me to tell me that I need a new ribbon on this machine—I'm going to get one tomorrow to save everyone's eyes.

Love,
Elaine

Letters from Joe (Joseph) Lewis Jacobs to his parents

9/29 [1961]

Dear Mom and Dad,

Hi. Classes started Wednesday, so now I'm in the full swing of things. There is loads of homework, but there is still time for fun.

I have enclosed an article from the Stanford Daily. It is, I think, self-explanatory. The question in brackets was asked by me. What I actually said was, "What method does Stanford use to lure so many top teachers from Eastern colleges? What does Stanford have that the Eastern schools don't, besides a good climate and coeds?" [President Sterling's] answer is essentially correct.[28] But he said, "We throw in the climate and the coeds for free."

After the questions were over, he played the piano at our request. And we all sang along. It was really great. Not many college presidents would do that. I don't think there's a person (student, teacher, anybody) who doesn't like him. Tell Barry he also did a solo of "I'm a gnu." Everyone was in hysterics during the song.

Well, I'm in the band. We practice two nights a week, plus Saturday. They lent me a lyre. But I have to buy suspenders and white buck shoes. . . . The formations are

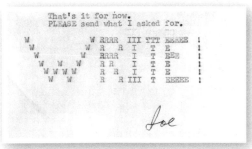

Courtesy of Stanford University Archives

complicated, and I don't know how I'll ever learn everything. But just marching again is exhilarating. . . .

10/7 [1961]

. . . On the 26th of September, the drum major and the student director of the band came up to my room. I warned them what the quality of my playing would be, and they frankly admitted that they were hard up for members. Therefore neither of us is under any apprehensions. The only reason I had decided not to join was that I was afraid they would turn me down. They also told me that it is rather easy to get an "A" in band, and that will help my average. So I'm in. . . .

I guess you heard about our football game this afternoon. There was a rally in the amphitheater and the dorms served box lunches. They attached a microphone to the radio and broadcast the game in the amphitheater. At halftime and after the game we had a direct phone to the Stanford locker room, and we all yelled cheers for the team. It made them feel good. . . .

I haven't gone to Hillel services yet. The reason wasn't a lack of desire on my part; it was simply the fact that for two Saturdays in a row I have had themes due in English. And you know your son, ye old procrastinator. . . .

. . . When you come up, I'll really give you a tour of the campus, but on foot. This campus has a beauty that is not immediately evident to the observer, and this is what I'll show you. The church, for example, is done completely in mosaic, and is absolutely stunning.

I have to go now, since, as always, I have homework to do.

Give my regards to everybody, and tell them that I'll try to write.

And you write. . . .

10/17 [1961]

. . . Slight problems on the matter of washing combs and brushes: There are no stoppers for our sinks, so I'll have to buy one somewhere. And I don't have a nail brush, but I will buy a toothbrush and use my old toothbrush for the comb. . . .

I almost died last Saturday. After getting in at 2:15 from a really wild house party Friday night, I had to get up at 7 to get to English. After English (at 9) the band rehearsed on the practice field. Then I had to dash to Civ at 10 (I was late). After Civ I put on my band pants (with suspenders) and ate lunch. Then I got the rest of my uniform, my clarinet, and my music, and went down to rehearse from 12 until the game. We marched to the stadium in full uniform (100% wool) and waited for the team and the other school's band to warm up and do a pre-game show. Then we did our show. And of course we also did a halftime show. And the temperature was around 90. After that game, I was ready to collapse, but we had to go to the gym and serenade the teams with a few numbers. What fun! . . .

That's all for now. WRITE. . . .

10/23/61

Sorry I didn't write over the weekend, but the past few days have been pure hell. That means that I have now had my first college midterms. On Friday I had one in French. I don't know yet how I did on it. And this morning I had my first Civ midterm. It was hideous. There were five different exams, but all the students of any one teacher took one exam. Here is the one I had: I (60%, 30 minutes) Analyze the influence of religious beliefs upon the political, economic, and cultural practices of the Egyptian and Hebrew civilizations. II (40%, 20 minutes) Answer two of the following: a) Discuss the major effects of the Neolithic Revolution. b) Compare the Code of Hammurabi with the Laws of Solon. c) "We cannot understand Greek civilization without an understanding of the city." Discuss.

Isn't that charming?!? I'm sure I flunked. . . .

My French teacher is real nice—not too good, but nice. I went to see a play here last week and she (along with her date) were sitting right in front of me. The first day she walked into class I thought she was a student. She's cuter than most of the girls. . . .

Yesterday afternoon . . . I came back to my room to find Tom asleep on his bed, and Doug Bruce (one of the guys down the hall) asleep on my bed. There were Civ books open on both desks. . . . It was so funny that I got Dwight and Les (in room 208) and they came to look. Then Doug woke up, but Dwight decided to put a little of Tom's shaving cream (aerosol) on Tom's nose. Of course Tom woke up, and it got smeared all over Tom, Dwight, and me. Later, Tom got Dwight, and then Dwight came back and got Tom. Unfortunately I fell asleep— barefoot. So Tom sprayed some on my hair and my feet. I woke up and, not realizing it was on my feet, stood up. SQUISH! All over the floor, my spread, my jeans, and everything. But it was funny.

Later, after dinner, about 15 guys ganged up on Walt (who is about 6'8" or more). But somehow someone tipped him off, so he didn't come in his room (they were waiting to ambush him in his room). But they went after him, dragging his bedspread to toss over him. We had artichokes for dinner, and Walt brought back a few to nibble on during the night while he was studying. But needless to say, they went flying all over the hall in the battle. It was really hilarious. Everyone got smeared with artichoke. Now that the first midterm is over, things will, I'm sure, settle down to a reasonable calm. . . .

That's all for now; I have to go wash clothes that I didn't get around to last week. I wash clothes about every ten days.

Write soon.
Love, Joe

Letter from Anonymous to her father

9-25-72

Dear Dad,
I am writing you to tell my first experiences. Please save the first few letters somewhere so I can have them as treasures. Saturday was a real long day. I got up at 6:45—had breakfast and took a Latin placement exam. Did really badly on it. Then I rode to the bookstore and bought some books incl. Cyrano de Bergerac. . . . I think I might like civil engineering. What type [of engineering] do you think I ought to take?

After that I went with my roommate to get a rug. She has different tastes from me and I was outnumbered.* . . . It's O.K. but not the best. . . . After that we went to a house BBQ where we were supposed to meet our advisors but we didn't. . . . At about 9:00 Sharon and I went to the Union to look for folk singing action; but we bumped into folk dancing. That was really fun. We learned about 5 dances—everyone in a circle jumping around. It's every Friday and really fun. It was about 10:30 p.m. by that time, and we again set out for folk singing but never found it, so we went to the coffee house. . . .

See you, Anonymous
*Her parents are still in town.

Letters from M.C. to her parents

27 Sept 75

Dear Mom and Dad,

I just got back from the SU–San Jose State game. I decided I had better things to do than watch SU get trounced so I left ½-way through the 3rd quarter. (Does that mean it was the ⅝'s?) . . .

Everything except the football game has been great so far. Well, not perfect of course, but I haven't regretted a minute I've been here. I think it's the people who really make a difference. It's still fascinating to me that so many people come from so many places. In my dorm there are people from India, Mexico City, Alaska, Hawaii, and from just about everywhere else, but not many from the South. . . .

She [my roommate] is quite nice, and she has a lot of records that I like! I'm beginning to be able to connect faces with names around the dorm now. . . .

You know, I really like it here a lot. I'm a little surprised that I haven't been more homesick or lonely. I'm meeting a lot of people, & it's fun. Maybe I can be independent outside the security of Stillwater. I know this is going to be a good experience for me. It's like nothing I've done before, & I'm learning a lot. Thank you for letting me come.

10 Oct 75
Fri.

 . . . Mrs. Sunseri, my Math 41 prof., is reportedly one of the best math teachers Stanford has. She is friendly & funny & also knows her stuff quite well.

I'm getting pretty well emersed (I need a dictionary out here!) in Marxist economics. It's interesting but I'm getting ready to move on. I think it'll be better when I know more about economics from a capitalist's view so I can compare the 2. You're right, Dad, I kind of like econ. I can possibly see it looming somewhere in my future.

I've only been to my writing requirement[29] once since class started for real. But I have a good feeling about it. There are 15–20 people in the class from all over, which makes it interesting. The prof. is friendly & helps relax everyone so it is an enjoyable class period. We are going to be writing on Tuesday & discussing books, etc., on Thursday. Some of the books I have to read are Pride & Prejudice (why didn't I read it in high school?!?), Madame Bovary, & Thomas Hardy's Jude the Obscure. . . .

. . . Do you remember this summer sometime when Pres. Ford was in California & visited a power plant? We went to the same one he visited. (Seems I'm following him all around; I walk by the law school which he dedicated every day). . . .

. . . Actually it hasn't been difficult at all for me not to spend money. Games & the flicks are the only things I've spent money on besides essentials like books & paper. Also, I haven't missed the car like everyone at home told me I would. It might be nice so I could go to the city (that's San Fran, not OKC!) or to the beach, but it's easy enough to find rides with other people & I really have no need for one around campus. At OSU[30] it's more necessary to have a car because of the way the campus & town are set up, but you don't need one here.

I've been noticing the people in my dorm & have figured out that only 2 out of the 95 people in the house smoke. That's not bad. I guess not all Californians are wild, right?

I'm washing my clothes now for the first time. Exciting . . .

Another "strange" thing that I've noticed about Stanford is that everyone (at least the kids) calls the teachers "Prof." . . . Nobody says Dr. or Mr. Smith, they say Prof. Smith. I'm not used to it.

This Sunday I'm going over to my advisor's house. He came & ate dinner at our dorm Wed. night. He says that they are going to have the fixings & recipes there for all kinds of breakfast foods & we all can make whatever we want for breakfast. They sure do a good job of trying to personalize the advisors to the students here.

That's about all for now. I've just about rambled myself out of things to say. . . .

I still really like it here.
Love,
M.C.

Letter from Anonymous to her family

October 5, 1980

Dear Family:
. . . Today I studied a few hours, but it is really hard for me to start concentrating and remembering what I read. Chemistry is going to be especially demanding and difficult, as well as Western Culture (philosophy). I really can't say I've gotten into the swing of studying yet, but probably no one has. I even skipped the beach trip all day just to get some reading done. I hope I won't be struggling in my classes, because right now

they are so overwhelming, and it seems that everyone here got straight A's in high school. I can see how the atmosphere here is intellectual and competitive, yet "laid-back" at the same time. I think the climate has a lot to do with that. It's like there's a definite time to work and a definite time to play, and you just have to figure it out for yourself. . . .

Anonymous

Letter from Natasha Pratap to her parents

PO Box 5983
Stanford
California 94309
U.S.A.

20/23 October 1990

Dearest Mom and Dad,
How's that to get you thinking about me right away?! Before you react predictably, let me remind you that I did use "How's that" when I was in Bombay, and it's not one of the cool American phrases that I've picked up! I don't mean to sound rude but I HATE it when people give that "we know" look and say, "Arre, Stanford and all hanh"![31]

Please don't get bugged that this is a printed letter. I'm not trying to cut you or anything—I just can't afford to write as much as I want to if I rewrite everything for each person. So it's either a common long letter or separate short-short notes. I thought this was a better option. . . .

The special retreat organized for international students was fun but actually in retrospect, it was no big deal.

By the way I don't think you'll [you all] should worry too much about my coming back with a heavy American accent because everyone here loves the Indian accent! Some of them say it sounds like the British accent, which of course is all B.S. My roommate finds the words "loo" and "bunk" damn amusing! Some other Indians have already started saying "control"! When I come home, I might just say "Hey, guys" and "That's cool, man" more than you expect but that's about it!

Also, don't worry too much about the foreign guys scene. (This is especially for Dad.) I'm simply not attracted to white skin. However, Stanford has a fairly large population of Indians. . . .

The four years of undergraduate studies are named freshman, sophomore, junior, and senior years respectively. All freshmen are expected to take 2 compulsory courses: Cultures, Ideas, & Values (Civ) and freshman English. My freshman English class begins next quarter. There are several different Civ tracks to which people get assigned according to their preferences. I am in the humanities track (includes the Bible and the works of Homer, Virgil, Plato, & Sophocles—sounds cat?!) . . .[32]

Now I can tell you which course I'm taking. I didn't want to start on the last page and then write half and half. So my classes are:

COURSE	*UNITS*
1. Humanities	5
2. Introduction to Logic	5
3. First Year French (Part 1)	5
4. How to Use the MacIntosh Computer	1

$$\overline{}$$

. . . We have a ping pong (well, table tennis!) table in our dorm so I play T.T. pretty often. Guess what, I DO GO TO THE LIBRARY!!!

The name of my dorm is Otero. It's part of Wilbur Residence Hall. The faculty member attached to my dorm is Dennis Matthews. He lives in a cottage outside the dorm. He's a nice, sober, peaceful man. We have 4 R.A.'s, or Resident Assistants, named Stephen, Corey, Karen, and Jennifer. They are senior students who live with us and help us with any personal or other problems that may arise.

Now, my room and my roommate. At first I thought my room was cosy. Then I thought it was dingy. But then, I bought a smart fluorescent lamp so now I like it again! My roommate's name is Jennifer, same as that of one of the R.A.'s. Just for your information, there are at least 3 more Jennifers! I really like Jen so far. She's no "whacko" American, in fact, she's pretty steady. She's MUCH more organized than I [am]. She falls asleep by 11 and is up by 6:45, and I go about leading my own "orderly" lifestyle—sleeping at 11 sometimes, at 1 most of the time, and at 3 or perhaps 5 on "one of those days"! She gets her h.w. complete a day or two before it's due, and I got the printout for my Logic work at 1:09 and gave it up at 1:25, ten minutes after class had begun. But don't worry, I finished my second assignment a day beforehand and actually, that worried me more 'cause I couldn't believe it and kept thinking I must have forgotten something! Jen & I are both generally quite accommodating and considerate, so we don't have any major hassles. But I really wish I got to spend more time with her.

She spends most of her free time with her boyfriend. . . . In short, although she might seem a bit intimidating at times, I adore her!

The food, I thought at first, is not as bad as they make it out to be. I was simply inexperienced. Now, inventing weird salad combinations is a way of life. My favourite combo is red beans and croutons topped with dressing and grated cheese.

The Stanford Quad is overwhelmingly romantic. One evening the freshman girls could go and get kissed by the senior guys at the Quad. It literally happened—I was witness! It was extremely embarrassing to see people stop to regain their breath!

The International Students Orientation Committee (ISOC) organized a "roll-out" a couple of days ago. And it was exactly as the term implies. We were woken up at 5:30, asked to roll out of bed, and go with them to the Quad for breakfast. No brushing teeth. No dressing decent! It was fun! We had another roll-out a few days later in our dorm but I didn't wake up for that. I should have because the guys were all dressed in tuxes or blazers!

. . . The workload has me pretty bogged down. It'll take me some time before I figure out how much of the work I have to do and how much I can avoid. I feel like this is the first time in my life that I'm studying. I can't believe how much I could get away with in Bombay. All that has been working against me 'cause it's really hard to get used to the idea of doing at least something constructive every day! My incredibly slow reading and typing rate don't do much for me either.

I went with a few Indians to play Dandiyas. I swear we had a ball! There was also a Diwali[33] dinner organized by "Sanskriti," an Indian association for undergraduates.

Partying so far is no big deal. Frat fun is exaggerated. The only diff. is that there's plenty of beer and loads of bare-chested, sweaty guys. The music isn't that great either. I think it'll be more fun when I get familiar with some gang to party with! But I don't think it'll ever be like home where you know nearly everyone and nearly everyone knows you. Even if I had doubts about getting carried away and going out too much, they don't exist anymore. You take responsibility for yourself and decide what's right. Sometimes I come home late because I've been chatting with friends in another dorm (Mom, they do walk me home afterwards!), and it's no big deal. Now, after having seen what I'm like without any external constraints I often feel that curfews and other disciplinary techniques are made such a big deal of at home, so unnecessarily. . . . It's not that I've come here and become defiant. It's just that if I never raised the issue before it was because I wasn't sure about myself. But now I am. My freedom far from overwhelms me.

[It] may be classroom discipline is necessary in the Indian atmosphere but looking at it from here it seems more like demanded respect. It appears as if teachers there seem to take offence at really silly things. I mean here if you wear shorts in class it's understood that you're just more comfortable in them, and it isn't even noticed. If you eat in class it just means that you're hungry and it's no big deal. The teachers don't think you're being rude. In fact if you eat you'll probably be able to concentrate more during the rest of the class. I don't know, maybe I'm wrong.

Adjusting is necessary but I'm putting up pretty well. I've been really friendly with other Indians and ABCD's (American Born Confused Desis, for those of you who weren't sure what I was talking about). I was hoping to set up a little support group before entirely venturing forth. I'm not sure how far that's worked out. The guys are easier to handle. The girls tend to be bitchy, nosy, and competitive. This girl in my dorm, Reena, asked me whether I was, and if I was why I was, oscillating between two guys. I mean, gosh, I hardly even know her. I'm not going to justify myself to anyone and certainly not her after the way she frames her question. And to top it all she says, "I'm just curious." Bloody hell!

The worst part about adjusting is dealing with people who don't know you. At all. Every action & word makes them form an opinion which could be really warped. At home everybody knows what you're basically about and they just keep building on or altering an image. To illustrate my point, one guy thought I was flippant and clownish and that I played around with other people's feelings. He thought it was difficult to have a serious conversation with me. Another girl said I came across as intelligent, persuasive, assertive, had strong opinions, participated in things, and was loyal. The first picture is simply disgusting and the second is too on the mark. I think I'm a mix. Tell me what you think when you write.

Mom, I got the couriered package today. Thanks. Tans, you must keep writing. I just freak on your letters!

Now I'm ending. In case you thought this was like a shopping trip for me, you're WRONG!! It's 1 a.m., and I have to be up at 6 to read a book and prepare questions for a seminar I'm supposed to conduct for humanities. I've been working on this since 10 p.m., and I had put in 2 hrs. a few days ago. That makes it about 5 hrs. in all. And everybody in the computer room thinks I'm working really hard on a paper!! . . .

Love you lots,
Affectionately,
Natasha

Fast Forward:
Natasha Pratap
(right) and her
senior-year
roommate, Jennie

Courtesy of
Natasha Pratap,
Class of 1994

Email from Nora Tjossem to her parents

From: Nora
Date: Wed, Sep 28, 2011 at 12:08 AM
Subject: I'm still alive!
To: xxxxxx

Hiya S'meesy and Papito,
I found out that the chem book materials are online, thanks to
the expensive program they made us buy, so I'm reading
chemistry and trucking right along. They ran out of the
i>clickers in the bookstore, so I hope that gets resolved, but I'm
keeping strong. We had a great Socratic discussion today for
SLE,[34] so that promises to be lots of fun. I also had an audition
for Gaieties[35]—the theater production performed before BIG
GAME that essentially makes fun of Cal for a great while—
yesterday, and that went pretty well as far as I could tell. It was
fun, in any case, whether I get called back or not. I opted out of

the a capella audition I was supposed to have tonight. It won't be the worst thing if I don't get into anything. Can't believe it's only Day 2. . . .

I miss you and the kittens. I've been googling [sic] pictures of baby polar bears therapeutically.

Lots of love,
Nori

Letter from Grant Glazer to his family

10/10/13

Dear Mom, Dad, Danny, Jane, Serena, & Sasha,
Thank you for the wonderful care package! Even though it came kind of late, the cookies weren't all that stale. I love the photo montage and have it hanging by my bed. Will says thank you for the "fruit snacks." Things are going really well. I'll try to facetime [sic] soon.[36] I love & miss you all! . . .

Grant

On the Approach:
Illustrated view of the
main entrance to
Stanford University,
Oct. 10, 2013

Grant Glazer, Class
of 2017

Courtesy of the
Stanford University
Archives

Email from David Weber to his mother

From: David Weber
Date: Thursday, September 18, 2014 at 7:16 PM
To: CHRIS WEBER

Subject: contact information and p.o. box

Hey mom here's my new address and my RA contact numbers:

My dorm is Junipero in Wilbur Hall, my room number is 323, and the P.O. box is 12292. I'm not totally sure what you should enter as a complete address, but I think it talks about it in the Approaching Stanford packet,[37] if you have that.

My RAs are:

Jazlyn Patricio [phone numbers withheld]
Logan Richard

My RFs are:[38]

Ari Kelman
Eva Jordan

Only call them if it's an absolute emergency and you haven't been able to get in contact with me for like 3 days.

Love you,
David

First Letters Home: Further Comments

"They already have electricity in the boys Hall and we shall soon have it but now we use candle light."

—Lucy Allabach, Roble Hall, Oct. 11, 1891

"We are allowed to petition for a change of roommates, and I am undecided what to do. . . . The group of girls whom I like particularly well seem to be concentrated in the other end of the hall. One of them . . . is urging me to move in with her."

—Alice Louise Clark, Sept. 25, 1935

"I guess you would call this another ordinary day 'around the Quad.' Some of the students in my English class are surely bright. Their vocabularies are straight out of Webster's and put mine to shame."

—Carol Hodge, Oct. 7, 1953

"There's a joke going around about the freshman who asked another freshman how he could manage to eat the Wilbur food. The other fellow said, 'Easy, I just take a teaspoon of Drano three times a day.'"

—Peter King, Sept. 29, 1961

"We have a dance this Friday over in the Cellar. . . . The theme is sort of juvenile delinquent combined with beatnik. We have a really good band, so the party should be wild."

—Joe (Joseph) Lewis Jacobs, Oct. 11, [1961]

"This place is really something. I've had dinner with the head of the School of Engineering; heard and seen one of the top jazz singers in the country. Big things happen around here."

—Phil (Philip) B. Laird Jr., [Late 1960s]

"The room is the pits—it's like a barrack."

—Anonymous, Sept. 25, 1972

"I haven't met anyone from Modesto yet but I know a guy
who knows a girl he thinks is from Modesto. (??)"

—(Jonathan) Chris Seaman, 1973

"[I made the mistake of] mentioning to one person that
I was making popcorn, and pretty soon the whole dorm
was knocking on our door and yelling out of windows
questioning me as to when I was going to make it."

—Alison Carpenter, Oct. 19, 1975

"It is the kind of place where you can sit in a circle
and play Conversions with words like 'philanthropist'
and 'map,' and two people instantly come up with
'cartographer'. . . just as readily as paint your
face and wear all red to go out and cheer at a
football game (even though we lost . . . again
. . . horribly. . .)." [Ellipses in original.]

—Christopher Lowman, Sept. 26, 2006

Chapter 2

Beat Cal

"All the same, I'm glad I didn't go to Berkeley."[39]

—Hope Snedden, Dec. 1, 1918

Letter from Lucy Allabach to her family

THE BALDWIN HOTEL
San Francisco, Cal.
March 19, 1892 [First Stanford-Cal game]

My Dear People,

This is indeed a memorable day, and I am so glad I have been here to shout and wave my red ribbon for Stanford, and we have won the day and beaten the University of California,— but perhaps I would better explain.

Stanford and U.C. had decided to have a match football game at Haight Street Park today. U.C. being an old institution and their men having been in training so much longer than ours, we could not expect to beat them, and yet our boys are not the kind to die easily. . . .

. . . At nine promptly we left Palo Alto and the [train] cars were all full. . . . We were a gay and hopeful crowd, but now and then our spirits would be dampened by a shower and the horrible thought that we might be beaten.

When we arrived at Valencia Street Station a number of cable cars were in waiting and we proceeded to fill them while some of the red muslin was transferred from the coaches to the streetcars. All the men wore red ties and had little red banners floating from their umbrellas and the women had red ribbons and banners. As we rode along the tin horns and college yell made it apparent that we were here. . . .

The grass was like a lovely lawn and the white lines were very plain and gave a pretty effect. In one part of the amphitheater cardinal was the color and in another blue and gold. On the grounds were elegant carriages and the gaily decorated coaches, as well as the ball teams, and more enthusiastic men of the two universities. The game was to begin at three but when half past three and nearly four arrived and they did not begin, we began to wonder what was the matter and at last the joke came out,—both teams had forgotten a ball and they must wait till one was sent for clear up to San Francisco. It was past four when they began at last. . . . The breathless excitement with which the friends of our team watched the whole, and the way they waved and shouted and blew their horns was very inspiring, and when Code, or Downing, or Clemans,[40] the last by the way is an Iowa boy who bids fair to win a great name on the coast, would make some fine plays, the noise would become deafening. Inside of ten or fifteen minutes our boys had made a touchdown and kicked the goal and thus scored six. Then we all went wild. At the end of the first half they had scored fourteen and U.C. nothing, but all the time they had to work so hard that it was not safe to count too much on their winning. It was terribly exciting in the last half as they would get almost to [the] Berkeley goal when Clemans would make a good run and bring them back, or when one of the U.C. boys would start with the ball and little Code would throw himself on him with such force that he would come down with the ball. Old and young shouted and waved the cardinal right royally. . . . Stanford won with the score ten to fourteen. My how proud we feel and how victorious. . . .

The boys very kindly sent the committee on decorations complimentary railroad tickets, and ladies were admitted free to the game so our expenses have not been great.

Senator and Mrs. Stanford telegraphed their hopes to the boys last night, and in some of the stores this morning we saw clerks wearing cardinal, while now and then they would wish us success; and the "Lick"[41] was decorated in cardinal. . . .

Such things inspire a college and unite its members wonderfully.

I do so wish you could be here. I feel real selfish to enjoy it all alone, and I want to be here so much next year that nothing but the feeling that duty bids me do otherwise can prevent my coming. . . .

Lucy Allabach

Letter from Francis J. Batchelder to his family

Palo Alto
Dec. 18, 1892

Dear Mother & All the Folks:
. . . Yesterday, the great football game between Stanford and the Univ. of Calif. came off—a day that everybody here has been looking forward to for months. We have had Walter Camp, the great Yale coach, here training our eleven, and the Univ. of Calif. secured McClung, the Yale captain, at the same time. For the last two weeks the two teams have been in such severe training that the men have not been able to attend hardly a single recitation. The Univ. of Cal. was overconfident of success (just as they were last year when they were defeated) but here we all thought it would be a close game, whichever side won, and it was, for it came out a tie, the score being 10 to 10. At the end of the 1st half the score was 6–0 in our favor, and our team was playing so much better than Berkeley that we began to feel

pretty certain of success, but our fullback failed to kick a goal by about three inches, and so the score stood a tie.

Half the proceeds goes to each university. Admission was $1 apiece and there were about 15,000 people present. One of the jewelers in S.F. had a life-size hollow silver football which he offered to the winning team, and this will now have to be over until next year.

Our fraternity rode out to the grounds in an immense stagecoach all trimmed with cardinal. We had cardinal flags at the horses' heads, S T A N F O R D in cardinal letters hanging over their sides, and cardinal flags floating from the four corners of the top of the coach. We invited the KAΘ [Kappa Alpha Theta] girls to go with us, which made up a party of twenty altogether—most of us riding on top of the coach, armed with tin horns four-feet long, and waving all the cardinal flags we had hands for. Then on the back of the coach we had ΦΔΘ [Phi Delta Theta] in cardinal letters on a white ground.

There were about a dozen of these tally-hos[42] on the field from Stanford & Berkeley, but everybody said ours was the finest there, it was so nicely decorated and had such a fine-looking crowd on top.

We didn't get back to Palo Alto till three o'clock this morning, and were all so tired out we didn't get up until nearly lunchtime.

With love to all,
Francis

Letter from Herbert C. Hoover to a friend

Leland Stanford Junior University
Nov. 9, 1894

Miss Hill.[43]

Dear Friend. I have treated your kind letter shamefully but you
do not know what circumstances I have been through since
writing you from Placerville in July. . . . Things are much as usual.
Jobbes [Jobs] are not so likely, and football absorbs everything—
all my time. My work during the past summer has been
especially beneficial. I enjoyed it very much. Learnd [Learned]
much and am better morally, physically & financially than 6
months ago. . . . Am Treas. of Student Body[44] you know and it
has proved a bigger job than I bargained for taking most of my
time, so that, to speak in the words of J C Branner[45] I must quit
at the end of this semester and go to studying. For as he says,
"You may be able to graduate all right but we are not turning out
A.B.'s but Geologists.["] I vertually [virtually] have control of
affairs and am making a hard effort to pay of [off] our old
indebtedness of $600.00 & conduct the present foot-ball season
successfully.

We will probably be beaten by Berkeley this year for we
have lost Walton, Whitehous[e] & MacMillan [McMillan][46]
and have not gained much, while they have gained much and
lost nothing. We have played the Reliance Athletic Club several
times and have been beaten every time. While Berkeley has
always managed to tie the score with them. They have Walton,
Whitehouse & MacMillan [McMillan]. . . .

The Team goes to Sacramento tomorrow. I shall not go long [along] as I must be in S.F. to complete arrangements for the Thanksgiving game.

We go to Los Angeles Xmas

We have a young lady taking Geology as a specialty now, a very nice young lady too.[47]

Wishing you the best of success I am Yours sincerely.

H C Hoover

Letter from Herbert C. Hoover courtesy of the University of Oregon Special Collections and University Archives

Football Absorbs: Image from Stanford-Cal game program, 1894 Courtesy of the Stanford University Archives

Letters from Fred (Frederic) Jewell Perry to his mother

**Stanford,
Feb. 5, 1899**

My dear mother:

A University of California man sits opposite me reading the paper. He is an enthusiastic collegian. He is revelling in Stanford sunshine, and is the recipient of much congratulation. He takes it all proudly and self-composedly, and then proceeds to tell the gathered Stanfordites how "we" did it. ("We" means U.C.) The man who is doing all the strutting you probably know by reputation if not by name. Arthur Perry is his cognomen![48]

Well may he strut! Berkeley has bested us again, and again Stanford objects and declares that if U.C. won it was not by virtue of the merits of the individual who got the medal. We should not have objected if Martin of U.C. had won the decision but we do emphatically kick against Warner. Any one of our men was as good as he. And all three of our speakers [debaters] far outshone the three representatives from Berkeley.

Arthur has been down here since Friday night and has been enjoying himself immensely. He has thoroughly explored the University campus, has visited Mayfield,[49] has seen our ancient club ["the co-op"], has traversed the Stanford estate, has witnessed our first game of baseball, has played tennis with me, has played pool and billiards in our Encina[5] club room, has attended a meeting of our literary society and others. He goes home on this morning's train.

Well, I am twenty-one this morning and have been such since last Friday. It's just Stanford's luck to have an intercollegiate contest on my birthday. Poor Stanford, she little knew the fatality of Feb. 3! On Feb. 3 it rained in the morning but about ten o'clock the sun began to break away from the storm cloud and by degrees peered forth from the gloomy background. At twelve it was shining with all its old-time splendor and making man and nature rejoice. At six the sun looked down on a motley collection of U.C. and Stanford men yelling and jesting for their respective colleges. The next morning Sol smiled and so did U.C., but Stanford, like the clouds of the morning before, wept great drops. . . .

April 30, 1899

. . . Our men drove around the bay in a wagon, struck the U.C. campus at 3 in the morning, and in 25 minutes had pulled up and packed in the wagon the Senior "C" of the Class of '98. The drive back to Stanford was a long and weary one and full of fear to the men. They did not know at what moment a contingent from U.C. might appear in sight to regain their fence and take its purloiners back to Berkeley as hostages or spoils-of-war. At Milpitas a telegram was sent by them to our campus stating that Berkeley was in pursuit and urged us to come on at full speed to defend our prize. We were to meet the fence at Alviso eight miles away.[50] Thirty students, myself included, engaged a bus, and hurried off to meet the fence. The telegram arrived at 9 a.m. Along the road the big four-in-hand rushed, the fellows singing songs and swearing vengeance upon U.C. for the theft of our Axe.[51] We were a jolly set and eager for a good "scrap." . . .

. . . Well, at Alviso we met our fellows with the fence and not a U.C. coward in sight. And then what a yell went up when we found that the fence was indeed ours, and effectually beyond the power of U.C. to recover it.

The homeward journey was a triumphal march. On our way back we met within the first mile five additional buses, reinforcements for the first busload no doubt. Every time we met a new bus we yelled and the newcomers yelled back. The whole five buses then got into line behind the dirty wagon which held the precious prize, our bus leading the others. We yelled and we sang and jollied up in general. . . .

. . . The procession, a quarter of a mile long, marched through Palo Alto and up through the University. All Palo Alto turned out to watch the parade. It was a holiday for Stanford. Enthusiasm was at its highest pitch. Old Palo Alto men yelled like young students. Women waved handkerchiefs, flags, and whatever they could lay their hands upon. . . . In the quadrangle the band met us and escorted the line around the Quad. In the center the procession stopped, and the "C" was taken out and put up. Standing upon it—our fellows made speeches and told how they stole the fence when sleepy Berkeley had forgotten the vigilance she had been exercising since Stanford's first visit in quest of the Axe. . . .

Good by—
Fred

Letter from Julia Hamilton Conkling to her mother

Sun. morning, [Nov. 12, 1911]

Dear mother,
. . . From 9:00 til 12:30 by night light I again crammed trig. and rose early Thurs. morning to stand in line at bookstore to

draw for tickets for football show.[35] Had my ex. in trig. Thurs.
morning, went to town in afternoon to order flowers for game,
came home, ate supper, & hurried to assembly hall so as soon as
doors were opened we could get in & get a seat. Well the
[Roble[4]] rally was wonderful. Never saw anything like it in my
life. Cheering & throwing of hats in air lasted for 15 minutes at
a time. My ears haven't been just right since. . . . Yells, songs,
band, & speeches were great. The assembly hall was so crowded
you could hardly move. When the team marched in I thought
the boys were going mad. The yell leaders couldn't control them
at all & they jumped up & down on the chairs till I wonder
there was no one left and someone wasn't killed. The girls in
galleries were all given yards & yards of red paper ribbon to
drop down, which gave a beautiful effect. . . . After this
performance all the men serpentined around the inner Quad
where red fire was burned then everyone went over to bonfire.[52]
The rain was pouring down but nevertheless it was the largest
fete I ever saw. I am sending you a little picture of the pile. On
top there is a boat with a fellow with a blue sweater with a
yellow C trying his level best to get in it. Below is the sign,
"Get on the boat, California." The band & boys serpentined
around the fire for about an hour when they became exhausted
& drenched. When we got home, we girls on the fourth floor
had a grand spread by the light of the moon. . . . Friday
afternoon I washed, & Gladys & I cleaned our room up &
decorated it with red geraniums and chrysanthemums.

Friday afternoon & evening guests began to arrive by the
dozens, the swellest machines and hats I ever saw, . . . [the]
huge machines decorated some with red pennants, others with
blue-and-gold ones. . . . Gladys' father, mother, & friend came
down in their machine from Los Gatos, so I had a ride over to

field & back in afternoon. We all went over early to get the full benefit of all the yelling & singing. I never said two words the whole time, I was so busy taking it all in. . . . Our men formed into a red field with a white block -S- and red confetti was showered upon all. . . . I wore my blue suit & hat & some beautiful red carnations. Both bands, yells & songs were grand & when our team came on the field, hundreds of red toy-balloons were sent up along with the cheering. Our men wore white shoes, red socks, little short white trousers, & red sweaters. The Berkleyites had blue suits with yellow-striped sleeves & socks. . . . Well, the game started. For quite a while neither side scored, then Berkeley scored three & soon after we scored our first & only three. Then from then on the game reminded me of a battle. One by one our men fell staggering on the field & the doctor rushed to the rescue with cold water. Sometimes they jumped up and went on playing, other times they were carried off the field and a substitute put in. In the California team only one man was hurt and not a single substitute was put in. I think it hurt me worse when those poor fellows were hurt than it hurt them for most of them were senseless. I felt so sorry for them I almost bawled. In the meantime California scored and scored and finally the gun went off and down came the California band, bear, rooters, & all, & around the field they serpentined while our poor wounded men hobbled into their dressing rooms and our rooters hurried over to guard the Quad & Palo Alto tree so that California would not hoist up their colors or serpentine the Quad. California did get over to the flagpole and half-mast the flag and Stanford colors. I never saw such a sorrowful looking bunch as the Stanford people in all my life. Well we returned mid the California Boola Boola & Oski Wow Wow[53] to Roble, had supper, and then went to the football show "The Follies of Stanford" at Assembly Hall. When the team came in, some limping & some with heads & arms bandaged, the whole house let off another loud cheering. . . . I did feel so sorry for the poor fellows. They have lost for three years now. I can't tell you whether the show was good or not for I couldn't keep awake. . . .

Love to all,
Julia

Letter from (Mary) Carol Stearns to her mother

Mon. a.m., [Mid-1940s]

Dear Mom—
. . . Right now Barb & I are in the War Bond Booth supposedly selling stamps—Of course at 4:00 p.m. there isn't any business—especially after the big drive they had last week. Did you hear about it? A race between Cal & Stanford with the Axe as the prize to the school that sold the most. We won. We had several Axe-teams to raise bond money—samples—1 pr. nylons went for $5,000; an old wreck of a car for $12,000, a date with the head hasher[54] $500 . . . [ellipses in original] etc. Really good . . .

Write,
Love,
Carol

Letter from Mary Allie Lesnett to her family

November 22, 1946

Dear Mother and Daddy,

This is the weekend of the "Big Game" with Cal. It is by far the biggest game of the year, and there have been lots of things going on. On Wednesday and Friday they have the "Big Game" Gaieties. . . . They asked me to stand in the queen scene. The position I had wasn't very important, nevertheless I suppose I should have been flattered, but I really wasn't too mad for the idea. You should have seen all the horrible makeup they put on me, it looked absolutely ghastly, although they said it looked fine on the stage. We had to stand on a platform which was about twenty-feet high and which you had to climb up some very high steep, wobbly stairs to get on. After it was over they rolled us out on this huge thing. It was sort of fun being in [it], but certainly not worth all the trouble.

On Thursday they had a parade of floats, a rally, and a bonfire. The parade was loads of fun. Every living group made a float on the back of a truck, there were about forty in all, and they drove past the front of the school. They were all about Indians[55] and bears. . . . The bonfire was a huge fire the freshman boys had spent three days building out in one of the fields, and on it was burned an effigy of the Bruin Bear. . . .

On Wednesday night, they caught some Cal men on our campus and took them over to Encina . . . and chained them up and shaved their heads. On some of the boys they even painted red S's on their heads. They marched them around campus the next day and made them bow to all the girls. I had never seen boys with their heads shaved before, and they certainly looked awful. They have been keeping all the roads entering Stanford blockaded, and every time you want to go in you have to show your student-body card. . . .

Love to all,
Mary

Letter from Carol Hodge to her family

21 November 1953

Dear Mom, Dad, and Grandma,
BIG GAME DAY! It had that fresh and footbally air, but the festive mood turned to one of gloom when the score ended up a tie. The game was exciting despite the outcome. Oh well, at least Cal didn't win either. C'est la vie.

The Stanford Axe turned up today. It seems it had been planted in Norm Manoogian's[56] car by none other than the Stanford Volunteer Fire Department. The story goes that it has hung on the wall of the Firehouse in plain sight the whole time it has been missing!

The SAE house won the prize for the best house decorations and well deserved it. Our partner, the Phi Sig house, was a disgrace to the good name of Roble. . . .

My date, Dave, called for me promptly at 6:30, and we were off. The traffic was awful, so we had plenty of time to discuss the game. . . .

Love,
Carol

Lean In: Beat Cal banner, Leaning Tower of Pisa, Oct. 22, 1960

Courtesy of the *Stanford Daily*

Letters from Elaine Lavis to her family

November 1, 1960

Dear Family,

Well, it was certainly worth getting up for breakfast this morning! The news in the Daily[2] was nothing short of unbelievable. In fact, it was so fantastic, that I've enclosed the article. (I knew you wouldn't want to miss this one, or have to wait until you got home to read about it.) As a word of explanation, the Campanile is a tower on the Cal campus, similar to our Hoover Tower. Each year, Stanford tries to hang a "Beat Cal" sign from it, but of course, the Cal students are always on their guard. Last year, however, some Stanford students did accomplish this feat. However, it will be mighty hard for Cal to top this last coup. I'm sure everyone will be talking about this for days. . . .

The rest of the news around here is pretty ordinary compared to our Italian triumph. . . .

Well, I better end here—I have some studying to do before I go to class. I'll write again soon, with more interesting news (although I doubt that I'll be able to find anything to top this morning's headline feature).

Beat Cal, Collected: Some things span generations, time zones, climates (Also see page 59.)

Photos courtesy of StanfordPhoto.com, (football players), the Stanford Axe Committee (U.K.), and the *Stanford Daily* (Matterhorn).

STANFORD ON THE MATTERHORN: Only the icy thin Alpine air 10,000 feet up the Matterhorn can reduce complex matters of Stanford life to their essential simplicity: Beat Cal! Left to right: Bob Ruth, Dann Boeschen, Jere Webb, all of Stanford-in-Germany, Group XII.

November 18, 1960

Well, only one more day until we BEAT CAL (we hope). If spirit is any indicator, we should be able to wipe them out! Everyone around here is out cheering, and rooting for the team. Last night the freshman men began work on the bonfire, and before they began there was a rally in the lakebed (where they build the structure). At midnight last night we all went down there, and with the band and the cheerleaders, urged the builders on to bigger and better things (the biggest structure built by any class, of course). The Wilbur[26] men worked all night long, and will be there until rally time tonight, completing the massive framework. Tonight, there is an all-school rally and bonfire with fireworks, and then tomorrow is the game itself. . . .

Love,
Elaine

Letter from M.C. to her parents

24 Nov 75

Dear Mom and Dad,

. . . This weekend was Big Game Weekend, & it's a good thing it was after my midterms. Friday night I went to the annual bonfire in the dried-up lake on campus. It was huge & impressive, but after they lit it, I kind of thought it was a waste. There has been a big debate over whether to have the bonfire or not. They probably won't have it next year.

After the bonfire, I came back to the dorm & ended up going to the city with some people from the house. Every year on the night before Big Game, the band marches (more or less, the

LSJUMB[57] is something else!) through the streets & plays at Union and Ghirardelli squares. We got there just in time to walk with the throng to Ghirardelli. It was wild walking/running through the streets of S.F. with a couple other thousand people. After we listened to the band for a while, we went to a deli and got ice cream.

Saturday morning I stood in line for an hour to get into the game. Our house all sat together & we had pretty good seats. There were 90,000 people at the game. The game itself was crummy but the atmosphere was neat. . . .

Love,

M.C.

Texts between Jason Seter and his mother

Jason [2014]

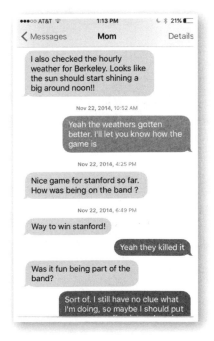

Beat Cal: Further Comments

"Professor Swain read a letter from Dr. Jordan[6] which expressed the sentiment of Sen. Stanford to the effect that whether we were defeated or not, all would conduct themselves with due propriety, and not visit the saloons etc."

—Lucy Allabach, Palo Alto, Cal., Dec. 18, 1892

"Well, we were simply frantic. We jumped up and down in frenzied joy. Some would be standing on the seat of a carriage and get so excited that he would fall out. I fell down myself in the bottom of our equipage and got up again only to have the same thing happen. I did not know what I was doing half the time."

—Austin Kautz, Palo Alto, Dec. 25, 1892

"If you come [to the big game], the females you know all sit together, so I will have to get your ticket when I get mine. I drew no. 14 so can get swell seats. Father & Joe[7] would have to sit in a different division. . . . If you can go please either answer immediately or telegraph me by next Tues. For Tues. we have to be Johnny-on-the-Spot[58] to get our tickets."

—Julia Hamilton Conkling, Oct. 19, 1911

"We play Cal here in basketball next Saturday. . . . Of course we're going to take them to the cleaners."

—Tex Bollman Allen, Jan. 15, 1930

"After we won the game, we all ran across the field to serenade the Cal. rooting section, and Governor Warren presented our student-body president with the Stanford Axe, which always goes to the team who wins the 'Big Game.' I'm sure it was a very impressive ceremony, but I was in such a crowd that I couldn't hear or see a thing."

—Mary Allie Lesnett, Nov. 25, 1946

"I got the tickets for the Big Game on Nov. 22. I bought
six of them at $5.00 apiece. . . . I am now the chairman
from our wing for defense before the Cal game. We defend
the bonfire & Campus from Cal raiders."

—*Bob (Robert) Lowell Swetzer, Nov. 3, 1947*

"This is to announce that Stanford is going to the Rose
Bowl next year. . . . No, we didn't Beat the 'L' out of
Cal (as the saying goes) but it was a great game. Stanford
spirit was at its highest peak."

—*Maryeda Hayes, "After Big Game," Nov. 21, 1954*

"May I PLEASE have the car Saturday night of Big Game
weekend?" Everyone takes a date out for dinner (tradition
says that they go dutch) and then to a dance. If Carl can
have the car when he's in L.A., why can't I have it that
one night?"

—*Joe (Joseph) Lewis Jacobs, Oct. 17, [1961]*

"Dad, I'll be the first one in line to get Big Game
tickets. There's a lot I want to show you up here."

—*Phil (Philip) B. Laird Jr., [Fall] 1966*

"It's actually quite a big rivalry. I'm happy I didn't
fly home before the [Big] game."

—*Mary Caballero, Nov. 2014*

Chapter 3

History at the Farm

"There were quakes all day & all night . . . . They say this will be the ruin of Calif. for 10 years anyway—folks won't send their children back here to college."

—Babe (Mabel) Bartlett, Thurs. a.m., Apr. 19, 1906, the day after the Great San Francisco Earthquake

Death of Senator Stanford

Letters from Lucy Allabach to her sister

Palo Alto, Calif.
Sunday, Sept. 1893

Dear Helen:

I have been to chapel and returned. There were a great many new people out, and Professor Thoburn delivered the sermon. Mrs. Stanford was out but I did not see her to speak with. . . .

Friday night was the reception to new students. . . . Dr. Jordan[6] gave a short address, also professors Marx and Miller. Mrs. Stanford was praised by Dr. Jordan and by all. The estate cannot be settled for two years, and affairs are in such a condition that . . . it seemed as though they must close for a while. Dr. Jordan felt that would never do so Mrs. Stanford has done all she could to cut down her own expenses. The Professors have consented to labor and wait, and here we are. It is going to be a very hard year indeed for the University.

About the first of August it seemed as though it would be necessary to close. The court had decided that no money could be used, except just what came from the estate, so the trustees, president of the Southern Pacific, and the Lathrops[60] all said the University would have to be closed. Dr. Jordan told Mrs. Stanford that that would mean virtual death to the institution. So she said it should go on, and has put at sale brandy, horses, and anything else that would bring money. She has turned off her head cook, and many Chinese help,[61] put her own money to the University, and with Timothy Hopkins as her chief encourager and helper is determined that things shall go on. As someone put it, Senator Stanford could not have died at a more inconvenient time if he had tried. . . .

Already as many have registered as were here last year and more are expected, but this only makes matters worse as of course that means need of more faculty. . . .

March 11, 1894

. . . Friday morning occurred the memorial exercises for Senator Stanford. They were very impressive and dignified. The only applause occurred when President Jordan, Harrison, and the other speakers appeared, and again when Mrs. Stanford and her friends came.

The music was simply exquisite and the [Memorial] Ode was very fine indeed. The speeches short and interesting. The exercises were in the gymnasium, and it was very nicely decorated with palms and ferns.

I must say good bye now with much love,

Lucy

Lawsuit against Stanford

Letter from Rose Payne to an older relative

Sunday Evening
October 13—1895[62]

My dearest Nannie:

Theodora tells me she has written her second letter to you this week & reminds me I am lacking in my record. No doubt she has told you all important events of the week so I shall act as

Bulletin Supplement. We are all excited over examination 1 in French Revolution next Tuesday and my mind is densely befogged in feudal rights & incidents not to mention direct & indirect taxation. . . . Saturday was the jolliest day of all. . . . At Palo Alto we found not a carriage as everything was at the University. There had been a great celebration on account of the decision for the suit—processions, honor brigades. Dr. & Mrs. Jordan had been met at the 5:30 train by the student body & pulled up to the University—the girls carrying Chinese lanterns, & the boys blowing horns and shouting. There was speech-making & bonfires & Dr. Jordan ended with saying that the "doors of Stanford University would never close." — — — Ra ra ra Stanford. . . .

Give warmest love to Aunt Tad and keep a big hug for yourself. I don't have time to discuss lectures with you much—

Your Toodles

Tax Exemption

Letter from Fred (Frederic) Jewell Perry to his mother

**Stanford,
March 5, 1899**

My dear mother:
. . . Thursday we have a holiday here. It is Founders' Day,[63] in commemoration of the great man who founded the greatest university in the West. . . .

Another great source of rejoicing to us here at Stanford is the passage of the tax exemption bill relieving Stanford from the onerous burden of taxation which the State has levied on the University estate.[64]

Only four states in the Union tax their universities, and California has taken the right step now. All that is left to be done is to get the people to vote on the constitutional amendment which comes before the people in the next election. The adoption of this amendment saves to the University annually many thousands. This enormous reduction in expenses will enable Stanford to educate the poor young people of the state free. Berkeley, as a state institution, pays no taxes. If Stanford did not exist the state would have to bear the expense of educating at the State University those who now attend Stanford. Since the State is relieved from this burden it might at least exempt Stanford from the excessive taxation to which this university is subjected. Every Stanford man in California will work like a Spartan to influence the people to vote for the amendment. The Cal is against the movement and is doing all it can to defeat the bill. We who love our Alma Mater will do all we can to overcome the senseless and unreasonable and unfair opposition to this act. Berkeley, I believe, is jealous of the great position which Stanford will occupy in the event of the passage of the amendment. A U.C. regent—an enemy to that progress and culture which he ought to represent—had the unkindness to vote against the proposition in the Legislature. This biased, ungenerous act reveals a meanness of spirit prompted only by envy and ignorance. Stanford is deservedly angry with the attitude which Berkeley has assumed in this uphill struggle of ours.

Good by—till Wed.
With love,
Fred

Jane Stanford's Funeral

Letter from Myron Carlos Burr to his sister

Mar. 24, 1905
Evening

Dear Gladys.—
The funeral is all over. Mrs. Stanford's body lies at rest in the Mausoleum beside those of her husband and son. Stanford University entertained more people today on the campus than have ever been here before or ever will be again for some time to come. The funeral took place in the Memorial Church.[19] Services were simple and quite brief. They began at 1:30 p.m. and closed at the Mausoleum at 4 p.m.

The church was jammed full, about 2,700 people being admitted where 1,700 only is regularly arranged for. Most beautiful music and brief but elegant speeches constituted the program of the church. The students and others formed in line and marched four abreast to the grave where the final services were held. The speech by Rev. Brown there was about the finest that I ever heard.

The floral offerings were magnificent. They came by the wagonload and almost the carload from everywhere. Many of them cost upwards of one hundred dollars apiece. Heard that the Alumni sent one which cost two hundred and fifty dollars. Seems like an enormous amount to pay for floral decorations, does it not?

Each class gave some floral decoration and Wednesday I went to Frisco to select one for the sophomore class. We decided on a wreath of white carnations and violets which cost twenty dollars. . . . Also went down to the docks and saw the big ocean liner "Alameda," in which Mrs. Stanford's body was brought from Hawaii. . . .

One of the floral pieces was a fine representation of the Memorial Church, all of flowers. Another was one of the arches at the ends of the Quad, beautifully designed in many different kinds of flowers.

The Rev. D. Charles Gardner, the chaplain of the University, Mrs. Stanford's favorite minister and the one whom she wished to preach her funeral sermon, was taken ill with typhoid shortly before Mrs. Stanford's death, and even now is quite weak and fearful of the results of the shock of her death. He has not been informed at all of her death, although he lay in bed not a half-mile away from the church all through the services. . . .

Yours very truly,
Myron C. Burr

Jane Stanford

Courtesy of the Stanford University Archives

The Great 1906 San Francisco Earthquake

Letter from Babe (Mabel) Bartlett to her parents

[April 18, 1906]
Wed. a.m.

Dearest Folks—

Strange to say I'm <u>still</u> <u>alive</u>! . . . I never heard such a noise in all my life & things were just flying all over my room. I seemed to be perfectly crazed—all the other girls have some thots but I don't think I thot a single thing.

[We are sitting out on the lawn now waiting for another shock. . . .] [Brackets in original.] Goodbye if the earth swallows us up. We're hoping for the best and are really quite cheerful.

. . . Not a soul in our house was even scratched but Mrs. Spencer was thrown from bed & sprained her ankle. It was about 5 o'clock that it happened. We chased out on the porch in our kimonos barefoot—some in their nightgowns & blankets etc. You never saw such an array & variety of clothes.

After the shock subsided we went in & put on clothes enough to go to the Quad. We could see that the church steeple wasn't to be seen etc. Every chimney on the campus is down—even the great big one. . . . It fell thru them, killed the engineer—those buildings are wrecks. The church is a mass of ruins, can see clear thru it. Simply can't describe its ruin. The Memorial Arch[65] is down—crushed the arches around. The arcades in lots of places are destroyed.

The new gym & library are utterly demolished. Nothing but the frame of the dome standing. These buildings haven't been accepted yet so guess the contractors will have to stand the loss. The big gates are just a pile of stone.

The chimneys fell thru Roble[4] & took the floors with them. Three girls fell thru the floor but no one was hurt over there. Joy, I'm glad I don't live there.

Encina[5] had the same misfortune, the air shafts fell thru taking all the rooms thru to the basement, with their occupants. The boys were working hard digging the poor fellows out. One was dead & the others badly hurt. Guess the hospital was full. I'll bet there was lots of heroic work done around by all the boys & everybody.

The Chi Psi House is the worst of the residences. It is shoved over to 1 side & all collapsed like a card playhouse. . . .

The earthquake could not have been at a <u>better</u> time—light, yet all in bed—just before the fires were started for breakfast, because the stoves & chimneys are all to pieces. We finally had some coffee & bread for breakfast—cook things on a campfire in the backyard. Just think if folks had been on the Quad 100's would have been killed. It is <u>perfect</u>ly <u>miracul</u>ous that any of us are alive. Sadie's bed collapsed with her. We are all planning to sleep outdoors tonight. Heavens I'll live in mortal terror of another. I forgot to tell you—[I got just this far when there was 1 horrid shock & I leaped wildly off the porch—it's over now.] [Brackets in original.] As I was saying—well, another terrible shock & off I leaped—the house was just tw<u>isting</u>. I'm on the lawn again now—there are lots of little shakers but I'm so brave now I don't mind little shocks. I was just about to tell you that the terrific shock predicted this a.m. didn't come—just slight ones like this p.m. . . . They say the earth is apt to open.

. . . I filed a telegram to be sent to you as soon as the wires are in shape. Heavens I'm praying you are all right & only wish you knew I was so. I know you're about crazy—no doubt you've heard terrible rumors. It certainly has never been equalled. Dr. Jordan said nowhere in the world [was there] such a demolition of stone buildings.

I had 5 pictures left in my Brownie Kodak so took it with me this a.m. before they shut off the Quad. Palie is in ruins so guess I couldn't get any more films—I was lucky to have that many. . . .[66]

I don't see when we can begin work—of course they'll have to inspect all the buildings before we can have class. Lots of the arches that are perfect otherwise have their keystones just hanging so you see nothing is safe.

Madrono[67] is condemned & not a soul can enter—poor homeless girls—I tell you there are lots homeless. The inspectors are just here.

. . . Say I want to tell you something really funny out of all this disaster. One of the big statues in the front of the zoology building took a headlong plunge & poked his old head right thru the cement & is standing there heels in the air.[68]

I never imagined I'd ever see ruins like these—just like old castle ruins. Whoever thot yesterday that this a.m. Stanford—all its wonderful, massive buildings—would be in ruins.

. . . Well, guess I'll quit. Can't do any good to rave on thusly—so good-bye. . . . Heavens how I wish I could hear from you.

The sky is all overcast with smoke from S.F. My it gives the atmosphere a funny—spooky feeling.

Lots & lots of love to all
Babe

[P.S.] Heavens this semester has been one continual round of troubles & to think this should be the climax or maybe something worse will happen tho i don't see how it could.

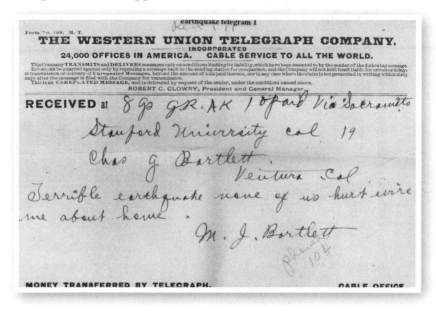

Telegram Home: Babe (Mabel) Bartlett, April 19, 1906

Courtesy of the Stanford University Archives

"The Bedroom": "Guess we'll sleep outdoors or on the porch again tonight." —Babe (Mabel) Bartlett, April 19, 1906

Courtesy of the Stanford University Archives

Louis Agassiz statue post-earthquake, 1906

Courtesy of the Stanford University Archives

Women and the Vote

Letter from Julia Hamilton Conkling to her mother

Wed. afternoon, [Oct. 11, 1911][69]

Dear mother,

. . . Dr. Mosher gave us a long talk, very pathetic indeed, this a.m. on how ashamed we, the educated part of the population, should be that the suffrage for women did not go thru. We have not done our duty, she says. She wept between speeches. She is so ashamed of herself, poor thing. She asked me about a couple of weeks ago if I was not for suffrage for women, & I said, "Oh of course." I knew it would save lots of time & trouble for both of us if I said that, so she gave me a little yellow vote for women button which I never once wore. . . .

The 12th Infantry Prepares

Letter from Julia Hamilton Conkling to her mother

Friday 7:00 a.m., [April 24, 1914]

It is so exciting here at college, I can scarcely sit still long enough to write. We have not slept for 2 nights at all. You know, I think I told you, the 12th Infantry has been camped just back of our house for about a week & they have been expecting word to leave any day & have been drilling every day in the field in front of our house. Their band was wonderful & believe me there has been some excitement. Night before last there was excitement started & the crazy fellows here all started to volunteer. Any fellow who volunteers gets his hrs. We sat up till almost 2, we could not go to bed. Yesterday they drilled all day & 8 o'clock last night orders came to leave. We were at a Catholic entertainment in the Armory[70] when a priest announced for the infantry to answer to their command at once. Everybody cheered while the soldiers left & a few minutes later when we left the Armory, we saw every one [of the] soldiers & all going for the encampment. We followed & found that orders had come to break camp & leave for Texas so we went on up to the camp & watched them pack. . . . By 12 o'clock everything was packed practically & the soldiers all sat around on the hills & the band played & they sang old-time songs you know. There were hundreds of students there & we all stayed & sat on the hills & sang with them. It was the most interesting sight I ever saw. But I was seized by such sadness I could hardly say a word. As they were not leaving till 6 we came home at about 2 & in our excitement tried to sleep but unsuccessfully. At 5 we got up & dressed & went back & found a huge crowd of students again & we watched them march off at 5:30. Before they left the college boys cheered for them loud & long & finally the whole infantry marched to the Mayfield depot.[49] It really seems like things you read about, it doesn't seem real. . . . How we will be able to study for finals I don't know. . . .

Tell me, is there any danger in El Centro [California]? Can we stay there all summer with safety? There are so many stories floating around I don't get the true drift of things at all. . . .

Love & Kisses
Julia

Quarantine

Letter from Hope Snedden to her father

Stanford Univ., Calif.
October 24, 1918

Dear Dad,

. . . Wilbur[71] quarantined us to the campus. . . .

I think the influenza is on the wane here. There are only 109 S.A.T.C.[72] men in the hospital. We have only had one girl & eight men die. . . .

. . . Just tonight the campus has suddenly blossomed forth in white gauze masks. Ruling from headquarters. You have to tie them on just below your eyes, & the girls look as if they had just escaped from a Turkish harem, or an advertisement for Fatima cigarettes. And you can't imagine the ludicrous appearance of a tall S.A.T.C. man sneaking into the library with one of them on, with the look of a highwayman. And you can't recognize your friends by their eyes. We're waiting for tomorrow to see our professors try to lecture in them. . . .

Much love,
from, Hope

Great War Over

Letter from Hope Snedden to her mother

"Great War Over": Hope Snedden, Nov. 12, 1918

Courtesy of the Stanford University Archives

[Below is a continuation of the letter pictured on the previous page]

schoolhouse. Already, all the S.A.T.C. fellows had turned out &
were there in ranks, with a band & all their officers. The parade
started & we marched to Palo Alto, down the Avenue from
Memorial Church. In the half light, the S.A.T.C. fellows with
their rifles looked almost like veterans, & there seemed to be
endless numbers of them. All along the way, people set off red
flares that lit up the palm trees & everything around.

In Palo Alto, all the electric lights were going, & the townspeople
were all out with flags, making all the racket they could. There
were quite a number of elderly couples walking around, carrying
American flags & service flags.

A fellow got up on top of an auto & led the cheering. Everybody
wanted to cheer. They began with the United States, & went thru
Pershing & Foch all the way to Captain Parker of the S.A.T.C.

Then everybody marched back to Stanford again, sort of calmed
down, & almost afraid such glorious news couldn't be true. It was
then about 3 a.m. All the fellows started singing: "Some day I'm
going to murder the bugler" etc.

Most of the girls didn't go to bed at all until morning. When I
went out at 6:30, everything was quiet. But the papers in front of
everybody's front door had in big headlines:

"Great War Over."

What did the "Times" say? Wilbur refused to give us a holiday
altho the Governor proclaimed one for the state. . . .

Last night the peace terms came out, & everybody hung around
reading them. All the girls were interested, altho some had rather
hazy notions. One asked me whether these peace terms had been
drawn up by the Germans.

The only thing that worries us now is that the German rebels refuse to accept these terms. Still, I suppose it would be easy to beat a divided Germany. But everybody surely hopes the fighting is done with.

The Clarks are hoping they can hear from Birge pretty soon. It is a month since they have heard from him. Mrs. Clark will be so relieved now. She has been reading everything on the subject of ballooning & knows just how they are shot down. . . .

. . . The minutes certainly do drag in . . . [history] class. But I see that there are possibilities for history to be about the most interesting subject in the college curriculum.

Last night, I heard Prof. Krehbiel. He had come directly from his S.F. Food Administration office to speak on "Modern France." I never heard a man speak in such a simple & informal way & yet say so much. People just naturally didn't notice how long he spoke because they were so interested. He had arranged three months ago to speak here, but then, he said, he had no idea it would be on such a momentous occasion. One thing he said that was rather interesting: last January, as we knew, we had exhausted our surplus of wheat, 20 million bushels. Hoover cabled this to Lord Rhondda, explained that all we could send England for the next six months before the new harvest came in would be what the American people voluntarily saved. It was then that Lord Rhondda pulled down the top of his rolltop desk, turned to the gentlemen around him & said: "Gentlemen, the war is over, & we are defeated." In spite of that, however, Krehbiel said that up to Sept 1st we had sent over 150 million bushels of wheat. Does that stand to reason? Krehbiel hopes people can still be as patriotic & unselfish as when the only thing in sight was to win the war.

William writes that he has been up with an instructor, & that there is nothing like it. Ruth & I may get a chance yet to fly.

It will be too bad if Francis doesn't get his commission when he deserves to have it.[73] Do you think he will?

Wonderful news we've been having the last few days. But I hardly dare buy a paper for fear there'll be some more lightning changes. Things happen so quickly. . . .

Hopkinton [New Hampshire] & everything about it just seems a dream here at Roble, & I come to believe I graduated from Horace Mann last year. It is surely joyful to be here with so many nice girls. Just in the three days I have been here, I have gotten to know quite a few.

Miss Gardiner, who is head of this place, recognized me because of you whom she knew.

The war is over!

With love,
Hope.

Dewey-Roosevelt

Letter from Mary Allie Lesnett to her parents

October 7, 1944

Dear Mother and Daddy,
. . . Everyone here is very enthusiastic about the election, so am I. I've decided now that I am definitely for Dewey. I've been having discussions with everybody about it and something [my piano teacher] Mrs. Bilenky said made me very convinced. I've decided that if Roosevelt wins the election, as he probably will, we will be proving to the rest of the world that a democracy is

not a workable government, because in a democracy it is the form of government and not the men in the government which are important. . . . They are saying that he is too indispensable to be removed now. In a democracy there should not be any man so indispensable that he can't be removed at any time, [and] if there is a man so indispensable, then the government is no longer a democracy—and I'm awfully afraid American democracy is at an end. . . .

Love to all,
Mary

United Nations Conference on International Organization

Letter from (Mary) Carol Stearns to her mother

Wed Apr 25, [Mid-1940s]

Dear Mother—
. . . While in SF we saw lots of interesting delegates [at the United Nations Conference on International Organization]—all in the costume of their country—Sheik Arabs, Russians with boots, Indians with head dresses. At the lobby of the St. Francis an American officer saluted a Russian—Instead of returning with any similar ceremony, the Russian stopped & grinned—then kind of sillily [sic] aped the U.S. salute with his left hand. Gee, the atmosphere is tremendous. Hope I get to go again. . . .

Write soon,
Carol

V-E Day

Letter from (Mary) Carol Stearns to her mother

Tuesday—V-E Day!
[May 8, 1945]

It's half-over. . . . At 11:00 a.m. we had a service in the chapel—Dr. Tresidder spoke—quite inspiring.[74] After lunch we all sat around the radio & listened to the celebration & speeches in England. No one here seems particularly hilarious—I suppose because of the false rumor & the talk going around about the end of the war. Everyone knew it had come, & so there didn't seem to be much to shout about when the final announcement came.

The week of the hellish midterms is over too. I don't know how I did on them yet. . . .

. . . Sunday he [Jake] came down about 12:30. I was working on a paper & didn't want to go sit around & watch them drink beer all day so I just didn't answer. . . . As I knew, we went to Rossotti's,[75] played cards—& they drank beer. . . .

. . . Friday night was the Soph Carnival over in the Boy's Gym. Each living group had some kind of concession. We had nail pounding—popular in spite of the drollness. Most of the houses had stuff like water dunking, mud-throwing—quite humorous. There were rat-races, fortune-telling, taxi-dances—I was dead—since I'd had both midterms that morning & had with 2 other girls that afternoon completely built our booth. That evening for supper we went out to Woodland's Hollow & had a hamburger fry. I sure had fun.

Did I tell you that the administration announced we'll have a Naval ROTC unit here—for sure—in Nov.—300 men from the fleet—so they shouldn't be too young. No football yet. . . .

Write.
Love,
Carol

Kennedy-Nixon

Letters from Elaine Lavis to her family

November 10, 1960

Dear Family,

Well, the events of the last two days certainly have been exciting ones. This election, if nothing else, will give everyone a lot to talk about for a long time. I know I'll certainly remember it!

On Tuesday night, early in the evening, listening to the radio, a Kennedy victory seemed pretty evident, and the margin seemed fairly large. Even up to the time I went over to listen to the T.V. set in the Medical Students' lounge with Victor, the margin was still a respectable one, and it just seemed like a matter of an hour or so until the final, winning electoral votes would be given to Kennedy. But, when I came back here to study, and was listening to the radio, the margin between the two in popular vote was becoming smaller and smaller. Then Nixon came on T.V. and made a statement that was not a concession, and then the Kennedy camp replied that Kennedy would not say anything until the next day, after Nixon again spoke. So, we went to bed, with the feeling that Kennedy probably had won. . . .

The next morning, the news said that he had won, but that the votes in such key states as California were still not all in, and the margin of the popular vote was still decreasing. By yesterday afternoon, it was pretty well all over—Kennedy and Nixon had spoken, and Kennedy was President. But the vote counters were still at work, (and still are, as a matter of fact) and as they progress the two candidates practically have the same number of votes. So, the way it stands now, we have a President who will have as many enemies as supporters, which is something to think about.

The one thing this election will do, hopefully, is set a lot of people thinking about the electoral college system. I hear that the Majority Leader of the Senate is already proposing legislation to abolish it, which is certainly overdue. . . . I heard an election official from California quoted on the radio as saying that it was ridiculous for a state as large and important as California to have to wait for so many hours before the vote was tabulated.

Well, enough for the comments on the election. We'll be getting them for a long time to come, anyhow, in the papers and on the radio.

Last night, I went to hear the poet Robert Frost speak, to an over-capacity audience in Memorial Auditorium.[21] He is an amazing man—he is eighty-six, but still has a remarkable amount of vitality, and certainly is as sharp as ever. . . . He made comments on the election, of course, saying such things as "It was a triumph of Protestantism—over itself," and "They don't praise ladies anymore; they let them vote." Along with some of his philosophy, he read several of his poems; some old favorites, and some more recent ones. Now, all Stanford has to do is to get Carl Sandburg out here to speak, and then my year will be complete. . . .

P.S. Please excuse the spotty look of this letter. I'm really not that uncoordinated, and can usually hit the right key. It's just that I've been having trouble with my typewriter—it sticks in several places. This has been going on for a little while, and seems to be getting worse, so I'll have to take it to be fixed as soon as I get the time. It's just awfully annoying. . . .

Saturday, January 21, 1961
. . . I had to leave for my English ten o'clock class before Kennedy was sworn in, or gave his speech. I read the text of his inaugural address in the paper this morning, and was very impressed, and sorry that I didn't get to hear him deliver it in person. But, I was happy to have been able to see all that I did—it was certainly thrilling. . . . But, actually, it was a little annoying to think that we didn't get a chance to get out of class and see the entire ceremony—such things happen only once every four years, and are of more than passing interest and significance, historically. But far be it for this center of higher learning to slow its pace for anything—except such earthshaking events . . . as football games, etc. . . .

Love,
Elaine

Orbiting the Earth

Letter from Elaine Lavis to her family

Tuesday, February 20, 1962

Well, we woke up this morning, and heard the man on the radio say, "This is history" and then we realized that they had shot the astronaut up into space, and that he was flying around up there. Pretty exciting, I must say—think, he's up there watching us! Now the radio is reporting on his orbits around the earth, and is giving reports from the different tracking stations that the capsule is passing. But, somehow, the flight itself seems anti-climactic, or at least in comparison with the take-off and the landing. Perhaps this is because at these two essential points in the flight, so much happens in such a short time, while the flight period itself is much longer, and as many things don't seem to be happening—the news commentator has to keep filling in with a bunch of non-essential but interesting side-lights. We'll have to wait now for the landing, which probably won't be for a few hours yet—perhaps we'll watch that on T.V. Like the man said, "This is history." . . . Well, the man in space is still flying around—he's over Mexico now, and fast approaching the California coast. It's time for me to go to my Shakespeare class now, so I'll mail this letter on the way, and perhaps I can wave to the space capsule on my way too! . . .

Love,
Elaine

Cuban Missile Crisis

Letter from Elaine Lavis to her family

Thursday, October 25, 1962

. . . I don't know how coherent this letter will be—I'm sitting here listening to the radio, trying to hear the noontime news, and see what has happened in the world since this morning. (It's a rather strange feeling going to class at nine, and not hearing anything for three hours, while knowing that so much can be going on.) From the way it sounds, the place to be watched now is the U.N. This afternoon's session will contain an important statement by Stevenson, and then one by the Soviet delegate. The student atmosphere seems to be much stiller today than it has been in the last few days—perhaps the shock of the crisis has worn off, and the students are going back to their usual apathy. Amazingly, the students did show quite a response the first few days, which is unusual for Stanford students in relation to any world events. The dinner conversations for the past few nights actually have been serious, but now I think we'll probably be back to the usual inane banalities—the next fraternity party, etc. Of course, the major concern of many girls the past few days was, unbelievably, that: "wouldn't it be awful if something happened, and all the boys had to go into the service, and we were here at Stanford without any boys? What would our social life be like then!" . . .

Love,
Elaine

THE PRESIDENT IS DEAD
GAME, ALL ACTIVITIES CANCELLED

Special
Edition

THE STANFORD DAILY

"The Peninsula's Only Morning Newspaper"

EDITORIAL OFFICE: DA 2-2166, BUSINESS OFFICE: DA 3-1301   STANFORD, CALIFORNIA, FRIDAY, NOVEMBER 22, 1963   VOLUME 144, NUMBER 46

Big Game On Next Week; Other Activities in Doubt

JFK Shot by Assassin During Dallas Motorcade

THE PRESIDENT

Johnson Assumes Office, Arrives in Washington

Gov. Connally Also Injured; LBJ, Mrs. Kennedy Unhurt

It Can't Happen Here

'Fair Play For Cuba' Leader Prime Suspect

Mourning on Campus: *Stanford Daily*, Special Edition, Nov. 22, 1963

Courtesy of the *Stanford Daily*

JFK Assassination

Letter from Gary to his family

Nov. 23, 1963
2:00 p.m.

Hi All,

The University is in a state of mourning. All of the classes for Monday are cancelled and all of the Big Game events were postponed until next week. There were to be many post-game parties in San Francisco on this Saturday night at the big-name hotels in the City. The ballrooms were reserved and now it is impossible to have them next week. Big Game spirit is very low, and many people expect a crowd of 60,000. On Friday morning before 10:00 a.m. Big Game fever was at a peak. Tickets were at a premium and some were sold for as high as $20. Now these same people who sold their tickets can buy from students that are going home for Thanksgiving for as little as 2 or 3 dollars. This makes a large profit for someone.

I enclosed a copy of the Daily[2] EXTRA that came out at about 10 p.m. last night (Fri.). You don't need to keep it as I have a couple of other copies. The TV in the lounge has been constantly operating since yesterday morning with news, pictures, etc.

I haven't received the clam shells, but I expect by the time you read this, they will have [arrived]. . . .

Otherwise everything is fine with me, and I expect to be home for Thanksgiving, at least for the dinner.

Gary

Protest after Protest

Letter from Phil (Philip) B. Laird Jr. to his family

5/8/68[76]
10:30 p.m.

Dear Family,

. . . I suppose you'd like to hear about the "sit-in" and such; so I guess maybe I'll talk awhile about that.

It has been pretty interesting around here, to say the least. You see, seven students are recommended for suspension for participation in a demonstration against the C.I.A. last fall by the Interim Judiciary Council (all faculty) after they had been pronounced innocent by the Student Judiciary Board (all student). Both of the boards were to be temporary until a combined judiciary board was established. (They have been working on the combined board for 3 years.) Anyway, the more radical element of students decided that this administration was not taking student attitude into consideration and decided that the only way to force the issue was to have a "sit-in" in the Old Student Union, which is the student services office, in order to force communication.

Well, I was really indignant about this, as were a great number of the more conservative members of the student body (mainly fraternities), and I'm sure you read about the anti-demonstrators, because for once we escaped our normal state of apathy and voted to get them out of the Union.

The point that I should make clear is that in principle, I agree with much of what the demonstrators demand. There should be more student participation in control of what goes at Stanford, particularly in student affairs. This is what is causing unrest in universities across the country—the refusal of administrations to recognize student abilities, student desire for participation in their own education, and the continuance of an administrative attitude tending more toward paternalism rather than equality.

I maintain, give the students (who you must admit are adults) more of a voice in what is taking place in universities— more of a voice, not all of it, but more than they've got now.

. . . I think you understand what I said. No, I don't like the tactics they chose to employ; but I am forced to admit that they in actuality did little harm and they did achieve a great deal—people are concerned all over campus and the administration is listening. . . .

Love you all,
Phil

Vietnam and Cambodia

Letter from Lanny Levin to his family

May 5, 1970

Dear family,
I haven't heard from you in a while, so I thought I'd write, especially since so many important things have been happening all over. Right now Stanford University is in the middle of a

strike. It is a strike <u>of</u> the University for the most part, rather than <u>against</u> the University. Although there is some coercion involved, I see the strike more as a suspension of "business as usual" for the purpose of directing energies, thoughts, and resources toward educating ourselves and the community about the war in Vietnam—particularly its escalation into an Indochine War—and toward organizing for action against the war.

The announcement of the invasion of Cambodia hit like a bombshell in the midst of a violent struggle to eliminate ROTC from the campus. Rock-throwing, window-breaking, and confrontations with police had reached crisis proportions by last Thursday, and the President's speech was the straw that broke the whole campus' back. Overnight, a strike was organized, and Friday class attendance was negligible—by Monday, Stanford was unofficially shut down.

The ROTC issue had really polarized the campus, especially because of the violence that accompanied it. The most recent events have at least partially united the campus. By Thursday I was not only in a great quandary about what to do and think personally, but I was getting a cold, and feeling miserable in general. On the spur of the moment, Bob and I decided to take off for Los Angeles for a much-needed rest. . . .

So far I have spent the week going to meetings, rallies, talking to many people; I have written to senators Percy and Smith, and have been doing a tremendous amount of thinking. I cannot write about all that has been happening, either inside or outside my head, but I would like to share some of my thoughts with you. I am anxious to be home so that I can express myself better and hear what you think. . . .

I believe that the use of the American Military in the last decade has been in many cases wrong, immoral, unwise, reactionary, and exploitive. I believe that with a military as large as ours these kinds of actions are almost inevitable. I see the draft as a device for ensuring an almost infinite supply of manpower for the military, and therefore the decision to use American armed forces is not as carefully arrived at as might be necessary were there not an easily available pool of men. I see ROTC as an extension of the military which I now deeply distrust, and as a relatively easily accessible pool of upper-class and middle-class potential leadership for the military.

Although I cannot honestly say that I am opposed to all forms of violence, I am outraged at the proportions of the violence being perpetrated by our country, and I seek a means to limit it. I am not so naive as to believe in any kind of devil-theory that claims military responsibility for all that diplomatically and morally ails this country, but military power and political power are very closely related, as are policy decisions and the size of the "military club." This means that both the political decisions themselves and the arms that make the decisions feasible must be criticized and changed. . . .

Regarding the President's decision to invade Cambodia, I will not launch into another long spiel. I am against our presence as policemen and reactionaries and anti-communists in S.E. Asia to begin with; I am in favor of the withdrawal of all American troops; therefore I am outraged at the re-escalation of the whole war, despite Mr. Nixon's feeble claims that this is not an invasion of Cambodia. I reject and am insulted by the emotionalism and the entire tone of Nixon's appeal to the nation on behalf of the United States' credibility, its continuance as a first-rate power, and so on. I resent his double-think, double-talk method of claiming that we're sending troops into Cambodia so as to ensure the withdrawal of troops on schedule and so as to protect the troops already there. The way to protect our brave American fighting men is to bring them home, not send them off to more battles. And while we're on the subject, I resent Nixon's labeling of campus protesters as "bums," and Agnew's meddling personal comments encouraging the ouster of Kingman Brewster at Yale for telling the truth that Bobby Seale or any other Black revolutionary cannot get a fair trial in the U.S. WHEW!!!!!!!!!

I know you have a lot of things on your mind, looking for a job and so forth, but I would like you, next time you sit down to write me a letter, to also write a letter to one of our senators, congressmen, or to the President. Would you let me know who our U.S. Representative is? Yates? Pucinski? I wasn't sure. I hope you are reading and talking about the issues of the day with all your friends, and that you will let them know that students are doing some real hard thinking, not just mindless violence the media so often imply. . . .

The strike is scheduled to continue through Friday at least—depending on local and national events, we'll have to wait and see what happens after that.

Love,

Lanny

P.S. Please save this letter.

Divestment from Apartheid South Africa

Letter from M.C. to her parents

18 May 77

Dear Mom and Dad,

. . . Hey, I almost forgot. Did you all ever hear anything about the protest out here a week ago last Monday? It made the CBS news Tuesday night, but not NBC. I was just wondering if it was in the papers or anything. It was a pretty big deal (1,500 people protesting; 700 sitting-in, 300 getting arrested) but it's too involved to go into here. . . .

Bye, will see you soon. Really. (Like 3 weeks & 4 days.) . . .

Love,
M.C.

Loma Prieta Earthquake

Letter from Dan Lythcott-Haims to his father

21 October, 1989

Dear Dad,

Not to be punny but that earthquake really shook things up. It's made a lot of people rethink a lot of things. When I saw people from the Marina District in S.F. risking their lives to save coffee tables and teddy bears from their condemned apartment buildings I just started to wonder. How can these things still be important to these people? They almost lost their lives and they're complaining about not being let into their teetering buildings. I wouldn't want to go near those buildings.

Nonetheless, down here at Stanford where the damage is a little less obvious, there are still many things to consider. After all, campus is only a mile or so from the fault, and there is no reason a quake wouldn't strike right here as opposed to anywhere else. When I saw freshmen sitting outside Branner[77] while the building inspectors checked the foundation, I just felt sorry for them. Only a few weeks into their Stanford careers and already many of them were talking about leaving. It was bad enough that the U.S. News & World Report survey placed us sixth again among American universities (just behind Duke!) but now this. There were a lot of pensive people on a lot of lawns around here.

Physiologically, the earthquake stays with you for long after the fifteen seconds they say it lasts. My legs were shaking long after the earth was still. But there's no way to really tell whether the shaking you feel is your legs or an aftershock. Seismologists have recorded over 1,500 aftershocks in the last four days. That's not a typo: fifteen Hundred!

Half of me wants to get a T-shirt printed and the other half is disgusted by the idea of capitalizing on such a tragedy. I think it'll be quite some time before I feel comfortable wearing an "I survived the quake" shirt when there are so many who didn't.

It's hard to imagine how the rest of the world is treating this tragedy. I'm sure if I was back East I would be rather nonplussed. That's the risk. Anybody living out in California knows quite well what could happen. Sure, but until it happens it's impossible to fathom just how it makes you feel. It's like living on a military target range. We are all sitting ducks.

I want to say "enough gloom!" and get on with things, but it just isn't that easy. There were quite a few irate students after Don Kennedy[78] announced that classes were to resume on Thursday. There are 500 students living in lounges and gymnasiums! There is no doubt a small part of me that's thinking "will my car make it to NY?" And that's terrible. The danger was always here. It just wasn't so obvious before. Well, now I have a heavy-duty flashlight.

Anyway, don't worry. I am O.K. Really.

Love,
Dan

Coal Divestment

Email from Nicole Bennett–Fite to her mother

From: Nicole Bennett-Fite
Subject: Stanford divests from coal!
Date: May 6, 2014 at 6:10:14 PM EDT
To: Victoria Bennett

!!!!!!!!!!

History at the Farm: Further Comments

"Last Saturday our basketball team played against a team from Castelligo Hall [sic] and were beaten. This is the initiation of public athletics for the girls here."

—Lucy Allabach, Palo Alto, Mar. 22, 1894

"Dr. Mosher is very happy over the victory of suffrage & so are all the girls. I never saw such a bunch of suffragettes as there are here."

—Julia Hamilton Conkling, Los Gatos, Oct. 15, 1911

"Dr. Jordan was the first president of Stanford and has been everywhere and knows everyone. He was in Europe trying to prevent a World War in nineteen fourteen and he lectured tonight on conditions in Europe. He says Poincaré was and is as eager for war as the Kaiser."

—Burnham P. Beckwith, Jan. 22, 1923

"Helen Wills Moody played an exhibition match here Friday afternoon and is she wonderful? She defeated the Stanford captain 6-2. I now am the proud possessor of a brand new personally autographed tennis ball from Miss Helen Wills."

—Tex Bollman Allen, Sunday afternoon, Mar. 2, 1930

"Wasn't Joe Louis's fight something?"

—Johnny (John) Murray Huneke, Encina Hall, Dec. 7, 1947

"Pierce Olson and I have been investigating the Reserves of The Army & the Navy—but I haven't decided anything. Pierce is enlisting in the Army Intelligence Reserve Corps tomorrow. I'll let you know if I decide to make a move."

—Bob (Robert) Lowell Swetzer, Jan. 18, 1951

"Well, since the world didn't end, I must be off to class, before I'm late."

—Elaine Lavis, Tuesday, Feb. 6, 1962

"It seems as if everyone is basing their choice on whom they don't like, rather than who they think is qualified, which is a sad state of affairs. That is, people will say 'I'm voting for Brown because I hate Nixon' or 'I'm voting for Nixon because Brown would be a disaster.'"

—Elaine, on the California gubernatorial race,
Tuesday, Nov. 6, 1962

"This all ties in with the 'sit-in,' which I'm sure you read about. I can't believe this big beautiful university—I'm continually more impressed with the people here and the fantastic ability of everyone to understand one another. Less than an hour ago President Pitzer[79] put his job on the line and really supported the students. I'm afraid that I keep becoming more radical—there's so much to change and so little time to do it."

—Phil (Philip) B. Laird Jr., Apr. 18, 1969

Chapter 4

Student Life in the Main

"Sorry the letter is so short, but if you get all the letters I wrote together, you'll have a history."

—(William) Russell Smith, Jan. 30, 1938

1890s

Letters from Lucy Allabach to her mother

Roble Hall[4]
November 7, 1891

Dear Mama:

. . . I don't seem to be thrown much with the boys anywhere, as I'm not that kind, and I guess it is usually shown in my manner and as report says there are many at Encina[5] who are not desirable and the faculty are going to thin them out so I'm going slow.

It is hard to tell who is rich here from externals. All dress well but not with much style, and there is not much dressing and no one dresses better than Minnie and I. They all seem to be able to be free and easy with money to go to Frisco or buy what they want but more in that way than any other.

We have addresses in the Chapel on Sunday mornings, given by some city minister or other proper person. Dr. Jordan[6] gave one and Professor Earl Barnes gives the address, his subject being "The Child's Religion." There are besides, Sunday classes for Bible study and a Sunday evening meeting. . . .

I have had callers but once and then four boys were here on Hallo'e'en, and they called on the other girls also, so don't worry about my Sundays or callers as yet. . . . The girls are very pleasant and the nicest have been very kind to us, and Mattie Haven who lives in Oakland was so disappointed that we were going home with Elsie Shelley for Thanksgiving as she wanted us herself. . . .

Last evening one of the girls from Sacramento had an elegant big cake sent her, and she had a dozen girls in to help eat it and I never tasted better. We get together in this way quite often for the purpose of devouring a jar of jam or cookies that some girl has brought. . . .

I fixed my suit this morning, and I've done some sewing nearly every Saturday morning and I'm tired of it. I shan't fix my blue dress till next spring. . . .

April 7, 1892[80]

Well, as Mrs. Barnes says, "she has me." And thus it is, or rather happened.

As her appointment does not go into effect until August, she asked Dr. Jordan if she might make any orders before that time so as to be sure to have everything ready. He told her to act as though she were queen and go ahead. Then she told him she would like some student to assist her and make charts and maps.

"Very well," he said, "there is Mr. Hughes who does such things very nicely, and you can get him to do it for you."

"But," puts in Mrs. Barnes, "I should like to have Miss Allabach do it."

"Can Miss Allabach do it as well?" asks the worthy president. Of course she did not know that, but at any rate there was no objection to me if I could do the work.

Then she proceeded to ask Professor Brown. He, in his usual manner, said of course he could not say till he saw me try, but that I had somewhat of an artistic sense and at any rate did not discourage her.

So I am to try.

"And so," she says, "you see just where we stand." The question that they ask is: "Will we do it as well as Mr. H., or some man?"

At any rate I told her we would learn all that those men could teach us and they at least cannot criticise. It may be that her health will not permit us to [do] anymore than get started this year, and it may be that we can do quite a good deal yet before school is out. She seems very glad that she can have me, for it will be so much more pleasant than to have a young man with her.

[Lucy]

Letter from Herbert C. Hoover to a friend

Palo Alto, Cal.
Aug. 30, 1892

My dear Friend,[81]
Find enclosed various documents bearing on several subjects of minor importance. Also will send you a catalog of the Palo Alto School. There is another famous preparatory school at Belmont—price $600 and still another at San Mateo—$400. Belmont graduates enter Harvard, Yale, & Stanford.

Prospects for 1,000 students. Snow goes.[82] No law department, no Horticulture, and no money.

Am going into baggage business at the beginning of school.

Got the encouraging news from my guardian that he has not a—cent & consequently am out with just $46.23 to get through the year. Dr. B.[83] says I can swim it if not he will throw in a cork.[84]

Halls open tomorrow. All white labor. No Chinese around anywhere.[85] Am working awful hard. Have considerable business worked up & 300000000000 schemes for making more.

May the Gods use you better than I.

Extra Hastily

H.C.H.

Letter from Herbert C. Hoover courtesy of the University of Oregon Special Collections and University Archives

Rock Study: Herbert Hoover, second from left (standing), geology class, 1894 Courtesy of the Hoover Institution Archives

---

Letters from Rose Payne To an older relative

Dec. 15, 1895

My dearest Nannie,—

. . . There has been great excitement over cheating. Through the very bold dishonesty of one girl and several boys in the Economics Department, it was discovered that cheating was a very general practice among the students. The girl was expelled as were three boys, and public feeling ran high both for and against. There was a meeting of the student body last

Wednesday when it was decided that a committee of seven students be appointed to be inferior to that of the faculty on student affairs. When anyone was reported as being seen cheating the name of the accuser and the accused was to be brought up in the lower court and judgement should be passed as to whether appeal should be made to the faculty committees. The meeting was a very stormy one and quite an experience in college life, but finally the vote was in majority for such a cooperation with the faculty in eradicating so grave an evil. We were opposed to it on the ground of its narrow, spying foundation but we were in the minority. . . . Friday night the chemical laboratory was burned out owing to someone leaving the gas lighted and the carelessness of the night watch. Of course, the building is not in the least damaged but the loss of apparatus was quite discouraging. . . .

Tuesday—Dec. 17—[18]95
. . . Oh I had a letter from Helen Lathrop asking me to spend the second week of vacation with her at her aunt's lovely home at San Quentin[86] and I have accepted—isn't that lovely— Christmas week we are going to be with the Myrick's and I am going to have a new dress. Theodora is loaded with exams and can't write—just now she is asleep.

your R

Letter from Theodora Payne to an older relative

January 1st 1897

My dear Nannie—

It seems very natural to write 1897. . . . I suppose Rose did not write you of the scrape a fortnight ago at the hall—You see Mrs. Stanford put a matron in who was thoroughly incompetent and when at the beginning of my vacation I came here Rose and Helen together with many other girls were most desirous of leaving the hall fearing something dreadful would happen and the cloud fall on all. It came sooner than expected in the form of 7 girls becoming intoxicated on the 4th floor and making [the] night hideous by their yells and screams. Two of the profs. were promptly summoned as the culprits defied Mrs. Clements and a few days after, all the offending girls were requested to leave the hall and were permanently suspended. Later Mrs. Clements received her notice that her place was declared vacant and she left the next morning on an early train saying goodbye to no one. And now Dr. Jordan with his usual aptness has chosen Mrs. Baker, chaperone of the Zeta-Psi Frat., to mother the girls and if she will only consent to it—will simply revolutionize Roble and give it an atmosphere of culture that it has never enjoyed even under Miss Thompson. You see Dr. Jordan was absent at the time and those were days of suspense but he is so prompt and decisive in everything he does. One feels so protected just to see him swing along to and from the quadrangle. . . .

Theodora

Hat Tricks: Fred Perry (likely second to left, standing) and friends in gear for the Plug Ugly[a]

Courtesy of the *Stanford Quad*

Letter from Fred (Frederic) Jewell Perry to his mother

April 9, 1899

My dear mother:

. . . This letter has several times been interrupted in the course of construction. First a fellow came in who occupied my time telling me about a wonderful recovery from baldness. At one time he was almost entirely bald, but he visited a specialist before it was too late, purchased some medicine, had his head closely shaved, went off into the mountains for several months, applied the remedies daily; and now he has a fine head of hair! I am thinking strongly of doing likewise in order to save my hair, which is coming out in great handfuls.

After my first visitor had departed, another friend rushed in to borrow my wheel.[87] My wheel, be it known, is a very popular convenience among my acquaintances. Shortly after my wheel left another friend called and immediately assumed the aggressive. He picked up a tennis ball and began to bombard my posters upon the walls. Seeing that he might do damage if he were permitted to go on, I called Joseph to my aid and the both of us tried to put the bellicose visitor out. But he didn't want to leave and he didn't. This precipitated a battle in which boxing gloves and tennis balls filled the air, and when the struggle was finished he was the proud owner of a black eye, . . . and I possessed a bruised finger. That was my last visitor, and when he was gone, I had an opportunity of finishing my letter. . . .

Fred

1900–1919

Letter from Fred (Frederic) Jewell Perry to his mother

**Stanford,
Feb. 4, 1900**

My dear Mother,

Your kind presents arrived yesterday morning and were the first reminders of my birthday. I thank you very much for the very toothsome remembrances. You and I, perhaps, were the only ones who knew that with the dawning of Saturday I should be twenty-two years old. I did not let the boys in the house know that it was my birthday, for had I done so this good right arm would have received so many enthusiastic punches that it would not now be able to direct the hand in this letter. I came near letting the secret out though. Mrs. Gillespie, our kind and thoughtful matron, the adopted mother of us all, asked me Friday night when my birthday was, having remembered that I had once told her that it occurred in the first week of February. She wanted to have a cake made in honor of the event. And there I was! I wanted the cake, Oh! so badly! Yet if I had told her, "on the morrow," every mother's son of the ones gathered around that supper table would have visited my room bright and early Saturday morning and would have conferred upon me many "honorable mentions" in the form of various, vigorous blows upon the said right arm. So I complacently told her that it would occur on the 23rd of February—and thereby saved my life—and lost my cake!!

Yesterday morning I studied and after dinner did a little manual labor. We have a lawn in front of our house and the grass needed cutting, so the freshman, one of the numerous juniors, and the two seniors went to work and shaved the thing. The poor freshman—claims that he came out to California to escape the drudgeries of the lawn mower, but we made him work it like a day laborer. The junior fixed the flowers & bushes, and the seniors— well, they principally bossed the job. . . .

Fred

Plea for Funds: Fred (Frederic) Jewell Perry, Mar. 1, 1900

Courtesy of the Stanford University Archives

Letter from J. B. (Jesse Brundage) Sears to his parents

Oct. 9, 1908

Dear Father and Mother:—

Got the card at noon today and feel much relieved to know that indications are so good. You have no idea of the strain under which we have worked for the past ten days or more. Wednesday was the 21st day, and as this is Friday and no telegram has come we feel that the great danger point is passed. But he is not well yet remember. He must be very careful. And you too must be careful that you don't get it. I have been so anxious to know where the fever germ came from & have asked in nearly every letter or card I wrote but you have not answered yet. I want to remind you that I have suffered as much for want of an answer to that question as for anything. That is the keynote to the whole situation. Is it somewhere where you have all had access to it or not? A germ is a germ and it has no respect for anyone. I really feel as though I have been sick myself. But now that the better news has come I feel much better and will hope that Dean will pull through safely. . . .[88]

Your loving son,
J. B. Sears

Letters from Hope Snedden to her father

Sunday, October 27, 1918

Dear Dad,
Enclosed find my account for moneys spent from Oct. 3–27 inclusive. It may not be made out strictly according to Hoyle,[89] but I hope it is plain & satisfactory. I give the itemized lists so that you can see whether I use good judgment or not in separating what you & I pay for.

Dad, I am also in a state of protest at the infrequency with which you seem to receive communications from me. Naturally, you think I am enamoured with Calif. & too lazy to write to my family which is obligingly putting me thru college. But, really, ever since I've been here, I [have] written you regularly every Sunday & Wednesday. It's . . . difficult to correspond across a continent. I'll have to number my letters as if I were writing from France. I am disgusted when I think of the questions I asked mother in the letters you don't seem to have received. But I surely am mighty glad to get yours. . . .

Yes, Dad, I'll try to work in some science courses. In the last Sat. Evening Post, it says: "The French Commission of the Red Cross wires that five hundred nurses are needed to a division, which is about double the previous estimate of fifteen thousand nurses for each million men."! . . .

Last Friday night, Uncle Ernest came for me. I had let them know. About eight of the girls were sitting around in the upper hall when the bell rang, & they all let out one howl, hoping it was for them. Much disappointment when the housekeeper[90] announced my uncle. But the girls just naturally kept shrieking. . . . Four of them tried to carry down my suitcase so as to get a look at Uncle Ernest. I never heard such a racket. But he seemed to enjoy it hugely.

Today we started out in the auto from San Mateo with our masks & a small lunch. We went down past the ocean & Half Moon Bay. Then we began climbing up from the bay on the famous La Honda road. It was just one series of turns after another so that my head aches. But all the time we were going thru redwood forests. It is like the groves we'd see on our trips with G.G., only there was much more wonderful timber all over those mountainsides than I've ever seen in N.H. When we got clear on top of the range, we could see San José, Stanford, Oakland all down on the flat land. Then we came down thru Woodside. . . .

This is a funny country here. It's like one pageant with its flowers & pretty houses. And everybody seems happy & well enough to-do to have an auto. And they all take them out on Sunday. Also, since I've been here, the sky has been always blue (I'm getting sleepy). California is almost too perfect so far, tho. No contrast. Too much like a World's Fair. I feel like Hamlin Garland's mother going thru the World's Fair at Chicago. . . .[91]

Sunday, December 1, [19]18.
Letters are just in from you and Francis describing the joint birthday celebration. It must have been great. Were there speeches, or anything? Ruthie's cake would naturally make everybody happy.[92]

It is a good suggestion of yours that I read North American Review, Contemporary, Nineteenth Century, & New Republic. I'll try to. At present, I read the N.Y. "Times" regularly. Of course, it is five days late, but it exactly keeps pace with your letters & any news you refer to, I have read that morning in the "Times."

The papers are awfully flat these days somehow, tho—This morning, the "Chronicle" featured in big headlines: "Two Chinamen Killed. San Francisco Race War." In contrast to the fighting in the Argonne forest.

I do read the Atlantic Monthly pretty regularly, too. If you have seen the November number, you have probably read the first story, "Birds of a Feather" by Marcel Nadaud, a story of French Aviation. It is very good, & I have just been reading, in French, another aviation story by the same author, published 1918, called "En Plein Vol." It's great stuff, & I begin to be glad of my French for the first time. If I thought Donald could understand French slang, I'd send it to him.

One thing I miss here, is your buying new books. My English professor said that long ago he decided he could save a fortune by not buying books, but by using a library wisely. I hope he has become rich. Anyway, the result is that he has read nothing modern. The "New Book" section of the library is as far up-to-date as "Mr. Britling." We were reading that before Donald went West. My . . . high school teacher—Miss Lewis—used to be quite remarkable in the way in which she kept up with contemporary literature. It used to be sort of interesting to have her referring in classes to "The Harbor," & Bryce's report on Belgian atrocities, books we were hearing about outside. But Evans, my prof. here, swears by Kipling, & states that at the present moment Kipling is a greater author than H.S. Wells. But he hasn't read "Joan & Peter," & doesn't want to. And I'd like to know what he's read of Kipling's lately!

Well, did I tell you I got one A in English? . . . Otherwise, he regularly gives me C's. But . . . my compositions are nearly always among the three or four that he chooses to read. It is always to illustrate some bad fault. He is fond of reading one of mine, saying how boring it is, & then reading a selection from the Atlantic Monthly, similar in thought, to show contrast in method of treatment. And the class never has any difficulty in seeing the contrast.

Dad, someday, if you can afford it, & want to do something nice for me, give me $10 to take a course in Russian literature here with Lanz. He is not paid by the University, hence the fee. I'm not awfully interested in "English Classics" but this other course would be fine. It includes reading & criticizing many volumes by Tolstoy, Dostoyevsky, Turgenev, etc. etc.

Following are some books I hope to read some day:
"Home Fires in France"—Dorothy Canfield

"Tales of War"—Lord Dunsany
  Capt. & 5th Royal Fusiliers
"Far Away & Long Ago"—W.H. Hudson
  Autobiography—So. America
"Out of the Silence"—Mary E. Waller
  Story of Indians & War of 1914.

If you should have any of these & get thru with them & could send them out to me, I'd be glad. . . .

I have been majoring in history here, but I am changing over into the pre-nursing course. Miss Stoltenberg is my advisor, & proscribes the science course that I am to take, & gives me my choice of the others. It is going to be very interesting; Stanford seems to have any amount of good science courses. There is very definitely here a five-year nursing course and, if you are willing to keep me in college that long, that is what I want to take. I would take three years work here. Then I would be supposed to go up to Lane Hospital in S.F. for two years more. But Stanford will give me my A.B. if I take those two years in a N.Y. hospital, & Miss Stoltenberg thinks N.Y. will credit my three years' work here. Then I would have both an A.B. & an R.N. If you approve of this plan, it is quite definitely settled & mother needn't think I'm to shift again. Teaching history & English was only a suggestion to satisfy Dad until I had really made up my mind. How long do you give me before I'm supt. of some hospital for the cure of tubercular children? . . .

Last night . . . about ten girls piled into my room. Two had ukuleles,—Peggy Carlsmith was one—& they surely did raise the roof. Those girls are what might be termed "roughnecks."[93] At ten, they left, so I went to bed. Yes, Dad, I get lots of sleep, especially in the morning.

Mother used to say I never could go to college because I took ¾ of an hour in which to dress, & college girls only took ½ hour. Well, I have found that I can dress in any given time. I have never missed breakfast yet, altho half the girls sleep right thru it. . . .

With love,
Hope

1920s

Letter from Hope Snedden to her mother

Jan. 25, 1920

Dear Mother,
. . . My, I am so homesick tonight. Francis wrote me the most beautiful letter that made me wish so much to be in New England. He surely appreciates the place.

Qual. [Qualitative Chemistry] is more interesting than ever. It is like a setting from a book, the long lab, with men working at all the long black tables; the atmosphere so thick & hazy that you could cut it with a knife; everybody whistling or singing; no assistants in sight. Prof. Lennox has his inner sanctum, attic office up a worn flight of steps. No one ever goes up there, but at the foot are two boxes,—one for the reports you hand in, & the other for the reports that come back corrected. People approach those boxes with trepidation, for it is sad to find a whole week's work come back marked wrong. I work very slowly, for I don't know what I'm doing if I go too fast, but I find that a lot of the men that were so far ahead are getting their "Acids" reports back not O.K.'d. I haven't handed in my anal. of that yet, but I have been getting pretty sure tests. . . .

The San Francisco Symphony Orchestra played here Thursday night. Leonard[94] had tickets for himself & Peggy, but Peg couldn't go so he asked me. Oh, Mother, it was glorious; I have been hearing the music ever since. Tschaikowsky & Bach; I don't know anything about them, but it was fine. And really I've hardly heard any music since the old Boston Symphonies. . . .

Saturday morning, chem. lab, no class is scheduled for Sat. morning, but if you go over there, you certainly find everybody hard at work. . . .

. . . You never can judge by appearances. A certain Cottrell [at a recent dance], with a half bald head seemed very uninteresting, until just by accident, I happened to find out that he was a pilot & flew for three months at the front. That is rare, even here at Stanford. . . . One morning he flew along the Meuse river, & saw the villages there but laid out so prettily in smooth meadows. And after being about an hour in Germany, he flew back to find all those villages in flames. I found out later that Cottrell is a graduate law student. . . .

Carl Henry called up in the afternoon to ask me to go walking in the hills. Carl is nothing if not conventional. He explained that he had grown up with a bunch of people who always called up a girl before calling on her. Then he arrived, attired very correctly with a stiff collar, a felt hat, & a box of candy under his arm. He feels it necessary always to bring a girl either candy or flowers. (It makes me laugh when I think of Peg & Don going out for the evening, & not even taking in the extravagance of a movie, but just bumming around, buying 5¢ worth of jelly beans, & eating them all!). . . He knew a good way out into the hills, where you could usually go thru gates. Once, however, I was forced to climb a fence, but he gallantly took my hand & I did it in style. He has a favorite tree which we found at last, & I sat on a wiggly limb while he sat on the ground. We ate chocolates & discussed a multitude of things. He really has a large variety of interests, & very fine ideas, if not very deep. But for an afternoon it is fine. . . .

Don says I am improving in Spanish. He is the second-best in the class.

Lots of love,
Hope

Letters from Burnham P. Beckwith to his father

Jan. 13, 1923

Dear Father,

. . . I have been trying out for the Dippy[2] again and have done much better than last time I think. I am determined to make it sometime as I believe I could develop some ability at newspaper work if I had the opportunity. I am trying to learn to use the typewriter a little as some of the courses require typewritten work and others prefer it. I have had to rewrite all my work for the Dippy on the typewriter, and it has taken me hours to do it.

In spite of the fact that I took castor oil last night I am feeling fine this morning. . . .

The students here are raising quite a howl over the fact that so many of our athletes were disqualified last quarter because of poor grades. Personally, I would be glad if twice as many were suspended. It is entirely too easy to slip thru Stanford without studying now. If requirements were lowered a diploma would only certify that the holder had lived near a college a few years.

I was slightly seasick the second day of my return voyage but enjoyed it nevertheless. I lost my new hat over the side of the boat when in the act of feeding the fishes. This disaster and the unpleasant circumstances under which it happened somewhat cooled my ardor and enthusiasm for ocean voyaging. . . .

Jan. 15, 1923

Today has been a day of most pleasant surprises for me. We had an examination in physics last Friday and as I had studied very little in preparation I was expecting a very low mark. Much to my surprise I found that I had received a very high grade.

I was delighted likewise to learn that I had made the Dippy on my second attempt. It looks like this would be a very interesting quarter for me. . . .

I received my War Saving Stamp check some time ago. It came very promptly. . . .

Your loving son,
Burnham

Letter from Burnham P. Beckwith to his parents

3/4/23

Dear M/Fother:[95]

How do you like my ambiguous heading? I don't believe you can divine to whom I am writing this letter. The lights went out for a while so I thought I would have time to write a letter when I would not be wasting time. They have gone on again however so don't blame me if this is a short letter. Blame the power house which gives very poor service here. . . .

I have been so persistently and continuously engaged that I have had to apportion out my leisure moments very carefully and systematically. Indeed my grades are lagging terribly; I fear I will not receive any "Bs" this quarter and I am very likely to be kicked off the "Dippy" any minute. They are only keeping me on because the freshmen on the staff are giving a banquet next week which will cost them about seven dollars apiece and if I were eliminated . . . it would cost about a dollar more apiece. . . .

Your loving son,
Burnham

Letter from Bob (Robert) Richardson Sears to his mother

Sun. nite, [1927]

Dear mama,
We're sort of beginning to miss you, do you know it?

I don't believe you had heard my latest honor when you left. I am now the Dramatic Editor of the Lit! I have charge of assigning all reviews, reading copy, making up the theater box, interviewing managers, and everything. Great stuff, eh? Each issue we run two full-length (400 word) reviews, and this month I am doing them both. Margaret Olsen, the editor, seems to be quite excited about the excellency of my style. Glad she likes it; sort of do myself. She's also running one of my book reviews this issue, and one next issue. . . .

I'm going up to town tomorrow night to see Taylor Holmes in the "The Great Necker." I'll have to write the review between the final curtain and 8 o'clock the next morning, when the magazine forms are locked, so don't expect to get much sleep tomorrow nite. Don't know who I'll get to go with me—guess I'll go on the train and write the review on the way home.

I just finished this week's story for Gray. It's not as good as last week's, though. The funniest thing happened last Tues. when we went to class! Gray was a little late, and when he came in someone suggested we all go to see a movie. Gray said, "All right!" And we did! Kinda dumb, what?

He made a little comment on the story to the effect that he liked it very much, and not a single word of criticism, so I feel pretty good. I haven't talked to him about it yet, but will. . . .

Well, have a good time, ma, for we won't let you get away again, right soon.

Love,
Bob.
(Dramatic Editor of Stanford Literary Mag.)
Heh, heh!

1930s

Letter from Tex Bollman Allen to his parents

Wednesday—10 p.m.
[January 15, 1930]

Dearest folks,

. . . Well, I hashed tonite.[54] I didn't hash much last week or the week before, but I've got about $5 earned this month, anyway. I had $10 in checks waiting for me when I came back after Xmas vacation. Hashing & serving punch one nite last quarter. I'm almost certain to get a job by next quarter—hashing at Encina. And I've got some more good news. I just found [out] that I can get what is called deferred tuition. I must pay my tuition the first quarter of each year, but the second & third quarters I can defer it for 7 years with no interest to pay. I guess that's what I'll do all right. Then I won't have to quit school. . . . I've seen enough of Stanford to know that I'm going thru here—if it takes 6 years or forever. . . .

. . . Lettering is a swell course.[96] They are doing just what Dad said all good letterers needed. Developing the letters first, then emphasizing the spacing. Believe me—you sure can letter when you get out of this course. I'm coming along first rate in it. . . .

Last week was wishing week for the sororities. They had a big time all around. 80 girls pledged. There was quite a fuss because some boy in girls' clothing had been attending all of the open houses of the sororities. Someone found him out at one occasion, but he made his get-a-way and his identity remains unknown. . . .

Signing off at 8:40 p.m.
Love,
Tex

ALPHA TAU OMEGA

Founded at Virginia Military Institute 1865   Beta Psi Chapter established December 1891

FACULTY MEMBERS

James Bradshaw
John Charles L. Fish
Edgar Eugene Robinson
Horatio Ward Stebbins
Graham Henry Stuart
Stewart Woodford Young

UNIVERSITY MEMBERS

Class of 1929

Robert Treat Paine

Class of 1930

Benjamin B. Frost
Charles Blaksler Smith
Donald Franklin Smith

Class of 1931

Albert L. Denney
Walter William Dolfini
Robert Parsons Forbes
Robert Irvin Gilbreath

Donald George Hare
Wilson W. Phelps
Robert Perrin Reynolds
Charles Clifford Weesner
Edward Campbell Yeazell

Class of 1932

Robert B. Filley
Willard S. Johnston
Richard James Keller
James Edward Kelly
Louis Jackson Owen
Richard Havelock Quigley
H. Kirby Schlegel

Austin Shean
Edwin Russell Smith
William Rembert Thigpen
Richard F. Webb

Class of 1933

John P. Allen
Tex Bollman Allen
Ernest C. Arbuckle
Samuel Tracy Clarke
Will Forker, Jr.
Kenneth Ross Hartley
Charles Henry Leavell, Jr.
Lou Phelps
Frank Stewart

Top row—T. B. Allen, J. P. Allen, Clarke, Denney, Dolfini, Forbes, Forker, Frost, Gilbreath, Hare.
Center row—Hartley, Johnson, Keller, Kelly, Leavell, Owen, Paine, L. Phelps, W. Phelps.
Bottom row—Querna, Quigley, Reynolds, C. B. Smith, E. R. Smith, Thigpen, Webb, Weesner, Yeazell.

347

Heads Up: Tex Bollman Allen (top row, upper left) and fellow members of Alpha Tau Omega, 1931

Courtesy of the *Stanford Quad*

Letters from Dick (Richard) Bartlett Gould to his parents

Sept. 25, 1931

Dear Folks:

I have some time to kill before lunch so I'm going to take advantage of it and type a letter to you and let you in on some good news—good to me anyway.

Day before yesterday the bum football players were taken over on the Goof[97] field and had a scrimmage. I was one of them of course. I got a lucky break and got on the defensive team and [it] went pretty good. John Bunn, one of the Goof coaches and [the] basketball coach, asked me my name, which is always a good sign, and [I] just prayed that he would remember it. Well, wonder of all wonders, he did.

Yesterday the Goofs scrimmaged the frosh, and he chose me and Bruce Tarver[98] as the two guards on the "first string." I did O.K., as I didn't get bawled out any, so I figure I have a pretty good chance to stay there. Hope so. All of last year's frosh team is on the Goof squad with the exception of a few backfield men. So I have redeemed myself in a way, from last year. I don't know how long it will last, but I hope it lasts for the year, then next year barring mishaps I may get a crack at the varsity. Well, here is hoping. Time will tell the story.

Dick Miles is playing end this year and had hard luck yesterday in the scrimmage. He dislocated his elbow. Lucky it wasn't broken; it was pretty painful but is O.K. now. I took him to the hospital this morning to get it X-rayed. The Dr. wanted to be sure everything was fixed correctly. The old School takes pretty good care of her worriers.

The hospital was the new one on the campus. It is swell, looks more like an apartment than a hospital; so I think I'll get sick and live there. . . .

Oct. 1, 1931
. . . The football squad has been officially divided now and Buck, Dave Packard,[99] and I are on the first string. When Dick M. gets out [of the hospital] again I think he can make the first-string end. Not bad for the Alpha Delts.

Pop is working a new system this year.[100] The Goofs are learning all the S.C. plays and formations that the scouts pick up, and we are to give the varsity [some] practice against that system. Pop sure is gunning for them this year. It is sort of now or never it seems. We have two real games ourselves and several practice scrimmages with J.C.'s. . . .

I registered this morning and everything worked out just as I had planned so I'm sitting pretty. Tomorrow classes begin and play stops. It will be sort of a tough change but after all that is what we are in college for. . . .

May 29, 1932
. . . Wednesday it was terribly hot and of course I scrimmaged the whole time. We put in as much time as a game without any quarters or halves to rest. Boy I sure was tired. I lost a little over five pounds in about two hours. Friday was a lot cooler, but luck wasn't quite so good. Bill Corbus was in L.A. and as I was the first guard that answered Pop's call I played in his place.[101] Did Pop ever give me Hell! I went pretty lousy on offence but better on defense. I scrimmaged the whole time anyway. Pop learned my name on Friday but I'm afraid the way he learned it won't

do me much good. He figured I was about the worst football player he had ever seen. I stand in pretty well with Tiny and Rabbit gives me quite a little help.[102] By the way Rabbit is going to be coaching the varsity next year and [Ernie] Nevers the Grays.[103] We only have one more week of football or three more practices. I hope I can give a good impression of myself on these last few days. . . .

I'm enclosing the annual A.D.P. letter with this. I thought you might be interested to know just what the fellows in the house do around school. . . . Ben Eastman[104] has been elected track capt. since the letter was written so that can be added to the list of achievements. . . .

Dick

Letters from Alice Louise Clark to her mother

November 5, 1935
Palo Alto, Calif.

Dearest Mother:
Yesterday's mail brought a letter from both you and father and two copies of the Ventura Star, in all of which I was very interested. Thank you all.

I have been trying to think of the easiest way to break this startling news, however I guess the best way is just to tell it. I have an opportunity to drive down to the U.S.C.-Stanford game if I pay my share of the gas. It is a small car and supposedly will not cost more than a dollar for each of us. . . . If you think it is alright, please write immediately and also send me a signed note that I can give to the housemother saying that it will be all right.

Now here's the rub. The boy whose car we are coming in, Marion Stekol, doesn't know anyone in the south. Dale and Cay Waltz are also going to be with us. They were all wondering and questioning about where they could stay. And to my own surprise, I found myself inviting them to stay with the Clark family in Ventura for Friday night. Then we could all go down to the game together Saturday; . . . Cay and I could stay at a hotel which is being reserved for Stanford women, and which will be properly chaperoned for a dollar apiece. (If you approve of the hotel idea, please send a permission for that too.)

. . . I can do it all, including a ticket to the game for less than five dollars. Midterms are all over, so the studies will not be a problem. I'll get to see my family as well as having the experience of going to an out-of-town football game, which is supposed to be one of the most thrilling parts of college life. I do hope you'll think it is all right. . . .

Please send a response to this babbling epistle right away. Maybe you had better make it a special delivery because there is not much time till Friday morning. I can keep all other news and the answers to the questionnaire you are going to send me until I can bring them firsthand. . . .

November 16, 1935
"The Oaks," Palo Alto[105]
When I got back from the city early this morning I found a message saying that you had called me from Ventura. I was much concerned, and I hope that the call was caused by nothing more serious than my exceeding negligence in writing you.

I am writing special delivery hoping that you will get this in the morning and so you can see how sorry I am.

I knew that Marion was writing you, and he would assure you of our safe return. And this week has been so full that there has hardly been time to eat or sleep, much less sit down and write a decent letter. That is the only defense I have to offer.

. . . Tuesday evening Jane Willis and I went with a couple of fellows up to study, and we really did study, at the home of a fellow, Doug Clegg, who lives in a large house up near Hoover's home. Their house is quite a novelty, exceedingly informal, they hold a sort of continual open house for all of their friends and their friends' friends. They have three dogs, one of them the hugest St. Bernard that I have ever seen, four cats, twelve white mice, and three monkeys. . . .

. . . Friday night I went with Marion's other roommate along with Marion and Cay, Dale and Mildred Warneke up to the Palace in S.F. where we danced, and had a good time.[106] Last night was the prize of all—a couple of days [ago] Elizabeth Lam, the Y:W secretary,[107] called up Mildred Warneke and asked her to go up to the city at a meeting of high school–age students and lead a discussion on a modern girl's ideal man. Mildred couldn't go so then Miss Lam happened to think of me living at the same place, I don't know why she asked me, but she did. I was very vague as to the type of meeting and what they would want, and I really don't know much about an ideal man. . . . They were quite a boisterous, hilarious bunch, and I trembled inwardly at the thought of the topic I was trying to present to them, but I did my best, and they listened, which is something. . . .

. . . Our room has become a regular gathering place for those who wish to lounge and talk over all of life's problems. There is hardly a girl in the house who hasn't spent some time there the last week doing nothing but knit and bull about everything. Do you wonder that my letters have been few and scanty? . . .

**Goodbye and loads of love, XXXXXXX & OOOOOO
Alice Louise.**

Letter from Alice Louise Clark to her family

**The Oaks, N. Melville Ave.
Palo Alto, California**

January 13, 1936

Dearest Family,
All morning and part of the afternoon I spent in classes. Since I feel particularly discursive, I shall tell you something about them. At eight o'clock I went for the first time to a class in the History of Japanese Civilization (which I am taking in place of the course in international law which I had originally signed up for) . . . taught by Prof. Ichihashi,[108] a very charming, suave, political, and cynical Japanese gentleman, who can make a remark beginning with a slight bow and the words, "In my humble opinion," such as "The American people have the biggest, best, strongest, wealthiest,—and many other superlatives—civilization, but are they truly cultured?" He invites everyone to question and quiz him and to not be afraid of exposing his ignorance, or our own. Taking him at his word I asked him something about the Vanity Fair cartoon of a few months ago. It made him mad just to think about it, but I think he was glad of a chance to express his views about a blundering

journalistic profession which had the brutality to caricature something so sacred to the hearts of a people as is the sanctity of the person of the Japanese emperor. All of this was just a sideline, one of the interesting diversions of the main point in hand which was a very sympathetic and delightful presentation of Shintoism and its expression in architecture, art, and literature. . . .

. . . I am afraid that you will think that I am getting too gay in flitting from department to department the way I am doing, but I'll tell you a good answer I got in conference with Dr. Wrenn—but that is another story. Dr. Cottrell's class in administrative organizations is pleasingly heavy like mashed potatoes and gravy. I like that simile, I'll carry it further. Ichihashi's class is a tasty hors d'oeuvres, logic—meaty and full of proteins, the psychology . . . a nutritious vegetable full of vitamins, vocal expression a dessert pastry rich and fancy, and music is—oh well, heck, I've run out of courses. . . .

. . . I went in to renew my contacts with Dr. Wrenn. . . . I confessed that I was rather ashamed of my last quarter's record. He went out and got my card, looked at it and said, "My gracious, child, what do you expect?" . . . First of all he said that I had made a mistake in signing up for three heavy courses, each of which had a great deal of reading all along similar lines. He emphasized careful budgeting of time, and urged me to be sure and get subjects about which I was enthusiastic. Besides this he wants me to get into more campus activities so he called up the man who coaches women's debating and obtained permission for me to sit in on some of the debates and perhaps learn to take part; found out who was the president of an international club, of which I had never heard, which seems to be fairly active, and advised me to get in touch with him if I were interested; and he also promised to put up my name for membership in a rather select and small discussion group in which many of the campus leaders both student and faculty are members. . . .

. . . My ideas are shifting in emphasis a little. Getting into the foreign service is a practical impossibility for a woman, at least without many years of menial preparation. However I don't believe that it is the difficulty which discourages me as much as it is the idea of living in a foreign land far away from family and friends, that objection had not occurred to me until now. Instead I think I had rather concentrate on the aspect of public administration and in the meantime explore around somewhat in the fields of economics and sociology until something opens up. At the same time I'll do my best to drag such good grades that the University will practically beg me to stay for a year or two of graduate work. . . .

Up until today I had only Mother's one letter of last week since I left home. I almost turned the tables on you one evening by calling you long distance. I was very glad to hear from mother today though and to know that her arm is better and that all the rest of you are behaving yourselves. I am going to take the medical examination form over to the gym tomorrow and see if I can't get the school doctor to fill it out for me, thereby saving three dollars. If she won't do it, I'll have to take it to some doctor downtown. . . .

Here's hoping that you will recover from the shock of receiving such a volume. This may never happen again, so cherish it highly. It's taken me all evening to produce, and such correspondence cuts huge holes in my time budgets.

Don't you like my fancy stationery? As you have perhaps observed, it is some that I have ruined in my typing, and I thought that you would be so glad to hear from me that you wouldn't be particular [about] what the letter was written on. . . .

Your loving daughter and sister,
Alice Louise

Letters from (William) Russell Smith to his father

January 27, [1938]

Dear Father,

. . . As you probably know, Dr. Nerad was up to see me, but I was up in San Francisco. I couldn't quite believe it, because it seemed so unusual. On our way up to S.F., we had a little trouble. There were five of us in the car of a boy across the hall. We were going up the big highway, (maybe a little fast) and some lady slowed up rather suddenly. We didn't slow up soon enough, and ran into the back of her car. It damaged the front of our car quite badly, but the insurance co. is taking care of it alright. Everything else was O.K. I guess the whole thing is of little importance, but I thought I'd mention it. Don't say anything to Mother.

Both typewriters are in use! The above was written yesterday. It is now 7:30 a.m. Jan. 28.

Last night I went to a very good school dance. It was just a little mixed dance, and I met quite a few girls. The Alpha Delt Boys helped me along very much by telling me who to and who not to dance with.

Dear Mother,

                                       <u>Wednesday</u>

I feel awful about the letter situation because you all have been so wonderful in writing. I never have written Rebekah; I guess by the time I get back, she won't even be speaking to me. Although not very cleverly shown, my sincerity is true. Your ~~sincerity~~ regularity in correspondence is astounding and appreciated no end. I realize I haven't shown it very well by writing, but I hope the future will @ more mail down your way. Things are in an awful state of aff you have to open all your apologies it is appa how it no

Alpha Delta Phi
Stanford University

Mrs. T. B. Smith
1222 Avalon Blvd.
Wilmington, Calif.

I was up at the house Wed. noon and night. We had pictures taken at noon. The more I go around there, the more I like them. They really are a swell bunch. . . .

I was certainly sorry about not letting you know about the fraternity deal early, but I thought that was pretty well-implied in the phone call. . . .

February 2, 1938
. . . It's about three o'clock now, and raining very hard. Of course that's the usual thing around here. In fact I haven't seen the sun for three or four days. . . .

I have two of my mid-quarters through, which shows that I have five more weeks till vacation. The time seems to go really fast around; I guess that's because I always have so much to do. I think that I already told you that I had a ride down for Easter with some San Diego boy who lives here in the hall.

. . . I do most of my studying in the Quad. At first I tried to study [at Encina], but the threshold into #345 is like a highway, so you can imagine how much I can get done here. When you do enter the place, you usually have to do it by a back entrance. If you walk in the front you're very likely to get a bucket of water; of course sometimes only the water comes down, and other times only the bucket. Also it's a good idea not to walk too close to the building, because anything you don't want, you just throw out the window. . . .

The Financial Situation

Money brought along in:

Checks	$115.00
	73.50
Traveler's checks	40.00

Cash 20.00

Money sent:
Received 7/20/38 ....25.00
Total 273.50

Money spent for:
Tuition.. $100.00
Community fees 15.00
Meal book 43.00
Room rent...13.00
Breakage deposit..10.00
Linen service 3.60
Club dues..1.00
Key deposit 1.00
Western Civ.[16] book..2.85
French readers 2.00
Chemistry lab 15.00
French course 1.00
History course 2.00
Bus trip.. 7.70
Aptitude test...5.00
Golf book 5.00
Western Civ. syllabus..1.00
Total $228.15
.... $273.50
.... –228.15
Money not accounted for $45.35

Love,
Russell

1940s

Letter from Mary Allie Lesnett to her parents

November 15, 1944

Dear Mother and Daddy,

Last weekend was a big success. The formal dance was just wonderful. I think the main reason why I had such a good time was the fact that I had spent four hours in the library and had accomplished a lot of work. Since it was Armistice Day the dance was a Paris Victory dance and they threw confetti. When I came home my dress absolutely dripped with colored confetti. . . .

Last Monday Mr. Tresidder[74] came back from Canada and the East where he had been visiting some colleges. All the students went up to his house to sing Stanford songs to show that we were glad he was back. He came out and made a little speech which was very impressive. He certainly makes you appreciate Stanford. . . .

We've just been hearing about all the rushing and pledging at U.C.L.A. . . . We were all sort of sorry that we couldn't be pledging something, too. As far as I can see, it really didn't do them much good to abolish sororities up here because the girls are awfully cliquish. . . .[109] So the situation is really about the same.

Love to all,
Mary

Courtesy of
the *Stanford Quad*

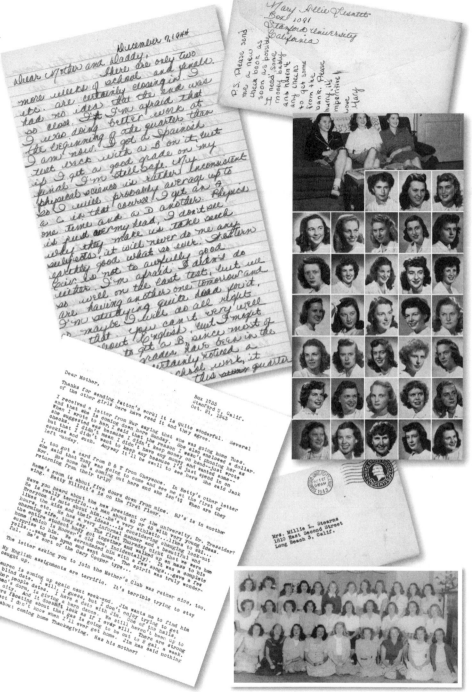

Storied House: Both Mary (Allie) Lesnett (fourth row down, far left, in head-shot photo) and (Mary) Carol Stearns (sixth row, middle) grew up in Southern California and lived in the all-female Storey House at Stanford. Today, the coed row residence is the Human Biology Theme House, and the diverse Stanford student body comes from all 50 states and around the globe.

Courtesy of the Stanford University Archives (correspondence) and the *Stanford Quad* (photos).

Letter from Anonymous to her parents

[Mid-1940s]

Dear Mom & Dad:

I am sorry that I didn't mention the things which you said you wished to know about, but I just wasn't as enthusiastic about them as I was about the campus and the success of my room. About my roommates; you can't exactly call them roommates because I never see them except when I use their room for a hall. One of them . . . comes from San Francisco. She is awfully nice and quiet and her parents seem nice too, but I have my suspicions about her being gentile.[110] The other girl is . . . also from San Francisco. . . . I really don't know them awfully well because I am never in my room except when studying or sleeping and there isn't any time then for conversation.

About my teachers: My geology teacher is . . . entirely devoid of personality, but he is very efficient. He is fairly young and is doing some research on something; consequently, he is not too awfully interested in the class. I am really glad of this because now I can get out of the class what I can without getting too-awful grades. My English teacher's name is Mr. Conley. He is the one who reminds me of Edgar Allen Poe; he has a rather dry sense of humor and is very intellectual. All the girls are in love (?) with my Western Civilization teacher (Mr. Grinnell). He looks like a combination of Frank Sinatra and George Murphy with a Bob Hope nose. He is a bachelor and only twenty-four, but he has developed his own ideas about things, which I guess is sort of unusual for a man so young. He is also very thorough. My French teacher looks like a Somerset

Maugham character. He is very jovial and everyone likes him.
His name is Mr. Naughton. . . .

Love,
Anonymous

Letter from (Mary) Carol Stearns to her mother

Tuesday [Mid-1940s]

Dear Mother—
. . . The train didn't leave till 6:30. But I stood in line—right at the
first of the line so that I wouldn't be so likely to be trampled on
when the gates opened at 6:00—& the mob stampedes thru them.

Betty Ann & I had a quiet trip—very few—only about 4
girls on the train headed for Stanford. Betty Ann had a deck of
cards & decided we'd like to play a little bridge. So we tromped
back & forth—in & out & back again thru all the pullman
cars—running into no one we knew—We did pass a soldier—
blond—hair sticking out in all directions—thought he looked
familiar so looked again. It was Mac—Johnny McClure—an air
cadet now. He rounded up some dumb sailor—who at first
didn't seem to know anything about bridge—but who kept
apologizing that he hadn't played much bridge lately—just
pinochle—"Yep"—he'd played lots of pinochle. . . .

I had such a good time at home, Mom. Thanks—

Write,
Love,
Carol

Letter from (J.) Fred Weintz Jr. to his parents

Room 203 Encina
August 31, 1946

Dear Folks,

I knew I hadn't written you in quite a while, but I was horrified
to find out in checking through my diary that I haven't written
since August 10th. I am sorry. I don't know where the time has
gone. The quarter is now over as of today, and I am now on
vacation until Reg. Day, September 24th. The last week has
been hectic; I haven't gotten to bed before one or at least twelve
any night since quite a while ago. Sometimes this has been for
extraneous reasons but the last week it has been for purely
scholastic reasons. Last week I found myself in the upsetting
state of affairs of being voted the man most likely to flunk one
and probably two courses and get low marks in a couple of
others, of the fellows in the immediate neighborhood. In short,
I was, to put it mildly, having grave scholastic difficulties. Now
that is all passed and I have good news to tell.

I don't know how I did in surveying, but I am sure I did
fairly well in the final in that; so I will pass the course, I hope,
in spite of 19% and 55% in two exams earlier in the quarter.
Then I really "cooled" (Stanford slang for getting a good grade
in a test) the calculus final. I found out from my instructor
today that I came up from a dismal "F" in the course to a lofty
"C," mainly on the strength of the final and my fine homework
average lately! O.K. Two down and four to go. In psychology I
outdid myself. In my wildest dreams I never thought of getting

above a strong "B," so what do I do? I only got an "A" in the long final, so I end up with a nice fat "A-" for the quarter! I'm pretty sure of a "B" in hygiene and ditto for choir. As for Spanish, that is not so good. All through the quarter I had been getting straight "A" grades but in yesterday's final I was handed a "C." But the test was not indicative of how much Spanish a person knew but of how well he had committed to memory certain chapters of the text and certain words that the instructor happened to emphasize. Besides that, the test was marked very stiffly—only a 100% rated an "A" and my 89% was only good enough for a "C." There were a lot of flunks too. I am sure of a "B" in the course, but that is disappointing inasmuch as I had always counted it as being one of my "A" subjects.

There you have it as far as I know now. My official grades won't be out for quite a while and my estimations of them may prove in some cases to be erroneous. But the total picture is good. . . . In a school where "brains" are a dime a dozen and ordinary mortals are few and far between, I am managing to hold my own, thank you. Don't forget that the average load per quarter is 14 or 15 units, and I just got through carrying 18 units plus extracurricular activities. This fall I plan to go back down to 16 (still more than average) and try to be asst. manager of the football team, a member of the glee club, and I-don't-know-what-else on the side. Don't ask me why; I haven't an adequate ready-made reason to offer.

Incidentally, my tentative program for the fall comprises the following: E.E. 100 (Principles of Electrical Engineering), Romantic Lang. S-22 (Spanish Reading), C.E. 99 (Statistics, a phase of engineering mechanics), and Hist. 112 (Russia). You might want to know why I'm making with the "hammer and sickle" stuff. Well, at the beginning of the quarter I petitioned

LETTERS HOME FROM STANFORD

to the Board of Regents to be relieved of having to take any more history here at Stanford on the strength of my Norwich credit. However, they gave me a bad time and said that I need five more units to fulfill a requirement; therefore . . . With Russia being in the news a lot these days and being moreover a big enigma to me, I figured a good way to "get hep" to the situation would be to take a course in Russian history! The guy who's giving the course Prof. Merrill Ten Broeck Spalding is a well-known recognized expert in the field. . . .

Sept. 1, 1946

You might think that with all the trouble I've been having in college I would be kind of fed up. . . . It is true that I am glad the quarter is over but I still like college a lot, and except for the wish that I could get home, do not have the feeling that I'd like to be as far from the Farm[1] as possible. . . . I like college, like Stanford, and think that this is the best school in the world. You can have your Princeton men, your Yale men, and your Dartmouth men; as for me, I guess I'll always be a died-in-the-wool STANFORD MAN. If I have a son, I hope he comes here. As a matter of fact, I'd like to see George come out here when he is ready for college; he couldn't do better.[111] For one thing, the climate would be good for him. There are lots of places in California where the climate is little better than New York's, but here it is ideal. In fact, there are so many lovely days that it gets monotonous. I've done my share of foolish things—kept bad hours, gotten overheated, etc. but have not had a cold since I got out here in March.

Well, I'll have to get busy and pack pretty quick. I have to move out of here and over across the road to Toyon Hall, where I will be between quarters.[112] Over there with me will be most of the football squad due to arrive here for fall practice on Tuesday. When the quarter starts I'll have to move again. And that brings up one thing that isn't so good. Room assignments for fall quarter have been made and I was assigned with about 2,400 other vets to live out at Stanford Village[23] in nearby Menlo Park, a couple of miles from the campus. As I believe I already told you, Stanford Village is the name chosen by the officials selecting from the entries in a contest conducted during the quarter for what was formerly Dibble General Hospital. Among the many clippings I am enclosing this time is one describing the place. It will be sort of like going back to barracks life, but after all, this is an emergency period and you can't have everything. The main trouble with it is the inconvenience of living at such a distance from the campus. This fall will be one time when I could really use a car. . . .

While I'm on the subject, I might mention what all the other clippings are about. "The Bull Session" clipping is a sample of a column that has been running in the Daily. . . .[2] It is always full of true campus humor, and I get a big kick out of it. Another clipping is on the contest results in picking the name for Dibble. I'm also enclosing some that you might be interested in on how they're going to work classes this fall when they have their record enrollment, about the Hoover Lib., and an interesting one on the "possibility" of Stanford being selected for the permanent U.N. Headquarters. I bet it won't be, but it's interesting anyway. The last clipping comes from the "San Francisco Examiner" of August 22, 1946. It lists the starting times for their hole-in-one tournament which Conrad Caprin, my roommate, and I took part in. It lasted over a period of days and the winner hit a ball that landed 2" from the hole. . . . "Cockie" and I didn't win anything in it but we enjoyed playing in it. . . .

After the tournament, our part of it that is, we went over to the North Beach section of S.F. near Coit Tower (It is the Italian section where Joe Dimaggio comes from) for dinner. "Cockie" introduced me to my first abalones. They are mollusks that have a taste like no fish food I have had and are good. I also was persuaded to eat my first ravioli there. . . .

Then we went to the State Theater on Market Street to see "Night and Day" with Cary Grant, Alexis Smith, and Monty Woolley. It is the biography of Cole Porter and prominently features his many famous hit songs. It is a musical well worth seeing. Other movies I have seen lately are Alan Ladd and Geraldine Fitzgerald in "O.S.S.," Lee Bowman in "Walls Come Tumbling Down," Danny Kaye in "Kid From Brooklyn," and a sequel to "Our Hearts Were Young and Gay" called "Our Hearts Were Growing Up." They are all at least fair to middling pictures and you will enjoy 'em. . . .

The football season is rapidly coming to the fore. I don't know what kind of team we're going to have because there will be a lot of new material out this fall that wasn't here this spring. I just saw two awfully big husky guys arrive this evening, whom I never saw before. It's conceivable that we could have a really good team, although I severely doubt it, Rose Bowl material that is. Anyway we're really back in big-time competition. I would even go so far as to say that the Pacific Coast Conference[113] and the Big Nine will be the two strongest conferences in the country this fall, taken as a whole. Speaking of the Big Nine, did you know that starting next fall (1947) we are going to play a four game home-and-home series with the

University of Michigan? Next fall's game will be at Ann Arbor. Boy, that will be a nice trip. You will all have to travel out there . . . to help cheer the Indians on.[55]

Did you hear [Walter] Winchell tonight (Sunday)? To hear him talk we'll be at war with Russia in a few months. The situation is serious, but I sure hope it will all blow over. Just from the selfish viewpoint alone, I don't want that. Give me a chance to get through college and get my degree.

I received your postcard today, Mother, from Maine. I'll bet you all had a wonderful time up there. I think it's swell that you were able to get away for such a nice vacation. How come you never did any of that when I was home? I think doing things like that is something that you should practice much more often, not every few years but every year or oftener. I can tell from the way you write that it does you a world of good.

Well, I am about typed out for this time and besides it's 1:00 a.m. and past my bedtime. I got very little sleep during "Dead Week." . . .[114]

Lots of Love,
Fred

Letters from Nancy Christine Smith to her mother

Wed., Oct 30, [1946]

Dear Mother,
. . . Had two exams today. Messed the first one up, but Scitovsky told me later this afternoon that most everyone did rather poorly and that I was better than some and not to worry

as it must have been his own fault in not making things clear. The afternoon exam was easy and I should have gotten an A. But that's an undergraduate course (statistics) and by rights I should get an A in it.

I still don't feel particularly bright, but perhaps I'll get by somehow.

The faculty (economics & sociology) gave a tea for the graduate students in those departments this afternoon. . . . It was quite a dull affair and I met no one particularly interesting, but it was a nice thing for the faculty to do. There's one old bird in the department whom I'd met at Haley's house with Lorie & Kenty just after we arrived. He's of the old school—over-expansive in his manner and extremely talkative. This afternoon I happened to find myself next to him at the refreshment table, and he decided to take me under his wing and introduce me to everyone. It was a scream. I met all the faculty wives, and while we were talking to a couple of them he said to me, "Well, and how do you like it here at Stanford? I hope you like it as well as those of us here who have met you like you"!!! I really choked at that one! Such an old fool, but he did mean well. . . .

Still haven't gotten the ribbon on my sweater. The Singer Sewing Machine shop said they'd make the buttonholes but wouldn't sew on the ribbon! Ridiculous! . . .

Thursday, January 9, 1947
. . . On Monday I got a call to the Administrative Office, and there was offered a job as resident assistant in one of the dorms, which would give me my room free.[115] I was quite flattered to have been asked, but it would tie me down a great deal, and that's what I wanted to get away from. I refused with thanks

and asked them to consider me for next quarter when I would know more about my capacity in economics. . . .

. . . It's really wonderful to be free—to be able to come home when I want, get up when I want, go to bed late if I want, etc. I'm correcting for two courses with about 50 papers in each, and they have exams every two weeks or so, so that will keep me pretty busy. I don't know yet about tutoring French, but will if I can. We're having our first French club meeting on Monday, and it will be interesting to see how it works out. I finally got an article in the Daily about it—after four trips down there to the office. I'll enclose it to show you your daughter's name in print, even though I don't remember telling them my name. . . .

. . . Gloria, who lives in the next room, just brought me up a hot lemonade—she has a bad cold, too, and we form a coughing duet in the middle of the night for our roommates. . . .

Sunday, Feb 16, [1947]
. . . .Went to the Tresidders Wednesday night for the record hour. They play records every week for all those who want to come. The program is announced beforehand, and never yet have they offered one I'd like, but I finally decided that I'd better go if I ever wanted to see the inside of the house. (He's the president . . . and lives in Hoover's ex-house, which is right behind Hilltop.)[116] It's really quite a nice house, although rather tomblike. . . .

Monday night, June 23, 1947
. . . My program for the summer has turned out to be a full one. The two courses I'm taking require a great deal of reading, and how I'm going to get my thesis done I don't know. But beginning today, I'm working in the library all day and come down at

night until it closes at ten, so I guess I ought to be able to do it. I'm necessarily limiting my social life, but I had such a fling last quarter that it ought to last me for a while. I'll go out on Saturday nights, but will try to limit it to that. No more of this three dates a weekend stuff for me. It gets monotonous anyway. But I did have a good time last quarter, and I've never been so popular in my life. But I suddenly feel ambitious, and interested in my work, so I'll really enjoy my summer. I don't have to worry about getting B's this quarter, since my marks were so good last quarter, but I do want to learn a lot, and these two courses promise to be fascinating as well as difficult. And I do like my thesis topic, and it doesn't seem like hard work, since it's so interesting. . . .

Monday, Oct. 20, [1947]

. . . My thesis is all done and turned in to the binder! What a relief. I worked on the damned thing every night until late, and it's a wonderful feeling to have gotten rid of it at last. It took me two whole evenings to do my diagrams—there were 25 of them, and every time I made a mistake I had to do the whole thing over again, as I was doing them in India ink—Then I had them blue-printed—4 copies of each—and took the thing down Friday night. Came back to work Sat. morning, had my hair cut & shaped at last, and went back to Hilltop for the rest of the weekend. . . .

Love,
Nancy

Letter from Johnny (John) Murray Huneke to his parents

[Late 1940s]

Dear Dad and Mother:

Due to the rushing, etc., my studies sort of rode along on hot air, and from now till the end of the quarter I will be very busy; however, I will write as much as possible. To supplement my letters for the rest of the quarter will be the Stanford Daily, which you probably will be getting about the same time as you receive this letter. I have really got to pour the coal on my studies now if I want to go any place.

. . . I will tell you about the boy in the room adjacent to ours. . . . He is a first-quarter freshman now. (You are not supposed to be rushed until at least a 2nd-qrt. Frosh: Interfraternity Council rule.) He was rushed by the Alpha Delts, Dekes, Sigma Chis, Phi Delts, and I don't know how many others. He had a whole drawer full of pins and, I believe, pledged several of them. Why couldn't . . . [my friend] be accepted by one of the many fraternities that [this guy] must inevitably turn down? It's a tough situation.

Our wing won its first basketball game last night by defeating wing 4E 21–14. I played the whole game (only 3 points). . . .

Johnny

Courtside: Johnny (John) Murray Huneke (fifth from left) at net, 1948

Courtesy of the *Stanford Quad*

Letter from Johnny (John) Murray Huneke to his mother

Sept 28, [Late 1940s]

Dear Mother:

Just received your letter and postcard today. Glad to hear about the new argyles and especially the Sunday Times. I would appreciate it if you would send up some clippings of the Harvard game as I would like to see what the Southland thinks about it. I like the Times sports page a lot better than the Chronicle besides.

Joe has seen the track coach (frosh), Ray Dean & varsity coach Jack Weiershauser.[117] He has a meeting tomorrow night about it. He knows that Criley is out for track—also is Bob Mathias.[118] Joe sure has changed a lot from being up here only a week. He has a perfect schedule for sports if he can only keep it the rest of the year it will be swell. . . .

Well, bad news: I flunked chemistry last spring. I got B– in geology, B in R.O.T.C, A in P.E., C in math, and B in foundry. . . .[119]

Love,

Johnny

[P.S.] . . . Just painted our room. Could you make some covers for our sofa? Very important. Please answer. . . . Do your bit. Thanx.

Letter from Bob (Robert) Lowell Swetzer to his mother

February 4, 1948

Dear Mom,

. . . Well, I have had a pretty busy week so far what with two midterms and plenty of reading to do. I don't know yet what grades I pulled in the two tests, but I think I'm at least good for a "C" or higher in both. Incidentally, the exams were in French and History. Monday the next, I have the geology midterm exam. It will probably be quite a stinker. I would certainly like to make a showing in it; so the midnight oil will be burned in my room this week.

My swimming is progressing by leaps and bounds. Already I can swim the length of the 60-foot pool underwater (I couldn't do that at home). My breathing in the crawl stroke has improved considerably to say the least. Although I am getting a proper amount of sleep, exercise, and food, it seems as though I become fatigued easily. Today I felt I had been wrung through a wringer.

I hope that this letter contains enough information for you. I have a horrible time remembering all this. When I finish some phase of life, I like to forget it; I like to be thinking about things ahead.

Much to my unhappiness, I discovered by checking my rebates that my funds for this quarter are running rather low. This is one Encinaman who is going to have to live a rather monastic life for the rest of the winter. I will definitely be home on the 20th of this month. . . .

Love and such,
Bob

1950s

Letter from Bob (Robert) Lowell Swetzer to his parents

May 24, 1951

Dear Folks,

Here is that long letter that I've been promising to write. . . . I beg forgiveness for not having written sooner, but you know how it is, I have been up to my ears in work. Consequently, there is much to tell you. I really don't know where to start.

The first item is of course my schoolwork. Although it seems to me that I have so many things to do in my studies that it is impossible to do them up right, it has been progressing satisfactorily so far, and will undoubtedly for the rest of the quarter. Right now I am in the middle of a short survey (paper) of the career of John N. Garner, dealing with his year as Speaker of the House of Representatives—that was 1931–32. Next week, for the same course, I shall have to read and report the Kefauver and MacArthur hearings. In Prof. Bailey's diplomatic history, I am reporting on American foreign affairs for the year 1872 as reported in "Harper's Weekly." I shall finish my exams and be home on either June 11th or 12th. I plan to use my entire vacation to gain some weight for the coming summer quarter.

Incidentally, I have been chosen to serve on the Executive Committee this summer (better known as Excom). This is the top body of the Associated Students of Stanford University, and is responsible for governing the student life of the some seven thousand people here. There are five on Excom, and it is considered quite a feather in one's cap to belong to it. John Motheral will act as Student Manager. . . . With the assistance of Jacqueline Miller, also on Excom. this summer, we will have a tight little political machine here.

John and I are progressing at a fair rate in the reorganization of the Chappie set-up. We will present a new constitution to the Hammer and Coffin tonight.[120] Without much doubt, the Chaparral will hit the campus as usual next fall—much better governed from within, and impervious to moral criticism.

I was planning to make this letter quite long, but I have apparently run out of pertinent things to write. I could ask a lot of questions about everyone and all at home, but I do that in most of my letters and get no satisfying answers; so, give everyone my regards and my inquisitions, and tell them I'll be looking around for them in a very few weeks.

Love,
Bob

Letters from Carol Hodge to her family

5 May 1955

Dear Mom, Dad, and Grandma,
Excitement today with a slightly humorous side. On Monday afternoon, Hugh and I happened to climb up and look into the fountain in front of the library. It was a slimy mess. Jokingly, Hugh said, "What a bio demonstration this would make!" Well,

later in the day, he told his friend Roger about it, and the idea got rolling. Soon they had made a very professional-looking sign which read:

ATTENTION ALL BIOLOGY 34 STUDENTS, DEMONSTRATION OF MOSQUITO LARVAE IN ALL STAGES OF DEVELOPMENT.

That night at 11:00, Hugh and I met Roger with the sign and proceeded to erect it on top of the fountain.

6 May 1955

Today the results of the sign were far funnier than we had anticipated! In fact, it caused quite a sensation. Some passersby caught on to the joke immediately, but others took it dead seriously. This second reaction provided hours of laughter. The comments were priceless, and Maryeda and I finally sat out on the lawn nearby, writing down some of the funny things we heard. The comments went something like this:

At first I thought it was a joke! But there are mosquitoes in here. So that's what the water has been left standing in there for. They're having an experiment.

Eek! We'll all get malaria. Are there really larvae in there?

For heaven's sake. Look at 'em all!

I'm a Bio 34 student, and I didn't even know about this.

Hell, they're not in all stages of development.

How do the mosquitoes fly out?

Two bio students, discussing the experiment quite seriously, argued whether larvae were supposed to swim above or below the surface. A professor walked up and said, "My, there seems to be more than one variety in there; I'd say several." And two fraternity brothers joked over the contents, saying, "Neat drinking water, yeah, neat mix for a Vodka Collins!" The other carried on, "Can't you just feel them sliding down the throat? When they're drunk they kick harder!"

One girl just about drank the water while looking in the fountain. Another fellow got so excited he got his shirtsleeve all wet, and several others helped brush the larvae off, saying, "Hey, you shouldn't get that stuff on you!" A guy with a high-pitched voice squealed, "Ye Gods! Look! They are in all stages of development!"

About 2:15 an old man came by and cautioned those standing near not to get too close since the mosquitoes would soon fly out and bite everyone. A boy promptly got his face so close to the water that he got his glasses all wet, but he kept right on looking. A highlight of the afternoon came when a very indignant fellow asked, "Who ever heard of such a thing at Stanford University?" And, of course, there was also a freshman boy trying to impress a cute girl by telling her in detail how the mosquitoes were developing. They stayed at the fountain about 20 minutes, poking their fingers into the water. He went on and on while she tried to look impressed.

Another funny result of this "experiment" occurred in Hugh's Bio 34 class. Many of the students really believed that the professor, Mr. Ferris, had put up the sign and that he would hold them responsible for the information on the coming midterm. There was a lot of discussion about it in the classroom. The professor was silent.

The end result and probably the biggest chuckle came much later when the sign disappeared AND a big truck pulled up beside the fountain. Three men in white suits and hip boots got out with their soap and brushes and began scrubbing out the "larvae."

The real goal of the sign was accomplished, and most people will never know the real story behind the "demonstration."

Love,
Carol

Eye for Detail: Looking deep for larvae, May 6, 1955
Courtesy of Carol Hodge, Class of 1957

1960s

Letters from Elaine Lavis to her family

Saturday, January 7, 1961

Dear Family,

. . . I guess that around here we have a choice of two alternatives—either it's wet or it's cold. So goes winter quarter, and the weather.

I don't know if it's the effect of the weather, or of grades from last quarter, or what, but it sure seems as if everyone around here is working much harder, already, than they ever did last quarter. The libraries are already very busy, and at night, practically everyone is studying. Last quarter, it didn't seem as if the people really started studying for about two or three weeks or so. I went to the Civ library[27] this morning, and it was very crowded, something that is rare for a Saturday morning. In fact, it is never that busy except perhaps right before an exam. I guess maybe people are reforming, or something, deciding to get all their work done early. Anyhow, it's a change, and not a bad one at that. . . .

Well, I think that I'm going to demand a refund of part of my tuition soon, if things keep up the way they have been going! The reason for my outrage is simple—my English class has yet to meet, even though we should already have had two lectures. It's like this—the room assigned for our class is too small, and not everyone can be accommodated. In fact, the class is so large that a room about twice the size of the one allotted is necessary. But, despite the demands of the professor, who is just as annoyed as the students, the powers who be will not assign a larger classroom. So, until some new development (which we all hope will come on Monday) the class can't meet, for the professor can't talk to the whole class at once, with half of them standing out in the hall, and he certainly can't give his lecture twice. The irony of it all is that this exact same thing happened to this professor last year, with this class. But the office that assigns classroom space obviously doesn't believe in learning from experience, which only serves to leave us poor English students uninformed and without a class.

Friday, February 3, 1961
. . . I told you that in biology lab this week we were going to be dissecting. Well, I had a mouse, and pretty well took the little thing apart. It was fascinating for me—I have never done any dissection of any kind before. The animals were killed just before we got them, but I found that I wasn't bothered by that at all. The only thing that is at all unpleasant about such an operation is that, since the animals aren't treated or preserved in any way, they begin to smell a little after about an hour or so. But even that wasn't too bad, and was made up for in the fascination that you get over what you are seeing. Next week in lab it's frogs—only this time we're not . . . dissecting the whole animal, but just working with his muscle.

Our lab instructor is a most interesting and scholarly fellow, and we were talking to him after lab this week for almost an hour. He is very adamant about the idea that the sciences should be an integral part of the humanities, and vice versa. He begins each lab section with a lecture tying the humanities and science together—often quoting from philosophy or poetry. I think that his viewpoint is certainly correct, and agree with him entirely. He was also telling us a little bit about himself—he was a history major at Harvard, and then went into biology after getting his B.A. He said that this is quite common among biologists—to get a degree in a different field, and then to go into biology. He was also telling us about the man who is lecturing this quarter for the course. He also is a brilliant man—and another Harvard graduate. (They all say that they are just sitting around and waiting to hear from Washington; and ironically enough, the lecturer's name is Kennedy![78]) But, anyhow, it seems that Dr. Kennedy was an English major, and even did some magazine writing, before he went into the field he is in now—neural physiology. He is doing a great deal of outstanding work in this field now—publishing three or four papers a year, and working on research—and from the reputation that he seems to have, Stanford didn't do too badly in getting him out here. He's quite young—only about thirty or so, and is an excellent lecturer, to top it all off. So, this is one of the reasons why the course is so interesting, and also quite difficult, this quarter. . . .

Friday, February 10, 1961
. . . Well, the whole dorm is now on a knitting binge. However, there is definite method to our madness—we are all knitting squares for afghans, to be sent to Africa, for poor children there. Each corridor has decided to make an afghan of its own, so that means that each girl has to knit about three squares herself. Our wool has come, for our corridor, and the needles are supposed to be purchased today, which means that we'll be starting soon. It's really fun to see—everyone brings their knitting down to the lunch or dinner line, and knits away while talking. It's amazing how many times during the day you are just sitting around and

talking, or not doing anything of importance, during which time you can knit. Let's just hope I remember how to knit—especially casting on. I guess I can experiment for a while, and it'll all come back. I'll keep you informed of our monumental progress. . . .

Tuesday, February 14, 1961

. . . We got our English papers back today—I got an A- on this one. . . . It was really funny to get the papers back, too; the instructor announced that they would be placed in his box in the English office. So, after class, all hundred or so students went over there, and queued up to get their essay back. It was almost like standing in line at the market, waiting to check out. You go up, and stick your hand in the box, and shuffle through the papers until you come to yours, and then remove it, and leave. It really gives you a feeling of personal contact, not only with the instructor, but also with the reader, who is some mysterious soul (male or female—sex unknown) who must sit up somewhere in some English office reading and chortling over all the undergraduate themes, and making sarcastic comments. . . . This machine-type technique operates fairly effectively, and the grades are fair and accurate, but you get such a feeling of lack of personal contact with anyone. Oh well, I guess when one becomes an upper-division student, one's sense of personal identity may return. . . .

Friday, March 10, 1961

. . . Biology lab this week didn't turn out to be the success I had hoped it was going to be. In the first place, the fish heads we worked on had been preserved in formaldehyde, and after you've been in a lab all afternoon with that stuff, it's none too pleasant.

In fact, you smell it for the rest of the day, and can't get the odor off of you, no matter how hard you try. Then, to top it off, whoever had preserved the animals in the solution had done an extra-good job of it, and made it much too concentrated. As a result, the fish were well-preserved all right . . . all the internal structures at which we were supposed to be looking were shriveled up, and unidentifiable. Out of the whole lab section, only one fish was anywhere near being normal, or good, so all our efforts at dissection were in vain. But, there's hope for next week—the lecturer is going to be putting on demonstrations in each lab, which should be interesting. And no formaldehyde, either! . . .

Tonight, as I mentioned, is the Branner[77] Carnival. And, since I'm going to shoot the evening, I'm going to do it completely. Mike asked me out to dinner, to the house of a friend of his who lives nearby. Then, after dinner we're going to come over here, and go to the carnival. The dinner part sounds really great— Friday night and fish is becoming increasingly worse. I think that it is a conspiracy on the part of the dining hall director—she must scheme all week to see just how bad she can make the meal. Either she doesn't want anybody to come to dinner on Friday night, so she can get the evening off, or perhaps she is anti-Catholic, and is looking for some conversions. But whatever it is, it's really bad. . . .

Well, the papers in English class were handed back today—or that is, most of them were. There are two readers for the course, and then the professor reads a few of the papers, at random. Guess whose paper was picked to be read by the instructor, along with about a dozen more? Actually, I'm quite pleased that chance worked in my favor this time—I'll be interested to see what comments he'll make. It may mean a lower grade, if he's more strict than the readers, but it's certainly worth it. . . .

Well, I must dash now, to anthropology quiz section, to garner whatever pearls of wisdom the section leader may have to offer. So, I'll write again soon.

Love,
Elaine

Letter from Joe (Joseph) Lewis Jacobs to his parents

12/10/61

Dear Mom and Dad,

. . . The party for New Year's is pretty definite. Donna's mother (Donna is Tom's girl) isn't too sure she wants them to drive home at that hour, so I said we could put Tom in my room and Donna in the den. If Clyde comes, he'll go in Carl's room and his girl will sleep with Donna. Les also might come up from San Diego, but we would have to get a blind date for him, perhaps Nancy. If necessary, some of the boys can use sleeping bags. Tom said he'd cook breakfast on New Year's morning, and I'll take care of making the beds, so it really won't be any problem at all.

Are you going to be home New Year's Eve or will you go to the Cornells' party? And could we just have a couple whiskey sours? Tom, when I told him about the one I had at the Top of the Mark, said they're his favorite, and I said Dad's are simply out-of-this world. Don't worry, nobody would get drunk. You, Mom, would probably be the first to get high.

Has Dad done anything on the shelves for the living room? What about the wine chest in the den you mentioned? Also, is Dad going to take any days off at Christmas? If he does, I don't think I want to go anywhere. I plan on doing some work for next quarter over the vacation (read about 1,000 pages in several books). I also want to see . . . West Side Story.

When will the Schultzes be back from vacation? Will Janet go? Does Janet definitely have mono? . . .

I got some . . . cookies from Grandma, but they were completely smashed. But they are still good. I have to write a note and thank her. I'm going to ask her to send me a salami. Isn't that a great idea?

If I get home early Friday night, I may put on a suit and try and get into Granada's Christmas Formal. If the same old teachers are guarding the door, I shouldn't have too much trouble. Leave the car keys in the tea-cart drawer. . . .

I have a list of things to bring back at Christmas. I want one of those coffee pots with the built-in heating element. I'll use it to cook soup and to make tea and cocoa. I also want to bring back more chocolate chip cookies. I will have finished the can I have now by then. And I want to bring back my voo-doo drum, plus a few assorted small items (scissors, paper clips, etc.), and some pills.

I've decided that instead of buying a red sweater, I'll buy a Stanford sweatshirt. Then I can wear it around Northridge. . . .

I just talked to Carl. He doesn't know yet when he'll be returning to Cal after vacation. He says you owe him a letter. I told him that I had a sneaking idea that I'll be the one to pick him up at the airport on Saturday. Am I right? He also said that there is a strong possibility that he'll switch out of architecture, but he's not sure yet. . . .

That's it for now. I have to study. UGH!

Love,

Joe

P.S. We get filet mignon for dinner tonight. It's the Christmas dinner, and supposedly the best one all year. I hope so.

Letters from Elaine Lavis to her family

[Early 1960s]

Dear Family,

. . . Anyhow—back to my classes. I think that the one I like the best is my Shakespeare course. Of course, I thoroughly enjoy reading all the plays, but the professor of the course adds even more to the class. It is taught by the head of the English department here, who is quite well-known as a Shakespearian scholar. He is an extremely interesting man. Physically, his appearance is rather surprising, the first time you see him. He is quite large and heavy, and really doesn't look like the "head of an English department" type (whatever that may be!) But as soon as he starts talking, you forget about everything else, and just wish you could spend the rest of the day in his class, listening to what he has to say. He knows the period we are studying so well that one gets the feeling he could fit in perfectly in Shakespeare's England if he were suddenly placed there. . . .

Sunday, April 29, 1962

. . . The big news here on campus is the student body elections. The primaries were held last week, and the final elections are this week. What is causing all the stir is that a graduate student—a fellow who is a political science teaching assistant and also working for an advanced degree—decided to run for student body president. He is a rather arrogant person, and he is running on the ticket that student government is all a farce, and to prove it, he will get himself elected, and then turn it into a quasi-dictatorship. He received the most votes in the primaries, and this week there will be a runoff between him and the next highest candidate (an undergrad). Now, a lot of people (myself included) are certainly agreed that student government is nothing more than a waste of time, and an ego-building experience for those people who like to see their names in the paper, and who like to act important. Student leaders can have no influence on the runnings of the University—and that's the way it should be. We are here to learn from the University, not to try to change it to our whims. But, even though I think it is not really that important who holds the student offices, I don't think it is the place of a graduate student—above all, one who is affiliated with the teaching staff also—to set himself up as the critic of undergraduate affairs. Also, word has it from some of this man's friends in the Poli Sci Department that he entered the race all in the way of a political experiment—to show how badly democracy can function, if given the chance. So, not only is this man setting himself up as a demigod over all the students, he is also manipulating all of us as if we were things. Well, I might get concerned enough that I might even go and vote— something I don't usually do, since I don't know the candidates, and don't care. But at least we now have a dinner-table conversation for a few days.

Monday, October 15, 1962
On Saturday afternoon . . . [I braved] it out into the deluge, all in the pursuit of knowledge. It was music-listening time, and we

went to the music library to hear recordings of English madrigals and other songs, for our poetry class. We have been reading the lyrics to many of these songs, but of course, in class, we couldn't hear them set to their music. However, Professor Winters strongly recommended that we hear some of them, and who are we to disagree with Yvor Winters? Picture the setting on Saturday afternoon: the music library is in an old, huge house—probably one of the original mansions on the Stanford property. You have to ascend this imposing stone staircase to get to the floor where the music library is. Then we sat in an old back room (calling it a hole-in-the-wall, or an extra storage space, might be more descriptive) to hear the records. We could look out the window and see ivy-covered walls, lawn, and rain pouring down. Now isn't that the perfect setting for Renaissance music-listening? All we needed was to have a knight come charging out of the bushes, to rescue the castle! . . .

Tuesday, January 15, 1963

. . . Classes are going along at their usual rate. Professor Winters is being as dogmatic as ever, and all the students who didn't have him last semester, or who have never read any of his works, are being as amazed and annoyed as ever. . . .

Many people . . . think that in a class, no matter who the professor, one should be able to disagree freely with the instructor, and should not be penalized for doing so. (If one were to write a paper or an exam advocating the exact opposite of what Professor Winters believes, the results might not be very good.) . . . It seems to me that if someone has devoted a lifetime to the intelligent reading and studying of a particular field, and if this critic has formed certain opinions, it's his perfect right to state them, and state them firmly. And students, who haven't even begun to do the amount of reading and studying someone sixty years old has accomplished, shouldn't feel that their opinions should be considered on a par with his. . . .

[April 4, 1963]
"THE BIG BLOWOUT"

'Twas the night of April 3rd on the relatively quiet campus of Leland Stanford University when all of a sudden surprises started bursting out in the dining hall of Paloma House.[121] And surprises there were—surprises for every single diner that evening. In fact, the excitement and astonishment has just now begun to wear itself down. To begin at the beginning . . .

Yesterday afternoon I took the candle that had survived all sorts of shocks between here and Los Angeles, including being lost for a time in transit between the two cities, to a florist to have him decorate it appropriately for the auspicious event. He bedecked said stick of twisted white wax with yellow flowers and ribbons, and made it quite beautiful—all for a slight fee, that is. The candle had a big bow of yellow ribbon at the bottom, and then three very full carnations around the base. Then six small yellow roses were arranged up the candle, the tallest of them reaching almost to the top of the candle.

My stealthy accomplice, who had driven me to the flower shop, and who had been bribed with ice cream while we were waiting for the piece of floral artistry to be completed, made all the arrangements for the safekeeping of the candle when we returned to the dorm. She made sure that it got down to the kitchen and was marked for the correct house. Then we all got ready for dinner and the big moment.

Suddenly, right before we were to go down for the festive meal, said partner in crime received an urgent phone call from the dining hall. She was informed that there was to be another candle passed in Paloma—another girl was also announcing some very exciting news! She was notified of this so that I could be told to be sure not to blow out someone else's candle. The other girl was also informed, and we were told that her candle (also for an engagement) would be passed first, and mine would be second. This evening, then, was really to be a special one.

. . . The honored guest was about to arrive. My English professor, Mr. Rebholz, was expected any minute, and of course he knew nothing at all about these last-minute changes in plan. My roommate Carol, in her usual sense of playfulness, decided that it would be fun not to tell him of what was to happen, and thus to let him be a little surprised also. She greeted him at the door with a stern warning: "Whatever you do, don't say anything at all until Elaine actually blows out her candle."

Dinner began. Not that any of us were really eating much of it, even though it was good. We all had our eyes focused on the doorway, through which the hasher would pass with the lighted candle. . . . The dining room was crowded, and it took quite a while for all the tables to be served. But finally the lights were flicked off, and all the girls gasped. The head hasher handed the first girl sitting at the head table a beautiful white candle with pink roses on it. Immediately the speculations began—who is announcing their engagement tonight? Only a few of us knew. (We had been told right before dinner, when we had been notified about the double ceremony.) The pink roses began their trip around the dining hall, coming to our table second. (This had all been carefully arranged. The first candle was to pass by me; the second was to pass by the other girl.) Carol got the candle first, handed it to me, and then I calmly passed it on to Mr. Rebholz, who was sitting beside me. He nearly dropped it in his excitement—his mouth fell open, and I had to kick him under the table to keep him from saying anything. But the candle went on, and as soon as he saw the other girl blow it out he knew what had happened. . . .

The hashers let a few minutes elapse, during which time they started serving dessert. Then the lights went off again, to the tune of really astonished gasps. "Another engagement!" "Who can it be?" Everyone oh'd and ah'd over the beautiful candle and flowers—in fact the unusual candle itself caused many comments. Finally it found its way home, and I got my chance at the "blowout." Congratulations followed, and the traditional song, "Felicitations to you," which even Mr. Rebholz joined in on singing. (They say that they sing "Felicitations" instead of "Congratulations" to a girl, because "Congratulations" sounds like they are praising you for finally "bagging him." I don't believe a word of it.)

Explanations to Mr. Rebholz and the other girls at the table followed immediately—both about the engagement and about the two candles. Then we passed candy and thus ended a rather exciting evening meal.

Actually, it was a lot of fun to have two engagements on the same night, especially since mine was the second. The girls were even more surprised when the second candle came into the room—they had already seen me pass one by, so of course no one expected what was about to happen.

[Love,
Elaine]

Postscript: The following announcement appeared in the Stanford Daily this morning:

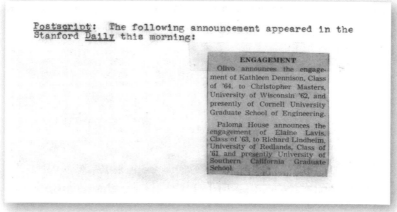

House Announcement: Elaine Lavis gets engaged, 1963
Courtesy of Elaine Lavis and the *Stanford Daily*

Letters from Joe (Joseph) Lewis Jacobs to his parents

October 28, 1963

Dear Mom and Dad,

You'll have to excuse the typing in this letter, but it's the electric that belongs to the IIR (Institute of International Relations), and I'm not really used to it. . . .

. . . I'm still going out of my mind with "Gaieties."[35] We are going up to San Francisco on November 10 for a recording session, and getting ready for that is going to be so tight it will be unbelievable. But we'll have to pull it off, somehow. I've tried to figure it out, and I'd guess that I'm spending 40 hours or more a week working on the show, which is a fair amount of time, and which leaves me totally exhausted, but which I love and wouldn't give up for anything. . . .

. . . Please let me (and Carl) know about when he has to return the car to me.[59] It's most important. I don't know what I will do if he doesn't have it back to me by Sunday night, but I think that homicide (justifiable, of course) might be in order. . . .

Incidentally, the curtain doesn't go up until 9:00 or 9:30 p.m. on Friday night[122] [Nov. 22, 1963]. . . .

1/18/65

. . . Oh, note the enclosed articles. The Mendicants[123] one was from the front page last Thursday, the LASSU one from edit page this morning.[124] Saturday I went up to meet Ida Mae. (We were going to meet Thursday but through a comedy of errors she couldn't make it, Ned's car broke down, and something happened to Mary, so I wound up standing in front of Hoover Tower for an hour waiting because they couldn't get hold of me.) So we got something to eat, then went shopping in Hillsdale Shopping Center, then over to Gisele MacKenzie's apartment for a while—Ida Mae had gotten little gifts for Gisele's two kids, who are adorable. And then to the theater, where I talked with Ned and watched the first act of "Auntie Mame." I came back, showered, changed, and went out to see "Stop the World—I Want to Get Off" at a theater in Palo Alto. It was quite well done—I'll send you my review after it gets printed. I went with Jim Briscoe—a friend from the Daily, and then we went over to the office, because there was supposed to be a meeting of the incoming edit board that night. Well, no one knew about it, but we finally got hold of Nancy—the incoming editor—at the Oasis [125] (a local beer and hamburger place where Nancy virtually lives),rounded up a couple of other staff members on campus and trooped off—along with Nancy's boyfriend and five six-packs—to one of the guy's apartments for an unofficial meeting that went on until

2:15 a.m. I got up yesterday, ate breakfast, wrote the LASSU article, came back, showered, changed, picked up my date and drove up to SF for dinner at Alfred's and then "My Fair Lady," which was good but not what it should have been. I'll send you THAT review when it gets printed, too. Tomorrow night I'm seeing "Mister Roberts" at Circle Star[126] (and am sending my jazz columnist Rick to see Nancy Wilson–George Shearing at [the] Hyatt in my place) and then next Tuesday I'm seeing Ella Fitzgerald and the Oscar Peterson Trio at the Hyatt. I'm sending John—my drama critic—up to the Actor's Workshop Feb. 1 to see Emlyn Williams do readings from Charles Dickens—I'm just not that interested. And so it goes—never a dull moment. Nancy will keep John, Rick, and me on next volume, and she also wants to expand the Daily's cultural coverage—i.e., book reviews, art shows, etc. (Nancy's an English major), so it could be busy. . . .

Almost forgot—I'm in charge of a play reading for Friday night.

P.S. Who pays for the battery, you or me? If it's me, tell Carl that I expect him to pay half of it. . . .

I guess that is it. I have to finish [the] "My Fair Lady" review before I go to class.

March 1, 1965

. . . It has occurred to me that the most intelligible and understandable letters I have written to you were those that I sent from camp at the age of 7 and that I have become progressively more disorganized and more incomprehendable (Or is it incomprehensible?) ever since. . . .

Also, I have decided to drive down the week of April 16–18,

which is Easter weekend. Terry will come with me, and we will come in his car. That way we can get together to celebrate Carl's and my birthday a couple of days late—which I think would be nice. God only knows when it will happen again. . . .

Love,

Joe

1970s

Letter from Wendy to her grandmother

11-27-72

Dear Granny,

. . . It's so exciting to go to the mailbox & get a postcard from you—& even more exciting when I get a pink card—that means something won't fit in the box—I really am glad to have the book Daily Strength for Daily Needs. I keep it by my bed & am trying to get into the habit of reading it every day. And the apples! All my friends say thank you!! I'd never seen such big apples & so sweet! . . .

I went to my roommate's . . . for Thanksgiving & really enjoyed it. She has a different background than myself—neither of her parents went to college, she's been working since she was 15, and she's spent a lot of time w/ "Drama People," people involved in school plays & musicals. We get along though & I enjoy being with her. . . .

I'm playing a lot of volleyball—6 hours a week—I'm on the intercollegiate team. . . . I'm really learning a lot though, from the workouts—not only about volleyball skills either! I was at the top when I left high school & now I must sit on the bench & dream about playing. . . . It's not really that bad, but I'm not on the starting team & I have to get used to not being among the top 6. Funny how we set such high standards for ourselves. Once they have been achieved, though on a different level, we must strive again to attain our goals. . . .

The only thing that gets me down is when I think about what I'm going to do after I graduate. I enjoy learning & thinking & growing, but where is it heading? Perhaps I should keep walking down my road & the answer will appear somewhere—Have you any suggestions? I'm interested in thoughts & ideas & reasons why? A philosopher? Shall I go live in the hills & wonder why? . . .

Well, Granny, I really just wanted to thank you & would love to see you or talk to you sometime but I imagine you won't have time till after the holidays—If not, don't worry—I love you

Take care,
Wendy

Letter from M.C. to her parents

10 Nov 75

Dear Mom and Dad,
I had an econ. test this morning and I think I did O.K., but I don't know. One thing about econ.—if I bomb a test, I can take another one to raise my grade. Thank you! Thank you! Thank you! . . .

. . . I don't think I've given much time to the food service here at Wilbur.[26] Well, generally I'm not too choosy and it isn't too bad.

We've had lamb twice & it was good. We have chicken a lot disguised in numerous ways. But oh how I long for your fried chicken, Mom. . . . There are big charcoal grills in the courtyards outside the dining rooms where they actually charcoal the steaks (medium rare or medium well). Several times they have also charcoaled hamburgers out there (again, not as good as Dad's but a passable substitute). All is not rosy and edible, however. Breakfasts during the weekdays are generally pretty dismal. I usually just have a bowl of Raisin Bran. . . . One main course that my mild-mannered, easygoing system has refused to accept: that is "Salisbury Steak." Now I don't mind soy-supplemented meat, but this stuff is terrible & you wouldn't believe the taste. Oh well, I eat salad when they have it. But when I come home at Christmas, I want to put in my requests for food. . . .

. . . People around here are getting Rose Bowl fever. The same thing happened last year and they blew it. . . .

. . . [My roommate] is interested in international relations (interested, because nobody majors yet, they just say they're interested in something). I'm not exactly sure what that is but I assume it follows the meaning of the name rather closely. She has taken French for 5 years and is taking French & German this quarter. . . . We pretty much think the same; I haven't noticed any glaring differences. . . .

. . . I'm getting bummed out on engineering & sort of science in general. I'm very tired of math & am not exactly looking forward to taking physics. I don't think I really enjoy the deep sciences that much. . . . [I've] admitted this "realization" & am now going to stop trying to be something I'm not. I have developed an interest in economics as I've gotten deeper into my class & think that something there is more in my line. . . .

Love,

M.C.

Letter from Alison Carpenter to her parents

Nov. 12, 1975

Dear Mumu & Dad,

. . . I haven't been able to get back into studying since midterms and the excitement of winning last weekend. I attempted to study in the dorm last night, but it was to no avail. Everyone else seems to do fairly well studying there so I decided to try it. I'm glad I did when the pressure wasn't on (there wasn't too much I had to do last night) because I finally learned once and for all that I can't study in the dorm. My schedule ran as follows: 5:30 dinner, 6:30 listen to stereo and try to take a nap (hopeless), 7:00 talk to two people from a local church for ½ hour, 7:30 talk to Claire for an hr. (we hadn't talked all day!), 8:30–10:30 read about 15 pgs., talk, run out in the hall to see how a dorm mate's chem. midterm was, etc., 10:30 exercise class. . . . 11:00 help fill wastebasket of water to throw at guy who's playing taps in the girls' bathroom, 11:30 get ready for bed, etc. I got accomplished in about four hours what I could have in about one at the library.

Tomorrow I'm really going to have to bear down and hit the books. I'm already two chapters behind in psych and four in art history. You just can't let things slide around here. However, do not worry about my burying myself in work. . . .

Love,
Ali

Letter from Anonymous to her parents

[Mid-1970s]

Dear Mom & Dad,
. . . I've been having slightly more conflicts with my roommate in that her boyfriend's in the room all the time and I don't feel that comfortable going in the room. She's told me that I'm perfectly O.K. being in there but I still can't help feeling slightly awkward sometimes. Also, I never spend very much time with her anymore. It's like all we do is sleep and change our clothes in the same room. Third, I feel we might as well have an "Off Limits" sign on our door. She always wants the door closed and nobody is ever in our room. I always have to go to other rooms to do my socializing. . . .

Anonymous

Letters from M.C. to her parents

4Feb76
Wed.
. . . Our weather has certainly been strange. For 2 weeks until yesterday we had temps in the 70s & beautiful sunshine. Last weekend I studied outside in my bathing suit. It was unbelievable! This is January?! . . .

[Thurs. afternoon, Feb. 5, 1976]

Hi again,

. . . This has been a truly exciting day today. . . . Just about every girl on my floor was out in the hall yelling, "It's snowing, it's snowing!"[127] And yes, folks, it was snowing. Not so much that I thought it warranted yelling at 6 a.m., however. It was amazing how wild people went. The Californians were especially crazy (because they know the significance of this long drought & then to have the first precipitation be snow, I suppose). People went out (at 6) & built snowmen (I saw them all over campus today), threw snowballs, "looked for hills" while wearing their skis, & ran around in circles yelling. The snow has been all anyone has talked about today & this afternoon it really snowed hard again (but didn't stick) for 30–45 minutes. . . . This is also the weirdest I've ever seen people get over just a trace of snow. It could have something to do with the fact that people have midterms this week & next. . . .

Snow it Goes: "The Californians were especially crazy," M.C., Feb. 5, 1976
Courtesy of Erik Hill, Class of 1979

19 April 76
Mon.

. . . Tuesday night I took a pizza (!) study break at 11:30 w/ Michael, Megan, Tom, Anne, and her boyfriend. Michael is Michael Jones (his dad is a doctor—just thought I'd cover all bases on the usual questions, Dad!) from Columbia, Missouri (he's a swimmer & hope-to-be engineer); Megan is Megan Larson (her dad's a lawyer) from Chicago (she's Michael's girlfriend and probably my best friend out here—she's in CE). Tom Smith (I'm not sure what his dad does—something w/ prefab building slabs?) from South Carolina (really from Indiana—he's very funny, & sort of reminds me of Mike Friedemann—he's a premed but doesn't really act like it); Anne Nichols from Pennsylvania (she's a creative writing major). . . .

Thursday night I participated in a Jewish Passover Seder in our seminar room. I was sort of wishing I could be home for Easter, and it was nice to be with other people who were wishing they were home, too! . . . I really enjoyed it because I learned something about Jewish customs & I also felt that, in a strange way, I was participating in a Maundy Thursday dinner service like we've had at the church for the past couple of years. I was deeply impressed by how seriously my dorm mates took being part of the Jewish faith. It was amazing that 3 people from NY, Chicago, & LA all knew all the Hebrew & the Jewish songs. I'm glad I went. . . .

14Feb77

. . . This afternoon it got up to 75 degrees and the "Stanford Country Club" officially opened to greet midterm-weary sunbathers, tennis players, etc. It was just like a day in late May at home. Beautiful. It's impossible for me to be able to imagine how cold it is back east. What's the weather like at home?

Unfortunately, this beautiful weather isn't as beautiful as it seems. Just about everyone out here (including sun-worshiping me) would rather see it rain for 40 days & nights. I'm afraid even that wouldn't make a dent. I've never been in an area so severely hit with such strict conservation measures. They are rationing water to the north of us (in Marin) & in the East Bay, & I would suspect it's just a matter of time for us. The University has cut back the water pressure in the showers (we now just get small trickles—very odd), has stopped watering the grass & in a token measure has even turned off the fountains.[128] People are actually trying to cut back but this situation is serious. It's really amazing how hard the U.S. has been hit weather-wise this year. Are you all pulling out of the drought yet? . . .

. . . I almost ran into SU's president the other day—literally. I was navigating my way through people outside the post office on my bike & this person made an unexpected move & I had to pull up short & turn my front wheel to keep from hitting him. He turned out to be none other than Dick Lyman. . . .[129]

3 March 77

. . . Speaking of money now, I'm getting ready to pre-reg so I found out how much I will be needing for next quarter. I would like to borrow $1,050 from you. I don't need quite that much for tuition but since I won't have been working long enough to have built up much money, I need to borrow a little extra to pay for books and other beginning of the quarter things. I set up my loan from Stanford the other day and I will be borrowing $500 from them at 3%, to be paid back when I get out of school. I'd say that's not bad at all. From what I remember of our previous discussion, you said you'd loan me the money at 7%. Right now I'm planning to try to make enough money this summer to pay you back by the end of the summer but I guess I'll have to wait and see about that. I'd really like to have it all paid back by the end of my junior year so I can finish my junior year only owing $500 for my schooling (to Stanford). Oh, I will need the money from you on March 28.

Still along the lines of money and Stanford, I found out (or brainstormed) something the other day. I've figured out how I may be able to save $1,500 or so my senior year. If sometime between now and the end of my senior year I take 10 extra units (that is, over the usual 15 unit/quarter schedule) I will be able to reach the 180 units required to graduate by the end of winter quarter senior year. That would mean I wouldn't have to register spring quarter and I would save that much money but still be able to graduate as a full-fledged, bona fide Stanford graduate. If I wanted to, I could stay here and continue to live in the dorm and work spring quarter, which is what a lot of seniors do. That way I could make some money to help pay things off. . . . Of course, all this is very tentative, but it is also a real possibility that could be worked out. Another chapter in my series on how to get that Stanford education and degree for the least amount of money. If I could come out of here owing only $500–1,000 everything would definitely be worth it. Well, everything will be worth it anyway, but that would just be icing on the cake. . . .

Love,
M.C.

Letter from Tom to his father

[From Stanford in Washington][130]
7/5/77

Dear John:

Thank you for your letter expressing your concern about your son, Thomas. I appreciate you sharing your views on this matter.

Hi, everyone! I'm at my desk typing out drafts for letters to constituents and thought that I'd write a quick note home. I spend most of my time in the office preparing and writing letters. Mostly, I just copy from similar letters on file. Being original doesn't make it when you're dealing with so much mail. It seems most people who write are crackpots!

Last night we (my roommates and other Stanford friends) sat in front of the Washington Monument and watched the fireworks over the reflecting pool which stretches out to the Lincoln Memorial. We picnicked on the Mall for the Fourth of July with about 25 Stanford and UC Davis kids. I walked over to the White House briefly to see the Marijuana Smoke-In which attracted a large crowd of young people and assorted hippie types.

The night before, we went to a progressive dinner hosted by Harvard interns, which was a great contrast to the crowd at the demonstration. There were also a lot of UC Berkeley people at the dinner, and I received the first razz about attending Stanford since I arrived in Washington. Those damn public school kids!! . . .[131]

We live right across from the National Cathedral; Ray, whom I know as one of my proctors from Zimbardo's class,[132] went to mass with me at a nearby church, then we went through the cathedral for a short visit, since there was a service in progress. I was very impressed by the architecture. It made me think of Europe and my desire to visit the Gothic cathedrals I've seen so often in classes since the eighth grade. . . .

There is so much to see in Washington alone. I have used the Library of Congress and will soon visit the Smithsonian Air and Space Museum. We just seem to be now getting settled in our apartment. . . .

Interns abound at the Capitol! An intern office has been set up and a regular program of speakers is presented each week. Most of the time interns are encouraged to roam around and visit whatever they'd like. I listened to almost all of the debate on the floor of the House the day they voted for the B-1 Bomber, before Big Jimmy [Carter] nixed the project. Most people I associate with (these damn liberal, young Democrat Congressmen and their staffs!) were very glad about the B-1 thing. Mr. Panetta had his 39th birthday last week and was selected as Chairman of the Democratic Freshman Caucus.

Mr. Panetta seems to be a very decent, intelligent man. George Miller has a reputation of being a flaming liberal. I've met two of the interns working in his office. Also, I'm fairly good friends now with one of the interns working for Pete McCloskey from Palo Alto. As an intern, I am entitled to just about all of the privileges of the regular staff persons, including getting into the buildings whenever I want. The lunchrooms are interesting places where one meets many interns from across the country, as well as students from Stanford who were unknown to you before. I think about 75 Stanford people are here this summer.

I think we are planning to get a telephone in our apartment soon. If you phone our room now, you'll get through to the switchboard, but often not reach us in the room. So it ends up as a charged call. The mail has been arriving regularly from Concord—all bills! Actually, I paid all my bills before I left so these all show positive balances. Money has been flowing freely and I think I'll end up going over my budget. I hate having to pay cash for everything. I wish my checks were good out here! I'm fine now though. . . .

Tom

Letter from M.C. to her mother

21Feb78

Dear Mommy,
I am very sick & feeling lousy. I have had a stuffy, congested head & chest, fever, sore throat, hacking cough, sneezes, aching muscles, headaches & depressed feeling since Saturday. I am trying to take care of myself (that, in itself, is practically an impossibility since I'm in school right now). I sleep as much as I can get away with, inhale lots of steam & take lots of aspirin & decongestants. Well over half of my dorm is also sick; they say the whole campus is hit hard. . . . I don't feel like doing anything except lying in bed. Too bad it's so close to the end of the quarter. If this keeps up too long, there may be some I's [Incompletes]. I doubt that, though. I guess I should just be glad I have all my midterms over. I imagine the "bug" bit me last week when my resistance was down from studying so long & late all week.

I hope I feel better by the time you get this. Don't get me wrong—I'm not writing to get you all worried. I'll survive (I think). I just wanted to say I wish I were at home and you were taking care of me. (I'd even eat homemade chicken & corn soup!)

Love,
(cough, sneeze, gasp, sigh . . .) [Ellipses in original.]
M.C.

1980s and Beyond

Letter from Mike (Michael) Clonts to his parents

10/29/82

Dear Mom & Dad,

I had a break in the action up here so decided I should write. Things are pretty busy up here. I've got only 3 midterms this entire quarter; however, they are all next week and two are on the same day one hour apart! Those are econ. (which I'm doing good in and I like a lot!) and geology (where we measure rocks, oh boy!). The next day I have a physics midterm, which will be tough. My favorite class is comp sci because we don't have any midterms or finals.

I got the care package last week and the food is coming in handy. I also got that bizarre letter about all the excitement down there. I keep waiting for the next letter to come up saying that you just made that story up to have something to write about! . . . Also, save any articles about it so I can read them when I come home. Were you guys all in the local papers and the TV news? I wish I hadn't missed all that. I also signed all the bank documents for the loan and sent them in. Right after I got the letter I went to "The Who" concert. It was their last concert in the Bay Area. . . . We barbequed steaks in the parking lot in the rain, which was a unique experience. We got [in] there pretty early so we were right in the front row on the floor level. Roger Daltrey, the lead singer, gave us high fives right before the end of the show; we were really close. We were also so smashed in by all the people that we couldn't really move but it was an exciting concert. . . .

Last Saturday I worked with this girl as a disc-jockey at KZSU,[133] the Stanford radio station. I ran the place for a little bit. It was great and I'm hoping to do it again soon. They have millions of records, and I told her all these songs to play that were new to her but which I had heard this summer. You should hear me, I'm a great DJ.

Monday was a strange day, the same day I got your letter and went to the concert I also got a letter from my high school friend who is still missionary-ing overseas. He said that the other day he had to perform an exorcism for this lady and her daughter on their house. The mother & daughter had been attacked by the evil spirits of the house and the girl had been on the floor kicking and screaming trying to get them off. This all happened in their back room where they had piles of gruesome crucifixes, pictures of Christ's crucifixions & saints, rosary beads, and hundreds of candles. He told them all these things invited evil spirits and they had to get rid of them to cleanse the house. The grandmother was there too. . . . The girl went into a frenzy and started destroying all the stuff. I guess it's O.K. now but I have to wonder, that's a little too much for one day: the Who story, his story, and your story. . . .

Love,
Mike

Letter from Natasha Pratap to her parents

1 October 1991

Dearest Mom & Dad,

Hi! I started writing this card, somewhere last year—but never finished.

Let's see, when I got here I was really happy to be back on campus—it's like a second home you know. The first week was busy & exciting—like last year. But it's after that, that you get to the point. I'm definitely better off than I was last year—more "at home" but I still have some similar problems. I'm an AA (Advising Associate) and I had/have a slight problem striking a rapport with a few of my advisees (6 in all). The American sense of humour is a little difficult to adjust to. Sometimes (a little more often than that!) I feel a pressure to be "cool," i.e. funny & entertaining. . . .

I'm really sorry we didn't get a chance to spend as much time together as we wanted to. Maybe it was my fault, maybe it was bad luck. . . .

Letter from Natasha Pratap to her family

9 November, [1991]

Dearest Family,

. . . I had a midterm in my automotive tech class—the second one—I think I did really badly although I worked very hard. It's just that [the teacher] docs mostly theory in class & the exam is mostly problems—so even though I understand everything I don't have practice in problem solving. I think I'm going to go speak to him next week. It's just that I don't want to be lame and drop the class. 'Cause I've taken it for 6 weeks now. Plus it's so easy to drop classes—it's like giving up too easy. Also, I think it's silly that every time you think you're not going to get an A in a class—you drop it. I mean what the hell. What's the big deal about getting a C once in a while—as long as you tried?! . . .

Love you'll [you all] lots and miss you very much,
Natasha

Email from Vanessa Hua to her parents

04-14-95
From: Vanessa Hua
02:27 PM

Date: Friday, 14-Apr-95 02:27 PM
From: Vanessa Hua
(lochness@leland.stanford.edu)
Subject: Entering the Information Age

Dear Mom and Dad,
I like typing in lower case -- it's more casual and friendly on e-mail. But if you insist, I'll write in with capitals. I have had a pretty good week. Classes are interesting. And I'm writing for the paper again. I just wrote an article on a man who can catch arrows mid-air. My next assignment is on two Stanford students who created a site on the World Wide Web.[134]

I have fun in my Chinese Conversational class, too. Although it is not very difficult, I am learning a lot. I don't really like the "Beijing" accent, though -- ending everything with an "r." I am looking forward to my birthday. I will be twenty! Doesn't that make you feel old?

See you soon,
Vanessa

Emails from Vanessa Hua to her father

04-28-95
From: Vanessa Hua
01:59 PM

Date: Friday, 28-Apr-95 01:59 PM
From: Vanessa Hua
(lochness@leland.stanford.edu)
Subject: life

Dear dad,
i will either come home tomorrow afternoon (saturday), or just come home next weekend. i am learning interesting things in my gothic novel class. i like being able to discuss the topics in a small seminar setting. my other classes are interesting as well. i am learning chinese -- i will talk to you and mom the next time we "jian mian" okay? :)[135]

05-02-95
From: Vanessa Hua
03:03 AM

Date: Tuesday, 02-May-95 03:03 AM
From: Vanessa Hua
(lochness@leland.stanford.edu)
Subject: teeth!

Dear Dad,

Depending on when summer school or internships start, i might need an earlier or later appointment. i tell you ASAP, okay?

So, is mom becoming less afraid of computers? now you guys can do e-mail at home. soon, our entire family will be on the Internet. I just wrote an article for the paper about World Wide Web. I will show it to you. i might come home this weekend.

Talk to you later,

vanessa

Stack-Up: The World Wide Web is here, but it can't do this. Vanessa Hua (top left) and friends, spring 1995

Courtesy of Vanessa Hua, Class of 1997

Letter from Anonymous to her aunt

From: Anonymous
Date: May 1, 2013, 7:10:40 PM EDT
To: xxxxxx
Subject: Hi!

Hi Aunt C,

. . . I'm very excited about Lakota, it's such a beautiful-sounding language and it expresses some really profound ideas in single words. . . . Lakota itself has about 3,000–6,000 speakers still alive, but the average age of a fluent speaker is 65 . . . so if it has any chance to stay alive young kids need to learn it right now. It's a very pivotal time for language documentation, in the next 10 years it's estimated that half of the languages around today will be extinct. My class is working to create language-learning materials to send to elementary schools on a Lakota reservation in South Dakota. I wrote a short-story book and now have to figure out how to illustrate it. . . .

In addition to Lakota, this semester I'm taking psychology, imaging (learning about how cameras, microscopes, telescopes, MRIs, and CAT scans work and the like), and a class on designing social interventions (essentially a class on how to create and run an NGO). So it's a pretty eclectic bunch, but I'm finding that Lakota is teaching me the most. New and beautiful ways to feel . . .

I love you or chante mitawa ekta ochignaka (which roughly translates to "into my heart I have put you").

Toksha ake (or, "until again," the closest equivalent Lakota has to goodbye),

Anonymous

Email from Kat (Kathleen) Gregory to her mother

From: Kat
Subject: Day in the life?
Date: October 9, 2012 at 12:25:19 PM PDT
To: Mom

It's too bad beautiful study spots are so difficult to find here. . . .
My Tuesdays are awesome. I just spent a half-hour in a one-on-one conversation to get to know one of my lecture professors and their research and am now hanging about the Quad until my next class. I'll write and run before a lab at 5, eat with my friends at Arrillaga . . . and then cram.

I've 150 pages of reading, a paper, and a midterm tomorrow, but at least I can study in style :). . . .

. . . Ok, I'll start working now.

Texts between Laine Bruzek and her mother

Laine [2013]

Texts between Laine Bruzek and her father

Texts between Jason Seter and his mother

Jason [2014]

< Messages **Mom** Details

game on sat. When/where does Stanford play?

Stanford plays Arizona state at 7:30 on saturdau

Away or home

Away

What are your plans for the weekend!

Work! Nothing but work ever in my life!

Not once you join the band and archery! What about inter mural soccer? Flag football?

Are you running at all

When I'm not slaving over my debilitating chemistry work, I've been able to go running. I'd like to start lifting too

Text from Anonymous to a friend

Anonymous [2016]

Probs not. Well, I just wanted to apologize for earlier. We're both very stressed. And I used to be very good at managing my stuff and when problems arose I used to have a better mindset. It's just... Stanford has come with all sorts of new challenges. Moving, being without you, transfer credit, class difficulty, roommate problems, and now--ugh, wisdom teeth. I just felt really overwhelmed. I'm sorry I called you so upset and I didn't mean to diminish any of the things you're going through. Thank you for being there and offering solutions,

empathy, and some humor

Text from Catherine Goetz to her mother

Catherine [2016]

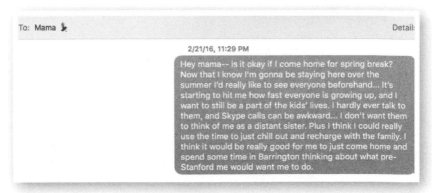

To: Mama   Details

2/21/16, 11:29 PM

Hey mama-- is it okay if I come home for spring break? Now that I know I'm gonna be staying here over the summer I'd really like to see everyone beforehand... It's starting to hit me how fast everyone is growing up, and I want to still be a part of the kids' lives. I hardly ever talk to them, and Skype calls can be awkward... I don't want them to think of me as a distant sister. Plus I think I could really use the time to just chill out and recharge with the family. I think it would be really good for me to just come home and spend some time in Barrington thinking about what pre-Stanford me would want me to do.

Text from Anonymous to a friend

Anonymous [2016]

ACTIVE NOW

Thanks querido. Rn I just need prayers bc honestly my life is a mess. Classes not going well, busy with other stuff like finding lab, internships, transfer credit still in progress, etc. Bike broke so I fixes it. Laptop not doing well. Mom freaking out bc dad was in hospital then George died now other fam friend has same cancer. To boot I'm also trying to figure out how to pay for the next two years but I have all these problems that cost money. So much of this stuff is out of my control. But God is good. I can manage and you can, too. Been through worse times (we both have).

Student Life: "Please Send, " Collected

"I think I'd better write a little paragraph on the things I need. (This seems to have become very characteristic of all my letters)."

—*Mary Allie Lesnett, July 31, 1944*

"That's the favorite way to dress-up down here you know—sweater & slacks. The sweaters I have now are O.K. for school, but I need a nicer one for dress. How about it?"

—*Bob (Robert) Lowell Swetzer, Mar. 27, [1949]*

My zither

Jeans material

One of my bungalow aprons

Flashcubes

My saddle oxfords

The Mastermind Game

The wallet with the cowboy stuff on it

The waffle recipe

Granada [High School's] football scores

List of family birthdays

Black loafers [for] practice—marching at night

Army blanket

My old pair of bermuda shorts

My picture of Stanford

American Flag

Gloves

Any good pictures around

Records

Red sweater that's in the sewing center

Some rugs

Food for me during dead week and finals

The brown shirt

White shoes

That lamp

Your white sweater

A lemon squeezer

Fur coat

Socks and shorts

Sheets

Tweezers

Sweets

Caricature portrait of me surfing

Camera

My formal

Money

My fairy costume

One or two good books to read

Anything to decorate this dump

My ration books

What I asked for

My French book

My address book

My book by Dick Gould on how to teach tennis

Cookies, raisins, honey bars, Twinkies, canned puddings

The world map from the last National Geographic

Clean laundry, so "I can send back dirty clothes"

Student Life: Further Comments

"My appetite is very good. Also, my digestion."

—Lucy Allabach, Roble Hall, [Fall] 1891

"Well with best of love I am your own faraway Lucy who loves her mother, father, and sister if she is a cross patch."

—Lucy, Roble Hall, Nov. 15, 1891

"There was so much water on the pavements and everywhere that even the bravest were dubious about getting over to Alvarado row, where we were all invited to an afternoon tea at the home of Mrs. Dr. Wood and Mrs. Professor Bryant."

—Lucy, Roble Hall, "December-no-more," Jan. 3, 1892

"I have only one real wish for Xmas . . . 'Frantique's Civil Engineer's Pocket Book, Edition of 1891,' published by John Wiley & Sons."

—Francis J. Batchelder, Dec. 6, 1891

"Here it is half past ten and I am . . . reduced from thirty-two candle power electric light to one single tallow dip. It is like going back a hundred years."

—Francis, Feb. 10, 1892

"I do not think our expenses will be any higher than they were last year—that is about 16 or 17 dollars a month. The board and rooms at Encina & Roble are to be $28 a month this year. The rise is causing a good deal of dissatisfaction among the students, and it may be lowered when the Stanfords return."

—Francis, Sept. 4, 1892

"Sunday, and letters!"

—Fred (Frederic) Jewell Perry, Feb. 19, 1899

"The excuses you give for not replying earlier are
incompetent, irrelevant, and immaterial. It would take
just fifteen minutes to dash off two small pages such as
you have used, and you need not assert that you have not
had a spare 15 min. since my letter was rec'd. Your
neglect is willful, perverse, culpable, and entirely
inexcusable."

—Fred, [one week later, 1899]

"During this week there will be more midnight oil burned
than has been consumed for the last year. These are the
times that try men's souls. Those who are behind in their
studies must make up their deficiencies in the
examinations, and only by 'cramming' and 'boning' night
and day during this week can they hope to pass."

—Fred, May 14, 1899

"We all hope that you had a happy birthday and that it
recalled the joys of a long list of such days. How we
should have enjoyed seeing you. Wouldn't we talk?"

—J. B. (Jesse Brundage) Sears, Sept. 23, 1907

"Mother, things are so interesting, this may be the enthusiasm of twenty-one, but Mother, interesting things just
crowd in on you from all sides."

—Hope Snedden, Sun. noon [1920]

"[I am] glad to 'sojourn in a world so fair.'[136] The
acacias and eucalyptus are both blooming and their
fragrance blends in an intoxicating way. Really, if
I start getting spring fever in January, what will
become of me by June?"

—Alice Louise Clark, Jan. 21, 1936

"I . . . did enjoy your long and detailed and interesting letter of a non-recent date. I know you all are pretty irked about my writing, but I really have had very little time, although I seem to find time alright when I need money."

—(William) Russell Smith, Apr. 12, 1938

"Sunday I spent most of the day on the lake. . . . You're not safe unless you have a bathing suit on; there were quite a few got tipped over, clothes or no clothes."

—Russell, Apr. 20, 1938

"The studies are going along alright without much of a mean deviation. I have been studying fairly regular with a little social on the side."

—Russell, May 8, 1940

"Hey! How can I send my dresses home if I don't have the laundry box up here?"[137]

—(Mary) Carol Stearns, Weds., Apr. 25, [1945]

"Tell dad that the first thing I want to do when I get home for summer recess is to drive the tractor like mad."

—Bob (Robert) Lowell Swetzer, May 16, 1948

"Roble food is good, but it is developing a definite 'Roble taste.'"

—Carol Hodge, Oct. 7, 1953

"Please try and write more often. I realize that my punctuality is nothing tremendous, but you must remember that if you miss me you can merely call up a friend on the phone. It's not that easy when I miss you, and I do miss you."

—Joe (Joseph) Lewis Jacobs, Oct. 31, [1961]

"Time for me to roar off to my daily one-o'clock wonder-education."

—Elaine Lavis, Wed., Nov. 8, 1961

"I miss you guys. I really do. You're a great family and I guess it's about time I admitted it."

—Phil (Philip) B. Laird Jr., [Late 1960s]

"I may have slaved over the paint bucket & may have a debt (which may not be so big, incidentally) but I still think it was all worth it."

—M.C., Fall 1975

STANFORD UNIVERSITY
OFFICE OF THE PRESIDENT

"Dear Mom & Dad, How do you like this stationery?"

—M.C., Nov. 3, 1975

"If you ever want to call me, most nights I'd probably be home except for Friday, Saturday, and Sunday, maybe Thursday sometimes."

—M.C., Feb. 25, 1976

"I'm afraid I'm going to be the typical college student and bring home my dirty laundry. It's not so much that I mind doing it, mostly it's because I'm cheap! Why pay 75 cents here when I can wait 5 days and do it at home for 'free'?"

—Anonymous, Mid-1970s

"The book on Oxford . . . had been checked out by a faculty member, and wasn't due for return until June next year. . . . I didn't think that volume four of the History of Oxford focusing on the 17th century would be in demand. . . ."

—Christopher Lowman, Sept. 26, 2006

Chapter 5

Letters from the Overseas Campuses

"At some point in Barcelona we had a real language network going—some Germans spoke to me about the hotel, I put it into English, which Johnny put into Spanish to the hotel owner! It took a while but the message got across."

—Chrissie Huneke, May 2, [1983]

Letter from George D. Green to his parents

April 28th, 1960[138]

Hello folks,

I have a few minutes before going to the Berlin Philharmonic so will start a letter to you.

We have spent both morning and afternoon in seeing the refugee situation. We began this morning at the main reception center here in west Berlin, where the refugees come first of all after crossing the border into east Berlin and then crossing again into west Berlin.

First of all we had a very informative lecture from the director of the center, himself a refugee in 1951. Some statistics he gave were well worth repeating: since World War 2 there have been 3.4 million refugees from east Germany, not counting those from other lands such as Latvia, Czechoslovakia, Hungary, Poland etc. Germany has a present population of about 54 million; of these, 13 million are refugees from somewhere behind the iron curtain—i.e. 25% of the whole population! That is a lot of people to absorb especially when three-fourths had another language, customs etc., and of course, none of them could bring more than a suitcase or so with them, many of them not even that much, so it was also quite an economic problem and still is.

Even more interesting are the most current figures: for example, the monthly refugee flow so far this year: January 5,300; Feb. 5,900; March 8,000; April to the 26th, 14,000. One reason for the rise since Feb. is that the Communists have put on a big push to collectivize the farms and also the hand-workers etc. who remain self-employed. This has, as the numbers show, driven thousands of farmers to make the very dangerous trip to Berlin to escape to the west, where they must now face the difficulty and hardship and uncertainty of starting life from scratch. The no. of farmers jumped from 200 in Jan. to 2,400 in the first three weeks of April, after the new laws came in. The psychological importance of west Berlin as an escape valve for refugees from Communism cannot be exaggerated!

After the background speech we split up into groups of ten to sit in on the actual interviews given to all new refugees. These people must show good reason for having left the Communist country in order to be granted refugee status in west Germany (this preventing infiltration and also preventing the complete flooding of west Germany with refugees to house, clothe, and feed), and hence they are questioned by a committee of three former refugees to verify these reasons. We got to listen to four cases, were permitted to ask questions when we didn't understand something—this was, I think, the most informative experience of the day, giving a unique insight into how Communism goes about its slow but relentless job of taking over the lives of the common people in service of the state. . . .

Love,
George

Letter from Lanny Levin to his sister

October 7, 1968

Dear Bryna Lee,
I received the birthday cards from all the family—early, even. (I got them both Saturday.) I was very pleased to get them, and it kept

reminding me of that glorious whipped cream birthday cake. Today's the big day, but I don't feel any older. We started Italian classes today. They'll be interesting I think. I also had my first lecture by Prof. Di Frederico, an Italian, on The History of Modern Italy 1860–1922.

The science-project sounds great. Do you think you can build it? Good luck (buona fortuna!).

The villa is interesting but not very comfortable in many places. The rooms are like cells. (It used to be a monastery (?). Firenze is the Italians' name for Florence.

There is a T.V. but I haven't watched it. About the only papers I read are The Daily American and the Stanford Daily,[2] mailed from California. . . .

Love,
Lanny

Letter from Anne Peters to her aunt

[1973]

Dear Aunt Betty,
It's a happy birthday to you. It's a happy birthday to you. It's a happy birthday dear Aunt Betty. It's a happy birthday to you. "What do you spose it is?" You will have to wait till I come home for your present (or until I get one, whichever's first). I'm late already—sorry. I got your letter today—with your present to me. Thank you very much. I think you know what it will be spent on: ris du veau, e oeffs au vin rouge (or ?) etc. I will give full details when I indulge. You were kind of extravagant—so

the meal may have to be stretched over a period of time—thanks a lot.

I hear the Giants are still doing really well. I wonder about the Warriors. You did say that they beat Bucks in 6. Wow! I never thought Mom and Dad were serious about getting a house. Jeez Louise. Sounds nice, but we already have a real nice one. Was denkst du? O ¿qué piensas tú? I am multilingual now.

I really enjoy hearing about Francie Jr. and Katy & Tony. I miss them. I think I'll write Francie a letter—I should have for Easter. I am determined to have an Easter egg hunt here tomorrow—I bought chocolate eggs already. I hope you had a nice one w/ good food.

Today I got back from a week + in Berlin on a field trip. It was really interesting. I took about 4 pictures of the wall. (I've taken about 20 altogether.) It was amazing. You can look over the wall from a platform on the west side and see the minefield—wire and everything—then there's a street with people & cars. Really eerie to think they can't cross. The whole city is fascinating, about the allies still occupying it and how the wall went up & who can cross. I went into East Berlin 3 times. The change is very noticeable—we had a tour thru East Berlin (for instance) & the lady pointed out a half-destroyed church and said that the conglomeration of architectural styles did not merit reconstruction. It's funny how no churches had enough architectural merit to be rebuilt but this square—seemingly boring-type styled buildings for govt. uses were rebuilt. The name of the newspaper there is "Freie Welt" or Free World. Weird. The trip was really interesting. West Berlin is really lively—best nightlife in Germany (none in E. Berlin)—all modern now. Only 1 old building remains (part of this church that has had parts built on now.) I would hate living there—it's all city. I think Tor's bday is around now too. Oops. Tell her happy B-day also. This quarter I'm going to study a lot—I like the classes and have decided that I should start working to get more out of school. I think I may be sick. Well, adiós and thanks again a lot for the present.

Love,
Anne

Letter from Alison Carpenter to her parents

Sept. 24, 1977

dear mumu & dad,

I feel like a zombie right now so I don't know how much sense all of this is going to make. It's now 7:05 a.m. Tours time and I've been awake since 2:00 a.m. . . .

So where to begin? The trip over was O.K. Slept a lot, cried a little, saw parts of 2 movies, chatted. . . . We stopped at Kennedy Airport instead of Bangor, Maine, as I had expected. That was kind of fun for me as I've never been to New York before—even though I obviously didn't get to see very much of it.

We finally got to Tours about 12:30 p.m. Thurs. I will never forget coming into town. Very foggy and dead—saw maybe 3 people & no lights on anywhere. The buildings are very close together—San Francisco–style—and mostly whites and browns— not extremely colorful. But by day you should see this place—a regular breathing, industrial city. I had some little provincial town in mind, but that's not the case at all. . . .

I am living in "Sanitas"—the dorm that is part of the university. This is where I wanted to live. At first I was in the Villa but I asked them if I could switch and they said O.K. . . . From my window I can see little European cars buzzing by and French women scurrying past. . . . There's also a fountain and a church off to the right. . . .

I didn't get out of my dorm yesterday until 1 p.m.—slept very late. . . . I was very nervous & not too psyched. Claire wasn't here yet and nobody seemed to be out and around in the hall, so I kind of said "Europe here I come" and jaunted out the door. I met a girl on my floor on the stairwell on the way down & we ended up walking around the city together. . . . I survived my first transactions at the market and P.O. At 3:00 our group met at the villa & we went for a walking tour of the city. Mother—the pastry shops are just brutal here. Haven't had one yet, but I'm sure I'll succumb fairly soon. After the tour, I had the unexpected but most welcome reunion with Claire. We had a heart-to-heart, went out to dinner, etc. Plans are already afoot for her, me, & this other guy . . . & who knows who else to go to the Oktoberfest this coming weekend in Germany. Claire & I had a bit of trouble getting dinner. Didn't know they didn't serve dinner until 7, sat in the wrong section of the restaurant, a drink almost fell on top of Claire, etc., etc. The adventures are already beginning. . . .

Today we had our French proficiency test. It's just to see what class we should be in, so I know I shouldn't be scared, but I am. My French is so poor that I'm convinced that nobody on the trip speaks worse or less than I do. It gets very embarrassing at times. I've heard that the other classes are given in French, which of course makes me nervous. If that is the case, there is no doubt I will take only one other class besides the intensive French. This language scene is probably my biggest concern right now.

I'm really glad I came here first instead of going to Cliveden[139] first and then here. Everything is much more of an effort here—classes, meeting people (both foreigners & Stanford students), the language barrier, getting meals, etc. Cliveden sounds more like a vacation than this, but . . . this will be a little more of an educational experience. . . . I still am really hoping to go to Cliveden next quarter though. . . .

Today after our test we have a meeting and are then going wine tasting. Tomorrow . . . we "chateau" it. I'm really glad i brought some French money with me—never got to the bank yesterday and I do need something to live (ie., eat) off of for the weekend. I want to review my French a little now before I get dressed & walk over to the villa with Claire. . . . Dad, one of these days we should put some money in my checking account so I can buy a plane ticket home. Not that I'm that anxious to get home, but I do hear you should take care of that fairly soon after you arrive. I'm in heavy pursuit of the ice skating rink, a piano teacher, and French children to take care of. . . . Take care and although I hate to bother you about this please do write. I can see "write" now that contact with the homeland is going to be crucial for me. Having a single will make it easier for me to get my letter writing done I think. I can't thank you enough for this wonderful experience you are giving me—

love,
ali

Letter from Wendell W. Birkhofer to his mother

October 9, 1977

Dear Mom,

I received your letter the day after I had "write Mom" on my list of
things to do. I was really happy to hear from you before I did write;
now I know what's going on and I don't need to enquire. But what
you want to know is what's happening in England, and I'll attempt
to give you a clear picture, although it is actually impossible to
communicate about my experiences accurately in writing. My trip
has been totally enlightening; that doesn't mean I have been happy
the entire time, rather that new doors seem to be opening inside
me all the time.

Where should I begin? . . . Munich is a magical place. The
people are cheery, warm, and often speak English. I had a great
time at the Oktoberfest, drinking several mass of beer a day (a
mass is equal to about a litre) and marveling at the Germans who
would be singing and dancing on top of the tables inside the
massive brewery tents to the Bavarian music being played by a
centrally located band. Just incredible!

Ah, Cliveden. You wouldn't believe it if you saw it. The
Cliveden house is a huge country mansion, originally built in 1666,
but altered several times since, containing over one hundred rooms.
I call it home. There is an enormous entry hall (really a living
room); a formal dining room which we don't use; a study; a full
library; an entire wing for our professors' offices and classrooms;
another wing for our living quarters (formerly for servants); a
basement level with the kitchen and dining room; a weight room;
T.V. room; laundry room; snooker (similar to billiard) room; ping
pong room; dancing room; a pub that is open every night and is

The Long View: As noted by Wendell W. Birkhofer, "Ah, Cliveden."

Courtesy of the Stanford University Archives

run by ourselves; and a piano room. Picture all this and a giant stone exterior that gives an impression of history, and you have the Cliveden House. But probably the most impressive element is the estate itself. The grounds cover hundreds of acres and include a formal rose garden, a water garden, a long garden with sculptured hedges, a soccer field, tennis court, and a swimming pool, and the River Thames with our own boathouse and a canoe. There are several cottages on the estate which are inhabited by the various staff members and their families—not to mention wooded forest and trails for running. Everything is so green—dark, light, all different hues, but beautifully green because of the wet climate. It does rain frequently, like almost every day!, though usually the sun breaks through for short periods daily also. You almost appreciate the sun more when you don't have it regularly, but I have always been grateful for the California rays. The Cliveden estate is located several miles from the nearest town in the English countryside, which is classically picturesque. It sounds like I'm over-describing, but I'm just giving you a small taste.

School definitely seems out of place in this setting, and the truth is that the academic program is very relaxed. I'm taking church architecture, history of London, and The Stage: 1400–1900. We take a lot of field trips (ha, ha, hee!). So far, Oxford (a beautiful town and college), Stratford-upon-Avon, and London many times. Friday night I saw A Chorus Line. . . . An introduction to so-called "culture" has been a big part of this adventure I'm on. Some people argue that California hasn't got any. I would say that we have a perfectly valid culture with different priorities than the East Coast of the U.S. or Europe. But anyway, the paintings, buildings, museums, and plays that I have seen do give me a feeling of pride in what humanity has done, even though I am very concerned at the same time about the disrupted balance between man and the environment.

Enough digression. The students here just don't take the classes seriously. A four or five-day "weekend" is common. Although many people have travelled around England already, I have been content to stay at Cliveden, or maybe venture into London for an evening. I'm planning a ten-day trip to Scotland during our "mid-quarter break." . . .

There is a volleyball club in a nearby town that plays in the top division in England, making it one of the top-ten teams, and I'm practicing with it every Wednesday night (the only night they get together). They play in tournaments on the weekends and have asked me to participate. However, I'm not sure if I will compete every weekend because I do want to travel a bit. Volleyball is on my mind—how it fits into my near future—and last weekend I went to London . . . in order to sort out my thoughts. I don't know whether I should finish school this year and play v-ball this season, or stop out until next fall and then finish school and play v-ball next year. In many ways I know the most sensible thing to do is graduate this June, but should one always be sensible? I have written my coach and asked his opinion, and I'll keep you up-to-date. Volleyball is definitely a high priority for me until I do graduate from Stanford; a national championship and All-American honors would be nice and possibly helpful for job opportunities. And who knows, the Olympics are coming up in 1980. I really was inspired by the Olympic Park in Munich; you could just feel the spirit of the Games in the air.

I have been doing some reading on environmental design and ecological consciousness. This type of work would suit me well, and in fact, Andy and I have been discussing just the same kind of business for a possible partnership when I finish school. We would restore old structures of cultural and historical value, creating a useful and socially beneficial establishment. Again, the balance between man and his environment is my interest. I feel that the modern city has in effect destroyed this balance, placing man outside of his true nature, and created unnatural stress in his life (you can relate to the stress factor, I bet). In the area of architecture and environmental planning is a partial solution to society's dilemma, I feel. I am also very interested in wildlife protection and wilderness conservation; today I spent five hours roaming the London Zoo, equal to San Diego's. These two very general areas, architecture and conservation, at least give me some direction for the future. At this point in my life I am somewhat reluctant to not have any potential careers on my mind.

It takes time to establish meaningful, or I should say emotional, relationships, and here at Cliveden I have been rather frustrated by the general Stanford student pretentiousness. A lot of people really seem to try very hard to be acceptable, but I can't say that I don't know what that is like. I have made some good friends—one of my roommates who went to Pali High, but whom I didn't know very well, and a girl or two. I think the source is me truthfully; I miss the people I love at home, despite all the fun I'm having. Tears came to my eyes too when I read your letter. I do love you and want you as my friend. I'm tremendously proud to have you as my mother. I have had some visions of us together when I was very, very young since I left L.A. I am also very proud of the rest of our family—we are all special.

Write me again when you feel like it. The letters I receive are a joy for me to read. . . .

I have always loved you,
Wendell
because we are love.
(I may be home for Christmas.)

P.S. I have a motorcycle here! Andy bought it last year and left it, and has given me exclusive riding privileges for the quarter in exchange for selling it before I leave. Don't worry. I'm very careful.

Letter from Chrissie Huneke to her family

January 29, [1983]

Dear Mom, Dad, Lori, Murray, Trapper, Ringo,
. . . Thank you for the telegram Lori & Murray—that was great. Hope finals went O.K. etc. It's Sat. morning—tonight is the "Doctor's Ball." . . . You asked [me] to explain this ball. . . . For this one there are about 80–100 couples—guys in tuxes, girls in white—all w/ gloves etc. All are young—17–22 or so approx. We are signed up by Stanford and I'm not sure how the others do it—maybe not sign up or are Dr.'s kids etc. I think those who are going [to] one for their 1st time are the 'deb' types. We had rehearsal twice this week. We march in after everyone is in the ballroom (300–400 people??). Then when the orchestra starts we have this dance/ceremony type-thing—where we curtsy for all the dignitaries/honored guests when they walk in (the Austrian Chancellor was supposed to be there last week but couldn't make it). This curtsy bit is hard—like doing deep knee-bends. Once again—my improper upbringing hasn't fully prepared me for the life of a socialite. We finish our stuff—[in] about 20 mins or so. It's really a beautiful thing—esp. when we'll all be in black/white. The

girls in ours have to wear these crown things and the guys carry these big sticks w/ vines and flowers on them—we use it in our dance. Then when it's done we all have the 1st waltz and then everyone else joins in. There are 4 or 5 bands in different ballrooms—the palace is incredible. Hope my pics turn out. We're all (6 couples) opening w/ Stanford people. Luckily my partner, Scott, is great in German so he can translate our dance routine instructions. This one goes till 5 a.m. but since we leave tomorrow I don't know how late we'll stay. . . . [My "Austrian family"] had their daughter's wedding dress shortened for me! It's beautiful. They are the nicest family. . . . Another girl, Julie, and I go over [there] for dinner once a week. Last week I learned how to make wienerschnitzel. They speak basically no English but we get on just fine. They've been taking in Stanford students for 13 years—have had 25 kids! Hope my writing isn't too small. . . . Sheila and I went to an English play in a theater around the corner. One night in a café we happened to meet the star of the play (Arsenic and Old Lace) and she got us great tix and had us backstage afterwards etc. She was great, and it was a nice change to hear a play in English!

Oh Mom—I know it's $$$ to send stuff, but is there any way you can send my V-neck beige sweater? If it's too much then don't, but I got some new boots that are that color and you want me to look "put together" don't you! The stores close at 12 Sat. so I'm off to get my supply of food for Russia—everyone says all they've got there was potatoes and cucumbers and bread that bounced. I'll smuggle in some oranges—or is that a western influence? Our teachers know we can't take any books in—so no homework can be done! Too bad! . . . Mit vielen herzliche Grüßen—

Deine—
Chrissie

Dressed Up with Someplace to Go: Chrissie Huneke (third from left) and crew, Vienna, 1983

Courtesy of the Stanford University Archives

Letter from Anonymous 1990 to his family

17 May '90

Mom—please don't worry about my grammar or sentence structures in this letter. I'm writing very quickly and am not trying to write a thesis.

Dear Fambly,

First of all, if you've been worrying about my finances, worry no more. I went to American Express and bought a pile of traveler's cheques with my checkbook. I had to pay only 1.16% for commission, which amounted to $6.00. . . .

I'm taking a bus tomorrow across the Andes to Mendoza, Argentina, where I'll stay for 3 nights. Hopefully I'll get to tour a vineyard and some caverns, and buy some choice leather products (very cheap). Huge steak meals in Argentina cost about $4, by the way. I'll also be paying about $5/night for my hotel room, possibly less. Next week I'm seeing the Talking Heads in concert. Musical groups are allowed to play here since the dictatorship was voted out of office. On June 1, believe it or not, I'm flying to Easter Island for about a week. To avoid having to pay any more money than we already are for airfare (which has been discounted already because we're students), we're bringing tents and sleeping bags. Hopefully we'll get to camp right next to the statues. I'm also bringing fishing line and hooks to catch meals. I've decided not to go to Buenos Aires because it's too expensive—even more than the whole trip to Easter Island will cost. After school ends, Machu Picchu and Peru is a possibility, but very uncertain. I'll have to see how the presidential election there turns out. . . .

. . . Our "parents" are only 27 years old. Sandra is extremely bright—she had the 2nd best college entrance exam scores for her year in Chile. Our dad is her slave, basically, giving her whatever she demands. It's kind of a bum deal for him, since he gave up a career as a mechanic in the Air Force to marry her against her mother's wishes. He had to give up his career (and he loves planes) because her mother had a relative in the Air Force transfer him to a place far away from Sandra to keep them apart. He married her to subject himself to a sort of affectionate totalitarianism, though they seem to get along well.

It's possible that we'll have the opportunity to meet President Aylwin while we're here. Our political science teacher is one of his friends. Neat! Also along the lines of politics, a political assassination took place here last week. . . .

Political assassinations are very common here, by the way. Romero is a good film about repression in Central America (much like South America) if you haven't seen it. I've seen a lot of movies here and many videos with my "parents." Sometimes they don't understand the humor of a movie or the jokes don't translate in the subtitles. Example: they only laughed for ¼ of The Naked Gun!

. . . I've been seeing a Chilean girl here that my mom set me up with. She's one of the best students Sandra has taught at the university. She came to our house to replenish the bird-seed supply for our canaries (12 of them), as her dad is a bird-seed & bird exporter . . . and because she's friends with Sandra, she gives her free birdseed. We hit things off right away, but I know I'll be leaving in a month and a half so we're mostly just friends. . . .

I went to a soccer game last week between the best Chilean & best Peruvian teams. There were a lot of faked injuries on the field, but the play was incredible, especially the goals. The fans were crazy, but there were plenty of cops there to keep them in line.

Thanks a lot for the birthday card—it's probably the best one I've ever received. As you know from the night you called me, my parents threw a BBQ for my friends and me. We went to bars afterwards, needless to say. I received a lot of candy from Chilean friends and more candy from our parents.

The books you sent have come in handy as I've shown them to a lot of Chilean students who ask me about Montana. Most of them have heard of the place from memorizing state names in English classes. Thank you again for sending them.

Lara: some answers to questions in your letter & comments. Tom & I made no money in the kissing thing at the flea market, but we managed to sell a $1 to somebody for 200 pesos, . . . less than it is worth. You said that I should sing American songs to people here. Most of the songs on the radio are American, though most people don't understand the words. There are few

Latin American rock groups. I'm taking economics, Spanish, political science, and cultural identity . . . taught in Spanish with mostly Spanish readings. The country western song I sang was about mama, trains, trucks, prison, and getting drunk. No one understood it (by David Allen Coe). . . .

Mom—there were so many questions in your letter that I'll also dedicate a section of this literary atrocity to your intellect. . . .

When I showed Sandra and Rafael the pictures of our house, they were pretty impressed. The house we live in is actually half of a house, the other half being inhabited by Christian Democrats, though Sandra says they're the same as Communists. Our guest house isn't fancy, but suffices. Most Chilean homes, like ours, don't have central heating. Thus we use space heaters. It's still cold when we get up in the morning, though.

21 May '90

I'm on the bus right now returning from Argentina. I didn't get to see caves or vineyards, but I ate a lot of beef. The food in Argentina is much better than in Chile. I ate good Italian food as well, including pizza with eggs and whole olives, as there are a lot of Argentinians of Italian descent. The empanadas were much better than the ones I've had in Chile. The girls weren't as good-looking as the Chilean ones, however. . . .

In answer to your question about the beach in Chile, it was a lot different from American beaches. People don't suntan and there are no outhouses, just a rocky hill on the beach that people use. The water was cold, though bearable. Chile has a Mediterranean climate, like 5 other small areas of the world, including San Fran. Thus it's exactly like Stanford in terms of rainfall, temp, seasons, and vegetation.

There are racial barriers in Chile, though I haven't learned much about it. There are less Germans in Chile than in Argentina or Brazil, but there are still a lot of them.

Sounds like you're learning a lot from your substitute teaching. With all the crap you're seeing, it should become apparent to you that you and Dad did something right in bringing us up. . . .

I haven't played any soccer in Chile, though I'm going to next week against the food service guys, who are always joking with us. Chile doesn't have a World Cup team for 2 reasons: they aren't good enough for one thing. Another reason is that they cheated in the final qualifying game against Brazil. They were getting killed by Brazil and the Brazilian crowd was particularly boisterous during the game, even launching rocket fireworks onto the field. When a rocket landed near him, the Chilean goalkeeper, who was among the best in SA,[140] faked an injury, cutting his face with something to make it look like he was really hurt. The Chilean team demanded that the game be replayed on another day due to the crowd's supposed injuring of their goalie. However, instant replay of the rocket and injury showed that the rocket didn't hit the goalie. He was banished from soccer, and the team lost any chance of being in the World Cup.

As for my summer plans . . . I'll probably go back to the U.S. at the end of June. I know that I'll have at least 7 ½ weeks of military training, 3 ½ of them with the SEALS in San Diego. I found out last week that I was accepted in the program, earning one of 32 spots nationwide among Academy and ROTC midshipmen. It may not have been too competitive, though—there isn't a lot of interest because most midshipmen are too afraid to apply. I probably got my first choice of sessions (from July 25 to Aug. 17), though it's possible I got the other, which runs from 27 June to July 20. Hopefully my cruise will run from the 3rd week in August to the third week in September. Thus I could be home as early as July. Because of at least 7 weeks of training and 2 weeks at the end of June in SA, there will only be about 3½–4 weeks left in my summer. Thus I probably won't have my job at Stanford, though I've written my boss explaining the situation. I'll have to see what happens, but it appears I might be spending those 3½ weeks in Helena and in Seattle with Rolf. . . . It's also possible that Jason, my friend in San Diego, could hook me up with a job for 2 weeks in San Diego before my SEAL training camp. While in Helena I definitely want to go to Glacier. When I go to San Diego, I think I might drive. It was rough not having a car when I was there for CORTRAMID last summer and I also want to check out the area, as I'll probably be stationed there after I graduate. I hope I get as good a cruise as Alex. I'll probably end up getting one in that region of the world.

I'm glad you guys will be in San Fran in October. The dates are perfect, as it's at the beginning of school and I'll have no tests. You'll get to meet Juli and my friends and see the slime-infested purgatory in which I dwell. . . .

Anonymous
P.S. Gorbachev is speaking at Stanford this quarter. I can't believe I'm missing it. He's one of the most influential people of this century.

Vantage Point: Looking below,
Easter Island, 1990

Courtesy of Tom Mondragon,
Class of 1991

Letter from Natasha Pratap to her mother

28 November '92

Dearest Mom,

First of all I must say that this time you've been just absolutely
great at keeping in touch! You write often & the letters are
long! Thanx a ton! Are you just travelling a lot more and getting
time on flights?!

I get mail very randomly here: for ages I won't get anything
& then I'll get 3–4 on the same day. We have pigeon holes by
alphabet here instead of mailboxes. So all my mail just goes
under P & often the box is full but there's nothing for me & I
get really bugged! But this one time I spent two days in
London & went back to find 8 letters!—plus a phone message.
Before I got to my room three people asked me if I had picked
up my mail 'cause it was bugging everyone to see it there!! And
of course it made my evening! That was when I got your
letter—but it took exceptionally long to reach me. I don't know
why. Anyway, I got the letter you sent w/ Dad, too.

Tomorrow (Saturday) I'm going to try & con Dad into coming w/ me for a movie—there are lots I have to catch up on. Let's see if he agrees. I'm dying to see Woody Allen's latest film—Husbands & Wives based on his life & it's no longer showing at Oxford. Actually it's not supposed to be all that great but I want to see it anyway.

So what to say abt. Oxford? This wk. has been very academic—stayed up till 5 a.m. on Saturday—all night on Sunday—midnight Monday—all night Tuesday! Yesterday my body was so screwed up I was forced to stay up all night & didn't want to study so I wrote letters! I turned in 2 papers— one 17 pgs long & the other 20 pgs. But I have 3 more to go, plus a final before the term ends in 2 wks. Oh, well!—But I've taken the last 2 days off to get a break & am in London.

Yep, as I was saying, there are times when the people on this program really intimidate me. They really know as much abt. painting as abt. politics! And last yr. I just got used to getting B's, thinking it happens—but these people get so many A's! Of course in a way I'm exaggerating because this is really the "cream of Stanford" & people do still get B's but in general everybody's Bloody Smart! Sometimes, I wonder what I'm doing among them & then I keep myself going by saying that if I'm among them—there must be something in me—almost by default. But I have to tell myself it's O.K.—you were one of the fifty who are here & not one of the 150 who are not! Chrissy (who I've gotten really close to—I think she's the first really close Stanford friend I've made—she's also on the program—dad's met her) says that it might have to do w/ the fact [that] this [is] a new system of ed for me—& it's literally foreign—i.e. not Indian that I am used to. Because she says she feels less confident in England so it's almost natural that I would feel less confident in the U.S.

For eg. I would "dhap"' a lot at home w/ confidence but at Stanford I don't feel confident enough to "dhap" & Chrissy says that everybody at Stanford gets away by "dhaping"—of course she calls it bull-shitting![141] By the way, I really like Chrissie—hope you meet her some time.

I don't know what plans are for Dec. We're considering seeing England instead of travelling to Italy. In any case why don't you book so that I can be back by the 23rd evening—so I get the next day Christmas Eve in B'bay [Bombay]. But I don't want to be there too much before that. So maybe if there's a flight [on the] 23rd morn. that gets there by night—and that will be only 3 days later than my travel limit which is the 20th. Keep in touch abt. these plans.

Anyway it's 3:25 a.m. I better go before I end up staying up all night again! Write again! . . .

Miss you more than you know! Love you lots,
Forever,
Natasha

Email from Tamandra Morgan to her family

From: tamandra
Sent: Tuesday, September 25, 2007 10:08 AM
To: Pauline Morgan; Carl Morgan; Jamelia Morgan
Subject: My first week at Oxford

Hello! It is currently raining here in Oxford, and we just finished a two-hour tour of parts of the university. There are 44 separate colleges within Oxford and about 17,000 undergraduates in total. On the tour they showed us places where the movie Harry Potter was filmed. We also visited the colleges where Bill and Chelsea Clinton studied, [also] Lawrence of Arabia, and Tony Blair. The city has so much history and beautiful architecture. It rains on and off here throughout the day. On Thursday we are going to Wales for a weekend trip. My room is large and with a lot of closet space. My roommate is a HumBio [human biology] student as well, and she is a senior. . . . I get free incoming calls. . . . Hope all is well! . . .

Love,

Tamandra

New Place, Old Building: Tamandra Morgan, Sept. 2007

Courtesy of the Stanford University Archives

Email from Erica Toews to her parents

READ THIS ONE (i think the other one got cut off)

Erica Toews Thu, Sep 4, 2008 at 10:07 AM
To: Ronald Toews

Dear mama and dad,

. . . I am in King's library, and I just now read your email—it made me very homesick! I miss and love you guys so much and am thinking about you always.

England has been a blast so far! The flight over here was a bit miserable because I couldn't sleep, and I had a window seat and felt bad asking the couple next to me to get up every hour so I could move around (I was terrified after mom told me I could die from blood clots.) But I caught up on journal entries and watched a couple movies. . . . I can't believe how beautiful King's College is: the buildings are so old, the architecture is incredible, and people go in punts (like the gondolas in Venice) on the Cam River that runs right by the building I am staying in. The whole seminar had dinner together the first night in the Dining Hall: the food here is pretty awful, I'm so sick of cafeteria food after being at Stanford, and it's even worse here because England as a whole does not have delicious food. Our professor, Peter Stansky, is a very old man with a mix between a Brooklyn (where he was born) and British (where he has lived for a long time) accent. He is brilliant, has published several books, and knows so much about so many topics. . . . There are 16 people in the seminar, so I am trying to get to know everyone. The first two days we spent just exploring Cambridge and getting to know our surroundings, and the first two nights we went out to pubs and had an amazing time experiencing (responsibly) the 18-year-old drinking age. On Monday, we had class in the morning and then our whole seminar went on a two-mile heartbreakingly beautiful walk through the British countryside to Grantchester and had tea and scones at Rupert Brooke's (a poet's) house. The scenery was too gorgeous for words: there were rolling green hills everywhere, and we walked along a river with willows on the banks and big pure white swans gliding on the surface of the water. The weather is always changing here: one moment it will be pouring rain (like right now) and the next it is lovely and sunny, but it is usually cold. On Tuesday, our seminar took a 2-hour bus ride to London and got there around 11:00 a.m. Our tour guide, an adorable, quirky, twitchy man named Stuart who is quite obsessed with Virginia Woolf, took us around and pointed out houses that prominent Bloomsbury Group figures lived in. It was a lot of walking, but it was very interesting to see the places that I have read about and that the Bloomsbury figures continuously mention in their writing. Then we took a bus to Sussex and stayed at John Maynard Keynes' (the famous economist's) country house. We had the most delicious meal that night (shepherd's pie), and I will never forget the hospitality of the British couple who lived there. (They had both been film students, and they rent out rooms in the house to as many artists as can afford it. I recommended they start their own Bloomsbury Group, which I think they liked.) Vanessa Bell's (Virginia Woolf's sister and a famous painter) grandchildren came to Keynes' house the night we stayed there and spoke to us about their childhood memories of the Bloomsbury Group that took place in that very house. The resemblance between Vanessa Bell and her female grandchild was uncanny. On Wednesday (yesterday), we had a guided tour of Charleston, the country house of Vanessa Bell and Duncan Grant (a painter in the Bloomsbury Group who was gay but had a daughter with Vanessa). Everything has been preserved very well, and it really maintained the feeling of a house rather than a museum. Then we went to Monk's House, the country house of Virginia and Leonard Woolf, which had expansive gardens with wonderful flowers and a ton of apple trees. (I ate one!) We took a bus back to Cambridge. . . .

Love,
Erica

Letters from Overseas: Further Comments

"A little more info on mail in Amsterdam. Write me c/o
American Express, Dam 9, Amsterdam, Netherlands. Then
after 3/19 write not to Köln (no office) but to me c/o
American Express, 16 Friedrich Ebert Allee, Heidelberg,
Germany. Then, after 3/28 change back to here on the
Burg. O.K.? O.K.!! Sorry it's so complicated."

—*George D. Green, Mar. 3, 1960*

"I'm staying at the youth hostel here in Vienna, formerly
a baroque palace in the woods at the edge of town and
very lovely and pleasant in the warm sunshine of early
summer."

—*George, June 6, 1960*

"Before we landed we circled a couple of times over Paris
and I can truly see why it is called "La Ville Lumiere"
(The City of Light). It absolutely sparkled, and there
was even a brightness visible in the air around Paris,
made by all its light. We were whisked through customs and
boarded our bus for Tours."

—*Barbara Armentrout, Apr. 5, 1965*

"My Italian has improved, but I don't think I'll be taking
an interpreter's job."

—*Lanny Levin, Oct. 28, 1968*

"I'm not one to complain about running on the beach,
sitting in the sun, exploring new towns and cities,
struggling with language barriers, and living cheaply!"

—*Chrissie Huneke, May 2, [1983]*

"[My host mom] speaks pretty decent English and is a complete sweetheart—when she heard I didn't have my luggage, she quickly offered me . . . warm clothes and T-shirts (many of which belonged to her father. "He is dead now," she laughed. German sense of humor. . .) Bis später."

—*Darren Franich, Jan. 11, 2006*

"There are several cherry beers that everyone agrees shouldn't be beer at all, and no one's ordered the strawberry one. Kyle, whom you met at the airport, tried one that was called 'smoked' which was interesting, but we all agreed tasted too much like bacon."

—*Christopher Lowman, May 13, 2009*

Chapter 6

Resilience

"You know, I'm having so many more and different experiences than last year and I treasure every one because I know they're all helping me expand."

—M.C., Apr. 8, 1977

Letters from Julia Hamilton Conkling to her mother

JULIA
Tues.—Sept. 5, 1911

My dear mother,

I'm afraid this won't be a very cheerful letter for I am terribly tired. It is now 5 o'clock and I have been reciting ever since 9:15 this morning and have been on my feet in the laboratory ever since 1:30. Believe me, college is no joke. I never found work so hard in all my life. Algebra and trigonometry and French are bad enough but chemistry! Gym is the only easy thing, and it makes me terribly tired. In the chemistry lecture class that I am in there are about 125 boys and six ladies, and I am one of those poor ladies.

All the freshmen are having hard times with their studies. I suppose it's natural they should but I have one piece of good news, and that is that I passed the English exam, and only 150 out of 400 did. My paper was perfectly punk and I never was good in English, but accidents will happen. I used to think I was good in chemistry but have changed my mind, guess I will drop chem. and take up the study of Eng. literature.

Tues. afternoon, [September 1911]
. . . I ought to be studying now, really, by rights, but I am too tired. Just came from chem. lab. Have been working there since 1:15 p.m. and it is now 5 o'clock. For two cents I would drop chem. and take something easier. I would drop it but it is against my principles to drop anything I once begin. I have to work again tomorrow. All the slow stupid ones do. . . .

Wed. afternoon, [September 1911]
I didn't have to work in chem. lab. this afternoon as I am ahead
of the rest of class now. It's getting easier but yesterday we had
an ex. in it, the awfulest thing, three of these terrible problem
experiments, with volume, pressure, temperature, & weight. I
got two of them I think but I could not do the third. Maybe if I
had had more time I could of but I couldn't in the time given so
that makes 66⅔ % I get if I got the others right. It's terribly
discouraging. I hope the others didn't do any better. I'll be sorry
for Lenna when she gets up here. You get such a comedown.
It's all I can do to stand it so I don't know what poor Lenna
will do. They say that freshmen always flunk in their 1st ex's.
But 60 is flunking & if I get 66 I won't quite flunk. We have an
ex. in chem. lecture course next Tuesday and one in French a
week from Friday. The professors are so kind, they give you
about 2 weeks to worry over your exams. . . .

I will have to stop and cram. I never did so much cramming
in all my life for such punk marks. I have forgotten what a 100
looks like; 80 looks mighty, mighty good. . . .

. . . Do you know that at Berkeley they have over 30,000
students & here about 1,700? They make you hike from here if
you don't keep your grades up to a certain standard. . . .

P.S. I may be at Berkeley next year.

Tues. night, [October 1911]
. . . I am so busy cramming for ex.'s I haven't time to write
much. Got 80 in that test I thought I got 66 in and all the boys
around me got 30 & 50. The one we had today in chem. I think
I got at least 75 in, maybe more. . . .

Nearly cut my finger off in chem. yesterday. Was trying to get a piece of bent glass tubing out of a rubber cork and it broke. I like chemistry fine though now. . . .

Los Gatos, [California]
Oct 15, 1911

. . . I got back my chem. ex. paper Thurs. Pride goeth before a fall. I was just thinking that possibly I might make Phi Beta Kappa[142] (the smart frat.) when I got that paper back with a big C. And there is no daily work to bring me up. Such is life. . . .

I have been meeting lots of the Delta Delta Delta girls and like them better than the Theta girls although I don't believe their standing as a national frat. is as good as the Thetas. I tell you the frat. I wish I could make and that is the Phi Beta Kappa. It is for boys & girls both who make certain grades in all their studies. There would be some honor to belonging to that and you aren't taken into that until your senior year. I'm going to secretly try for it but I don't expect to make it so won't be disappointed if I don't. . . .

Tues. morning, [October 1911]

. . . And mother, don't say anything to Nickie or anybody about me trying to make Phi Beta Kappa, because he would think me all together too ambitious & I don't expect to make it, I'm just going to do as good work as I can during my first two years & then if I don't make it I can slow up anyway during my last two years. I do wish I could make it. . . .

Thurs. night, [December 1911]

. . . I have my French ex. in the morning. Crammed from 6:30 till 10:30 last night on it and have crammed all day today. Not through yet. Am almost dead & just to think this is just the beginning, I haven't even had a single ex. The ex. tomorrow lasts from 8:15 till 12:15. After that I will have to start in cramming chem. I have one thing to be thankful for. Because of my good work in algebra, Prof. Green excused me from the final so I will only have four. I wish some of [the] other profs. would come through. But that was the only ex. I was not dreading & did not intend to study much for. That's always the way.

The ex. tomorrow is terrible. You know one semester's work in university in a language is equivalent to a year in H.S. & this ex. is over the whole thing, verbs are just sailing before me now. I'm almost dead. . . .

Everybody in the hall is cramming their heads off & everybody is complaining of sore eyes. I don't see how people live through it but I suppose a week from now I'll be all through & alive and almost home.

Friday 5:00 p.m., [Oct. 31, 1913]
. . . I have two exes. next week, on Mon. & Tues., so am spending the weekend cramming. I am so ashamed I haven't been to the Nichols but you see I am so busy now making up my week's lost work. If I were to miss another week I would have to stop college. It is just terrible. This university is getting so hard. They are just trying to flunk people out so that they can have only the best students. Every single prof. works you to death almost.

If I were starting at Stanford again I would take 4 ½ years to [do] it. I am so tired by 6:30 at night I can hardly hold my head up & simply have to go to bed by 9 & don't get any work at all done. Everybody is completely worn out. . . .

Love & kisses,
Julia

Letter from Julia Hamilton Conkling to her father

Wednesday night, [April 1915]

Dearest father—

A very hurried note before I lay me down to sleep to tell you I was elected to Phi Beta Kappa tonight. Isn't that grand? I haven't heard yet how many made it. But about 18 I think. . . . I'm awfully tickled. I think it's wonderful. Incidentally—

Initiation fee .... 5 bones[143]
ΦBK pin .... 5 bones
Total .... 10 bones

Believe me it's worth it. Emerson is a frat brother of mine. Emerson wrote "The American Scholar." O yes! I am the only girl (or man) in the math. department who made ΦBK.

Please tell mother. It is really true.

Love & kisses
Julia

Letter from Julia Hamilton Conkling to her mother

Friday, [April 1915]

Dearest mother,

. . . I am sending you a Daily Palo Alto.[2] Please save it as I want it. I am very happy for I have certainly deprived myself of no pleasures here at Stanford and have not by any means boned all the time. Neither have I wrecked my health. And am happiest of all on father's account as I feel like I had in a small part repaid him for some of what he has done for me as that is the highest honor I could have gotten. . . .

I always thought when other people made ΦBK that they should [not] worry about studying anymore but now I am ashamed [not] to hand in my best work. It's awful living up to your reputation. . . .

Much love & kisses
Julia

Letters from (Mary) Carol Stearns to her mother

Mon. a.m., [Mid-1940s]

Dear Mom,
. . . The quarter seems to go on & on & I still feel as if I'm centuries behind—I get so sleepy that I just can't stay up & study. I suppose I'll be saying, "Well, next quarter . . ." But I was talking to Bones the other day (the fella who goes with Roxie) & he said he's had a scholarship all along—& only a B average. The only trouble is I'm afraid I'm going to have trouble getting B's. . . .

Tues—[Mid-1940s]
I just got my econ. ex. back with a big fat F—at least I got a 35—High was 93; Median 52 ½ & low—21. I don't know what's wrong with me, Mother. I just can't do it. I studied for it—hard—& I just missed the point on all the questions. Then people in the house who skim over the reading the nite before

& never go to class came out with a 58 or so. Am I just dumb? It sure looks that way.

It isn't just this course—my grades in everything are poor— at least not what they should be. My average for Econ = 50— Class average = 55—So I have a C so far—but what if I get another 35 on the next ex? I just don't know how to learn it any better.

If things go on this way, maybe I'd just better go to J.C. next year—or something drastic.

Or perhaps I should move out of the house next quarter. I hate to—but I hate worse to get these lousy grades. These girls are wonderful—but is it worth it? Then on the other hand, is the house the cause of it? I studied 33 hours last week—at the libe mostly—so it was fairly concentrated study & should have been plenty to pass me on that exam.

What'll I do, Mother? I certainly don't like to admit I can't do the work at Stanford. . . .

Please write soon—
Love,
Carol

Letter from (Mary) Carol Stearns to her mother and sister

Tues. Eve, [Mid-1940s]

Dear Mom & Mur—
. . . I don't think my little geography course is going to be such a snap as I once might have [thought]. The prof is new—& impressed us with how hard he was going to be. He seems to

know his stuff, tho, & he's interesting. Another reason it might not be so easy is that Betsy . . . is in there—& she's one of those straight A persons who doesn't look the type. In fact, they say she'll be the next pres. of Tri Delt. . . .

Love,
Carol

Letters from (Mary) Carol Stearns to her mother

Monday—5:00, [Mid-1940s]

Dear Mother—

. . . Incidentally—prepare yourself for a shock! I went in & got my Contracts final back. 80 is an A. I got 78—a high B—& second highest in the class! Ain't it terrific? I was awfully pleased.

The campus is absolutely seething with men. 125 new ones in law school. I walked into the usually vacant law libe—& searched for a seat. 4,200 students registered so far. . . .

Friday—Oct. 5, [1945]

. . . Yesterday I went to see about getting a job. The only likely prospect is working in the library—which pays 50¢ an hour. I went to see the guy in charge of the library and he was out for the day and so I have to go back and see him some other time.

In the mail yesterday I received a letter from the Committee on Scholarship congratulating me on receiving Lower Division Honors. That means I'm on the list for being in the upper 10% of my class. It goes, they tell me, on the permanent record. . . .

. . . A couple of days ago in the law libe a girl came up to me and asked me if I were I . . . and since I was, she asked me to come to a tea that she was giving yesterday for all the women in Law School—which means 10 or 15. She was giving it in honor of Lucille Lowman, a girl who just finished serving as the law clerk for Justice Douglas. It seems that each of the nine justices have one law clerk to do their research. . . . The justice writes to the dean of each law school asking for recommendations . . . and on this basis he chooses his clerk. Lucille just finished her year. She was the first woman ever to be appointed to such a position . . . and 'twas quite an honor. She was terribly interesting—told us how she happened to be chosen, what kind of work she did, how she liked Washington, etc. She was graduated from U. of Wash. Law School—the only four-year law school in the west—with honors . . . and just finished her year as Douglas' assistant on Oct. 1. . . .

Thurs. Eve 9/26/46
. . . Classes are kind of scary, as they always are at first! My law classes are huge. In my section there are 125—& 3 girls (including me). . . . Nor does this large class have the informal & friendly air of my classes last year. Luckily, I feel very conscientious—so far—& as yet am not very anxious for dates. . . .

Friday Noon 10/4/46
. . . The other guy is something on two feet that sits beside me in all my classes & drums his fingers on the desk during the lecture. His first words to me—even before he told me his name—were: "I have quite a record to keep up. All the rest of my family went thru here & were first in their class." Modesty got him nowhere. . . .

Tuesday Eve, 10-15-46
The worst has happened—& thank G—it's over! Mr. Osborne called on me for a case. It all began yesterday—"Well, let's have The Six Carpenter's Case, Miss Stern." I gulped, waited a couple of

minutes & then barged into the case. I just opened my mouth—& he interrupted, "Evidently there is a Miss Stern & a Miss Stearns—but very well, Miss Stearns, proceed." I said about one sentence when some jerk in the back of the room raised his hand & said, "We can't hear her." Of course the room is huge—as it would have to be to hold 125 people. . . .

My hand was shaking like a leaf as I held my brief—I felt violently ill—& proceeded—my voice sounding to me very strange & strained. Osborne interrupted me again—asking for a very simple (& unessential) fact which I had not included in my brief. When I couldn't answer him, he asked Miss Stern for the answer. Miss Stern suddenly developed a case of laryngitis the boy sitting next to her repeated to the class. "Very well," said Osborne, "Whisper the answer to your neighbor, Miss Stern, & he'll say it aloud." He did & we proceeded. Osborne kept firing questions at me for 25 minutes—keeping us 5 minutes after the bell had rung. After class & all yesterday I read & re-read my case—knowing I'd be called on today to finish up. I consulted Pete[144]—he read it, looked up his old notes; I asked several others about it. So today I felt quite prepared—& I was! Osborne spent a full ½ hour on me—& I survived without a blunder—& now feel more confident than I ever have. . . .

Write. Love,
Carol

Letters from M.C. to her parents

23 Feb 76
Mon.

Dear Mom and Dad,

Things aren't really going all that well. I'm sorry to say but I didn't feel like telling you about it on the phone the other night. I really hate having to tell you at all. I did very poorly on my econ midterm (about a D). The grade alone upsets me but what really disturbs me is that I studied so hard for it. The problem is, I don't really know how to take the tests here. In high school I did well because the tests were mainly memorization. . . . I know it's mostly my fault but it's kind of scary to think that I went through 4 years of high school and never really learned how to think. I had studied but just not the right things in the right way. I thought I knew what was going on but I guess I really didn't. I'm pretty depressed now, although not as much as right after I got the test back. I have never felt like a complete failure & it's hard to accept a failure. It's hard not to completely discount any abilities that I may have because right now it seems like I can't really do very well at anything. . . .

I feel much better now that I've "spilled my guts" to you. You can't imagine how hard it is to tell your parents who are so proud of you & your former success that you've failed. I really want your opinions but I hope you won't be too stern or anything. (I realize it's unfair of me to put conditions on your response.) It's kind of like when I lost something when I was a little kid—you didn't have to get after me, I already felt terrible. I feel terrible now. And Dad, please realize that I fully know that I am going to have to head for & decide on a career. I'm afraid I know that all too well & that's one of the things that torments me most now. I am struggling to cope with a failure in something, the realization that I don't have a major, consequently a career, and the feeling that I just want to quit it all. I'm doing better mentally now, but sometimes it's harder. . . .

25 Feb 76

. . . Since I last wrote you, things have improved somewhat (which is why I'm writing so quickly—I don't want you all to worry or anything). . . . I found out today that I was just a few points below a B on the econ midterm. The prof graded very liberally which helped me immensely. . . . I'm still a little down but am getting so busy I don't have time (or can't take the time) to think about it.

Face in the Crowd: M.C., freshman dorm
Courtesy of the *Stanford Quad*

28 Sept. 76
Tues.

. . . I've been filling out various things today that I put "sophomore" on & that's kind of neat. I'm finally getting up where it sounds respectable! . . .

Tonight four guys from my last year's dorm are having a big trailer-warming party (they live in the trailers—across the street from Wilbur[26]) and a lot of Rinc people are expected. It should be a lot of fun. . . .[145]

19 Oct 76

. . . It's kind of a weird life that I am leading. In the morning I'm a student & go to classes. In the afternoon I'm a working person & am part of the workaday world. But when everyone else goes home at 5, they go home to their leisure time—I go home to being a student again and to my studying. . . . So far I've found that I can handle this situation. I've always got a zillion things to do, but I guess I like it better that way than not to have anything to do (ask me if I still feel like that during midterms!) . . . I have to work at it to find time to mess around with friends, relax, run, & go to the flicks[22] as well as go to all my classes all the time. (I think I only missed a class twice all of last year—it's generally a frowned-upon practice by peers more than pressure from profs.) . . . When I look at the things I'm doing I realize they really aren't earthshaking things. . . . Still, they're all I've got. . . .

. . . More and more this is feeling like "home." My best friends are here, my educational goals are here, my lifestyle & attitude is pretty tied up here. Of course, nothing can replace my home, Stanford doesn't replace it, it just complements it. I am an extremely lucky person to be out here. I may take a lot of things for granted but I never forget how much I have to be thankful for for being here. Of course, there are a lot of times when I wonder if it's all worth it, but deep down I decided that a while back and know it's still true. I think it's really something to have something to work & struggle for so much. Would Stanford mean as much to me if I were on a full ride? Don't worry, I'm not immortalizing or idolizing S.U.—I, of all people, know all too well many of its shortcomings. But I also know it has a lot of good points—points that make it one of the top schools in the country in an honest evaluation. It's just kind of neat to think that I'm a part of that. And it sort of makes me feel good that I'm overcoming all the odds I am & I am working my tail off to get it. Well, enough of this soliloquy. I didn't mean to get so carried away. Tomorrow I'll probably be damning Stanford. That's kind of how my mind works. . . .

14 Feb 77

   . . . I laughed when you said a course in philosophy would scare you out of your wits, Dad. Sometimes I think the same thing (like when I sit down to write a paper!), but I guess I figure it's something I've got to hit head-on & shouldn't hide from if I'm to come out of here "a well-educated Stanford graduate." (That's said in a deep, reverent voice. Just teasing!) Actually, I'm finding it easy to follow the class so I guess I am learning something. Most people seem to excel in one field or another (science or humanities) but I don't. . . . I do about equally well in sciences & humanities, although I never blow the top off either. That can be a little frustrating sometimes but I try to look at it positively & realize that at least that means I truly can be a better-rounded person. . . .

You asked about my sleep & dreams class. Mostly we are learning about sleep more than dreams. . . . The other night I had a terrifying dream which woke me up (it's very rare for me to have nightmares) & the first thing I did in my groggy state was to look at my clock & say to myself, "I've been asleep an hour & a half so I'm probably in either stage 4 or REM sleep. I wonder how long I've been in REM." . . . One-third of our lives is spent in sleep and yet only one doctor in 100 can correctly state the 2 major causes of sleep disorders. . . .

. . . It's a little hard to believe that soon it will be spring quarter, though. . . . When I decided to come out to Stanford almost 2 years ago, I thought I would only be here for 1 year. You never can tell what will happen. . . .

8 April 77

. . . All in all, I'm beginning to feel what it means to be taking 5 classes—20 units. I have an immense amount of reading to do—17 books this quarter. Luckily, about ½ of that is novels, but even novels take time. I think it's probably good for me, though. I'm definitely learning to handle classwork a lot better now. That's one thing about Stanford (& other places, I'm sure), they make you work hard with a lot of work, but eventually you get used to it (well, sort of . . .) & you can handle it. Maybe that's why my grades are improving. . . . My perspective has changed a little since high school & although it would be nice to have a 3.95, I guess I'm still pretty happy about having an overall grade average that's superior (B) at Stanford. And best of all is the fact that while I'm not worrying about grades anymore, I am learning a lot. Took me 2 years to figure that out, though.

2 July 78

. . . I'm glad I finally got to tell you about my grades. When I picked them up I was amazed. I had picked up my final exams a couple days earlier & found out I had an A– in money & banking. That was a real surprise. I sort of figured I would get an A– in Marx on the basis of the final exam. I really thought I'd make a B+ in underdevelopment because I didn't think I did all that great on the final. But for once, all my finals pulled me through. I made the median score on all my midterms—which means a solid B. But the finals count ⅔ of the final grade & I guess I did well enough on the finals to pull in A's. That's a first. You know, I have finally, after 3 years, learned to accept myself as average at Stanford & accept the B's I make as decent grades. But precisely because of that, it's all the sweeter to make A's— straight A's. . . .

Love,
M.C.

Resilience: Further Comments

"As I go on I presume it will be easier for me to get the substance of what I study in a shorter time."

—*Lucy Allabach, Roble Hall,*[4] *Nov. 1, 1891*

"She as all freshmen has been having trials & tribulations. . . . You find you are nobody when you get up here or at least it seems that way at first."

—*Julia Hamilton Conkling, Nov. 11, 1912*

"He [said] that it is one of the hardest courses given, especially in regard to the time & application it required, but he didn't know what they could do about it. . . . But Mother, it is a splendid [class], one of the very best I've ever had. It is teaching me chem. thru & thru.
. . . I hate being second-rate. . . . the skies are so blue, Motherly, so much nicer than they were."

—*Hope Snedden, Monday night, [1920]*

"The chemistry test this morning was murder. I seemed to have studied all the wrong things. Write as soon as you can."

—*Bob (Robert) Lowell Swetzer, Nov. 12, 1947*

"I have done homework all day and still don't have my Western Civ[16] assignments or my bio finished yet. I guess I have to learn to study all over again with different methods."

—*Carol Hodge, Oct. 1, 1953*

"I got a 'B-' in that psychology class (from the same guy I got a 'D' from last quarter). So there!"

—*Alison Carpenter, Apr. 16, 1976*

"I think Stanford really has done me a lot of good and even in my darkest times I knew I'd rather be here than any other school. It's still worth it."

—*M.C., Jan. 23, 1977*

Chapter 7

Ruminations

"I just thought I'd let you know there was a little depth to be found; and sometimes it is easier to write how you feel than to talk about it—it would just be embarrassing."

—Phil (Philip) B. Laird Jr., 11:45 p.m., Mar. 19, 1968

Letters from Fred (Frederic) Jewell Perry to his mother

Stanford,
Mar. 19/[18]99

My dear mother:

Outside the rain drizzles down drowsily, inside it is pleasant and warm. The clouds are one vast expanse of mist, the landscape is partly hidden by the drizzle, and all nature is taking a day off to enjoy the moisture and quench its parched throat. All California has been sighing for rain and last Wednesday it came. Every farmer in California was rejoicing at the downpour and every farmer's son at Stanford took part in the general jollification. Said one rustic young friend of mine to me, as we watched the great drops form streams in the quadrangle, "Every drop means a dollar." His father runs a prime ranch. Said another rural individual to an agricultural acquaintance, "Let's shake, old boy, and give thanks." And they mutually congratulated themselves and "gave thanks." An Oregonian remarked in a tone of condescension, "You can tell the Californians on the campus, they're all smiling." The Oregonians, you know, have web-feet because of the excessive rainfalls up there, and the necessity of wading through countless rivulets. . . .

Kappa Sigma House
Stanford, Feb. 11, 1900

. . . The drift of all this is simply: Claude must go back to school.[146] If he is desirous of getting into a bank or an office he must have some school training. He must learn to write, he must learn to spell, to use correct grammar and to speak good

English. He must learn to think and act quickly. If he can gain these precious acquirements I am sure he can get a position from which he can rise to be a good, useful, and prosperous citizen. . . .

. . . He must have much backbone—sticktoitiveness <pertinacity> in studying. I shall help him all I can. Claude, I believe, is a bright boy. He is not a mature fellow for his age. He does not see the proper perspective in things. He lacks judgment & concentration of purpose. If, when he once begins to study for office work, he continues his "grind" for six months steadily, there is much hope for him. . . .

Feb. 19, [19]00

I am glad to hear that you have at last reached an agreement in your estate interests. You probably have your money safe in [the] bank by this time. I hope so. . . .

. . . The first thing you should do with your money is to move!! We need not attempt to be anything more than we are—Perrys—until we get away from 1214 H—When we get into a more respectable neighborhood, then we shall show the Jewell in us. . . . We shall be able to be clean and choose good companions. We shall not be compelled to select persons beneath us as companions. Claude will be able to be a better boy, and I shall have a home to which I should not be ashamed to invite the boys from my fraternity who are all sons of parents who live in good homes.

Please look around for a new house right away, won't you? . . .

Fred

Letter from Michitaro Sindo to a friend

November 24, 1901

Dear Miss Cone:[147]

It is very kind of you to take interest in my work here, for availing me to write about it. I am afraid my letter is already too long and is tiring you out but availing your kindness I wish to confide to you something about my future.

. . . There lies before my future a vital problem, and I am at a loss how to decide it. Dr. Jordan[6] persuades me [to] take up zoology and specialize in fish work for my future and remain with him permanently. For this he almost promises to pay me gradually up to something like fifteen hundred dollars a year, after I should graduate . . . [from] college and become able to do independent investigations. This he thinks I am on a fair way to do; and beyond this it depends on my ability and diligence. This is inviting in a way, but the field is so narrow, although I am pretty well assured of a comfortable permanent position. My inclination is however to take up [the] medical profession. This is . . . long and hard work, but the future field is very wide and there is a chance of doing some great things, also a chance of flat failure. I asked Dr. Jordan to wait [for] my answer until next summer. If I decide on medicine probably I have to get out [of] my present position in favor of a permanent man and transfer to Physiology Department. Dr. Jenkins recommends this course and offers to me a position in his department enough to earn my expenses. He thinks I can succeed in this branch of study, but as you know I am getting rapidly older. . . . So do you see I am in a dilemma, and do not know what to do. I wish to hear your opinion about it.

As I am so busy I am not taking my English lesson; and am missing it so much. The continual reading of scientific subjects, hard and dry like lava flow of the Hawaiian mountains, from morning to night, days in days out, simply fossilizes one's brain. It is [the] rarest pleasure to divert the weary mind to some refreshing poems or prose of the masters. . . .

Ever faithfully yours,
Michitaro Sindo

Letter from J. B. (Jesse Brundage) Sears to his parents

Palo Alto, Cal.
May 17, 1908

Dear Mother and Father:—

. . . I can only mention that our trip to see the fleet was one of the greatest treats we have had since we left home two years ago the 30th of this month. When the first ship poked its prow through the Golden Gate the last one in line was not yet in sight. . . .

. . . So you have put the farm up for sale have you? Well it made Harry[148] feel a little bad when I told him, but, while of course I shall always feel that that is home yet I realize that it is by no means a valuable investment for you. There is too much expense, work, and worry, and too little income. Gov't bonds would be fully as good or even better I should think. Of course we are naturally wondering what you are asking for it, who has it in charge, and what your plans are if it sells. . . .

. . . I hope you'll both live to see what comes of all our college training. Maybe we are not fools after all. I surely hope not, and I must emphatically believe we're not. And so however ridiculous it all looks to you, you must try to enter into it with our enthusiasm and see from our point of view, for I can tell you that anyone who goes through the grind that a poor man has to go through to get through college believes in it with all his heart and soul or I tell you truly he would not live through it. . . .

We three out here have been exceedingly fortunate all the way and yet it has not all been play and trips to see the fleet etc.

There is not a little of the real grind mingled with it all, and yet we are not ready to say quit by any means. We'll get there someday.

I should be very glad if you could get your money invested in some way so you could come out here this fall and stay & see me graduate next May. You have a standing invitation. . . .

We were well pleased at Dick's success. . . . I think you might both go down to see him graduate. It would cheer him along quite a little more than you may think. Not by any means the least joy of our success is the knowledge that it brings joy to you. We never quite forget to share our pleasures with those in the old west.

We have very little news to write so you see I have a little tendency to grow reflective.

After grading a stack of papers nearly a foot thick which I finished after several day's work you may know that I felt rather glad that vacation was near. . . .

With love from us all to all at home,
I am, Sincerely your son,
JB Sears.

Letter from Alice Louise Clark to her father

Stanford Library
Nov. 26, 1935

Dearest Father:

. . . I can't tell you, nor is this exactly the time or the place to tell you, how much I appreciate the father I have. In this academic, ambitious atmosphere that I am living and breathing, I realize how much I owe you for the foundation of learning and philosophy of living that you gave me while I was developing from a brown-eyed baby on your lap listening to your lullabyes of poetry to a grown-up (more or less) young woman able to know and love her parents as people to be admired and respected not because of what they are, but because of the personality and character within them.

You will probably be surprised at this sudden breakdown to sentimentality, but the best and most fitting birthday remembrance that I can think of is just such a feeble and halting expression of my love and affection for you. . . .

Work here is about as usual. I am spending some long hours in the library in order to get my term papers into shape.

My best wishes to the family for a joyful Thanksgiving. And again, a very very happy birthday to my Father from—

Your loving daughter,
Alice Louise

Letter from Phil (Philip) B. Laird Jr. to his family

3/19/68
11:45 p.m.

Dear Family,

How do you like this—a letter, and I actually hadn't planned on writing this week; but since I'm in the mood I may as well talk to you for a while.

Well, I've finished my history and political science finals and have only two more finals to go. Now I know you've heard this before, but I have honestly worked harder for the last two weeks than I have ever worked before. Nobody, not even I, believed I was capable of doing it—but darn it, I have.

It really has paid off; I feel pretty confident about the two tests I've had. Yet, around here, with the competition in everything you do—well, I've learned not to expect too much; so let's say I'm hoping for B's though I'm sure that at any other university the two papers I've done would have been solid A's. I'm not depressed though; I'm finally coming to realize the true value of being in a situation like this—it's good for me. It's good because I'm learning to fight for every goal against the toughest competition anyone could face. It poses an interesting problem at times; but I still feel that if I continue to improve and grow I'll be a match for any one of the people around here—yeah, it's a heckuva challenge.

So that's how I feel right now—rather peaceful, rather tired— and a bit older than I used to be. Yes, after two years around here you're not really better prepared for any particular occupation; you're not any better prepared after four years; but you've grown and learned to see things and feel things that the vast majority of humanity miss throughout their entire life—so I guess there really is a reason for being here and doing what I'm doing.

Alright, enough of that, I guess I was beginning to sound an awful lot like our cousin—but I just thought I'd tell you how I felt—you won't see any change in me, I'll be the same clod as always; I just thought I'd let you know there was a little depth to be found. . . .

Hey, Gerry (I'm sick of "Gerri"—it's too "cute"), guess who's going to be one of the guides when the C.S.F. group comes to Stanford—yes sir, your very own brother. . . . [. . . and on the left here we have the chapel . . . any other questions, Little Girl?] [Brackets and ellipses in original.]

Actually, I'll never forget that when I came here with the C.S.F. group when I was a junior my one dream was to be able to someday guide people (preferably for the . . . C.S.F. group) around Stanford like our guide was. So you see—it's going to be one of my private little dreams come true.

I've been talking too much—it's time to climb back into the shell. . . .

Love you all,
Phil

Letter from Wendy to her father

Spring [Early 1970s]

Lieber Vater,
Have you ever noticed how many times we search for answers & create systems to facilitate understanding when in fact the "answers" lie all around us? . . .

Yet we are not content when just sitting for hours (unless we learn to use our senses). Our moments of relaxation, if extended, approach boredom & so we avoid total leisure & pursue some methods of giving meaning to our lives, to put some purpose on our behavior. . . . Closely tied to that desire & need is a need for personal expression—We must manifest ourselves in some concrete way in the world, thru human creation, & interpersonal relationships, in order to reconfirm a belief that we exist at all—

Every individual begins his existence involved in a relationship, though on simplest, biological terms—& as a product of a relationship & as a human creation himself. . . Feeling little warmth from those around him, he may look elsewhere (away from life & persons) to find (or put) meaning into his life—He may jump on the donkey of achievement & ride for a goal—He will climb the mountain of success & arrive at the top, alone, knowing only to search for another mountain to climb because achievement made him feel good. (And there's no reason it shouldn't, for achievement is a tangible reflection of our existence & worth.) But the individual who climbs mountains all his life many times misses those aspects of life which give life a lasting meaning, not one which is felt only when he arrives at the top—He misses what is basic to any existence: life & creation & relation—So hard does he look at the top that his eyes cannot see, his ears cannot hear what life consists of w/out ornamentation—the simplicity, yet grandeur, of this world—So full of answers, if we would only open our eyes—So full of meaning, if we let ourselves have relationships, . . . but everyone has relationships . . . or do they? . . .

Am i speaking only of those very few ideal relationships? what of everyday encounters? i believe this idea of relationships of encounter can & should be extended to the times shared w/ any individual—The total self as such is not laid on the table, so to speak, but what is shared, be it a smile, a thank-you or hello—is shared fully. . . . It is not an experience or a utilization of another but a reflection of the fact that we share a common essence, "an innate you" as Martin Buber would say—Persons are ends in themselves, not means to another end. . . .

. . . The other element which i mentioned is human creation—It seems like the idea of "putting something into a meal" has been transformed to putting a meal into something—The T.V. dinner into the oven—No more homemade cookies . . . just buy one at the bakery—or if you feel a touch creative, buy a box mix and add the eggs—NO TIME. . . .

Everyone knows how important the personal touch is, so why has it dissolved? People run around doing things, & feel at the end of the day, perhaps that they have achieved something . . . but so many are unhappy—They must live someone else's life, through television, or movies, because they are discontent with their own—Or else they only see their own & again are unhappy, though many don't know it—Funny how once you get on the donkey, & are reinforced for whatever you do, you lose sight of yourself & your position & just keep on moving—Away, or towards, but not usually stopping to BE, & therein being content—

Many philosophers have written about the dissolution of language—& about God being dead—Primarily, the concept involved is that of the death of old categories—old systems which have lost their meaning. But instead of abandoning the old systems, we retain them, although the content has changed. . . . Hmmm . . . but structures are hard to break down— Nevertheless, i feel we must begin again to sense-out what is around us, what things are basic to life & the environment in which we live (were born) & from there, given that content to establish new forms—To create order from the given chaos & harmony instead of beginning w/ a system as a grate into which we must force our varied experiences & encounters—

> "Love is most nearly itself
> When here and now cease to matter."
> T. S. Eliot

Fortunately, love is something which knows no categories— which needs no specific focal points, for it involves whole beings & acceptance of a total person as a person—The essence which is shared knows no boundaries, for it is its own modality—& so, though our perspectives may differ, as [do] our experiences & personalities, the relationship remains—

i love you
&
God bless you,
Wendy

Letter from Wendy to her grandmother

February 1973

Dear Granny—

. . . It was especially good to talk w/ you, Granny, for you hold a very dear place in my heart, among my close <u>friends</u>. Though we have had diverse experiences & hold different perspectives, I believe we live within a similar world.—one of loving, giving, sharing, patterned after or rather—guided by Christ's teaching. Seeing you gives me faith that that is a good, enriching, fulfilling way to live. And so I strive to follow God, to give to many & be open & honest—But I wonder, is there a limit to how much one can give? is it impossible to be close to many? or does the supply of love never give out? I hope the latter is true, but at times I feel empty, & I need to be alone or go sit in church that my well be refilled. Thank you again for everything. May God be w/ you always—

I love you—
Wendy

Letter from M.C. to her mother

8Dec76

Dear Mom,

. . . As you know, I've been finishing up my psych readings lately & a part of them have been on the psychology of sex roles. My prof, Sandra Bem, is a leading researcher in the country on that topic. Today she & her husband (one of the top social psych researchers in the country—I'm taking his class next quarter) gave a talk in class on an egalitarian marriage & sex roles. Besides having read several articles & going to class, in the past week I seem to have become engaged in several conversations (with guys) about sex roles & "a woman's place." So this is really a topic on my mind recently.

I have gone round & round trying to decide how I feel about all this—on the one hand it would be so much simpler to plan on just getting married & having a family but on the other hand, I am at a highly competitive university that encourages people to be the best in their careers. Basically, I feel that each person should be free to follow whatever course in life they choose. In saying that, of course you know I realize that there are some physical limitations as well as other "non-sex" related considerations (economics, etc.) But by that I mean that men & women should both be able to do whatever they choose. I am not about to put down any woman who wants to be a housewife. If that's what she wants, that's right. But if she wants something different she sure shouldn't be made to feel guilty about it.

This morning as the Bems were talking about how they are raising their daughter, I had to think about how you all raised me. I think you brought me up to be as autonomous as possible. She gave the example that when her kid wants something to eat, she often suggests that she (the daughter) push a chair up to the counter. I was immediately reminded of all the hundreds of times I pulled out the bread drawer so I could reach a glass & how I learned to handle a gallon carton of milk at age 4 or 5! It's interesting looking back on your own childhood and trying to figure out certain motives & such. I often wonder about the influence you had on me, as opposed to Dad (or vice versa). It's difficult for me to keep things in perspective about Dad now, as a result of several conversations we had this summer. I had always felt that his attitude toward me (a woman) was, "You can do anything you want in this world." But this summer the words I heard him saying didn't back that up in a general sense (or put qualifiers on them). I always thought him to be nonsexist, but this summer, that turned around to a degree. That's his right of course, but it was kind of a surprise after all these years. I know he believes I can do anything, but women cannot. . . .

I think back to when you decided to go back to work—I was very dead set against it, for purely personal, selfish reasons. Now that you're not working, though, I can see the turmoil you're going through searching for something meaningful to do. That probably has a lot to do with my current feelings that I want to have a career & not just be left "without a job" when my kids leave & I'm 45. Of course, my goals for my life are different somewhat from yours but you, as my main female role model all my life, have a great influence on them.

A couple things I've sort of wondered about—what your feelings were when you were my age and what your thoughts were about bringing me up. I've heard you say that you would have liked to have gone to med school, but I believe you said there wasn't enough money (I think that was what you told me). At that time, wasn't it a little odd for women to think about being doctors? When you were in college, what kind of goals did you have for your life (particularly with respect to sex roles?) I guess I'm kind of wondering what kind of latent feelings you had, if any.

. . . A survey done a couple years ago asked kids what they wanted to be when they grew up. The vast majority of the girls said housewives &/or mothers, with only 2 or 3 mentioning nurse or teacher. The little boys mentioned a wide range of occupations. I started thinking about myself then. The earliest thing I can remember wanting to be was a P.E. teacher. I'm sure that was mainly due to my athletic abilities. I wanted to be that for several years. Then when I was 11 or 12, I decided I wanted to be a stockbroker. I've always known it was a little odd for an 11-year-old to want to be a stockbroker, but I see now it's even more unusual for a girl. Thinking back, I saw absolutely no reason why I shouldn't be able to be a stockbroker. . . . I played all-boy games & played mostly with boys & was always trying to prove I was just as good as the boys (a very difficult concept to get over even in adulthood). Another factor may have been slightly opposite—the fact that I came from an all-girl family. I believe some studies have indicated that women at all-women colleges are more assertive than coeds, because they are not intimidated by men in classes, clubs, etc. And when they emerge into the "real world" they remain more aggressive & assertive. Perhaps in the same way I became more assertive growing up in an all-female house (or as an "only" child). I guess what I am ultimately asking is—did you ever consciously (or unconsciously, now that you look back on it) try to instill traditionally male characteristics (assertiveness, aggressiveness, independence, etc.) in me, or try to blind certain sex roles?

. . . I am quite fascinated with this subject now—from both objective & personal viewpoints. I'd like to talk with you about it at Christmas. There is so much to be said and letters are lousy for discussions! I'd be interested to hear your opinions from a personal vantage point & also from a professional viewpoint. . . . Well, I must go now. Too bad my tests aren't just on the psychology of sex roles (which by the way, I'm taking as a class

from Sandra Bem spring quarter)—I've done lots of reading &
discussing on that lately!

Love you,
M.C.

Letter from Anonymous to her father

[May 26, 2015]

Hi Daddy,
I'm glad you're doing better. A lot has been going on for me
this year, all good things. Mommy probably hasn't mentioned
anything because I don't think she really understands the
transitions I've been making or doesn't really approve.

In terms of my personal life, I've [been] going through my
cliché college growing-up faze. I cut my hair and got my nose
pierced and deactivated from my sorority and am moving into
the vegetarian co-op on campus where I'll be living in a
commune with five other people, etc. I realized last year I wasn't
really being myself or around the kinds of people I wanted to
be around. I realized my relationship with John hindered me a
lot too. (Wow, why doesn't anyone tell you it's a bad idea to get
into relationships so young?) I came into Stanford assuming I'd
be similar to other people but I guess that's not the case. It
seems like most of the people here are very privileged and are
here for the name/eventual money, fame, power, etc. Not a lot
of people here care about helping others or their morality, or
are really that smart/genuine/impressive to be honest. There are
still some really incredible people though, of course.

I took a philosophy class at the beginning of this year that helped me realize I wanted to do more with the humanities. I also hated being around CS majors all the time because all they talk about is money and how many interviews they have lined up for google [sic] or whatever else. So basically I've switched majors this year from computer science to symbolic systems (mix of philosophy, CS, linguistics, and psychology) to philosophy to public policy. I realized that advocacy was actually a career, but I wasn't too sure about law school until yesterday. Mommy met this successful advocacy lawyer who works in DC and owns his own firm. He convinced me to go to law school and wants me to come intern in DC next summer. (I'm studying abroad in Cape Town this summer/doing a public service program in gender rights while i'm there.) My lawyer friend says that good lawyers in advocacy are rare because they have to be really ballsy/have really good morals and fortunately those are my only 2 unique-ish skills, so I feel better about the fact that I hate public speaking and will probably hate law school. You're probably cringing because you always shat on lawyers and discouraged me from pursuing the humanities. Sorry not sorry. I'm not going into corporate/criminal law if that makes you feel any better. Not sure if you know what advocacy is but basically I want to represent minority groups or maybe run a nonprofit, something along those lines. Deciding that I want to go to law school also helped me realize I won't really ever use the econ that the public policy program includes, so next quarter I'm just going to take a bunch of classes that sound interesting and then figure out something else to declare at the end of the quarter. I'm considering history, African and African American studies, comparative race and ethnicity studies, and feminist/gender/ sexuality studies.

I haven't quite decided on my final class schedule for this quarter, but classes I'll be shopping next week include solidarity and racial justice, civil rights and education, human behavioral biology, free will and responsibility, African American women's lives, and creative nonfiction. I haven't actually been engaged with any of my classes here until now so hopefully now that I'm taking classes I'm actually interested in I'll be more engaged. I've only ever done assignments the night before and don't normally go to class but I still have decent grades so it'll be interesting to see what I can do if I actually put effort in.

Best,
Anonymous[149]

Text from Anonymous to a Friend

Anonymous [2016]

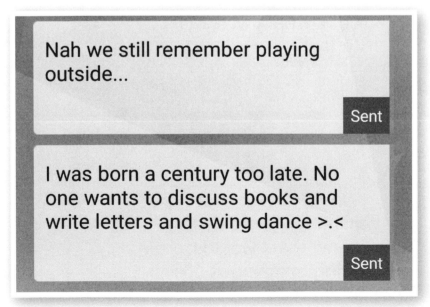

Nah we still remember playing outside...

Sent

I was born a century too late. No one wants to discuss books and write letters and swing dance >.<

Sent

Texts between Sydney Larson and her mother

Sydney [2015]

Messages (1) **Sydney**   Details

Look what I walked by today!

That brings back some memories, do you remember it as fun?

Would have blown my mind in 7th grade to know that I would be living on campus 15+ years later!

Ruminations: Further Comments

"When I was a freshman I took it for granted that I had to
do a great deal of sitting up of nights, etc., but now I
take it for granted that the one thing to do is to go [to]
bed & get plenty of sleep. . . . "

—Rose Payne, May 17, 1897

"Already I am joining hands with the future and can feel
the rushing waters of that stream into which in a few
years I shall hurl myself to sink or swim, to live or
die, to survive or perish."

—Fred (Frederic) Jewell Perry, Stanford University, Feb. 3, 1898

"My birthday comes Wednesday. The year has been so short.
Yet it has been full to the brim for me. Time flies but
still there is time for me to do a good deal that is
worthwhile."

—J. B. (Jesse Brundage) Sears, Sept. 23, 1907

"You have always done everything for me & I don't seem to
be very grateful."

—(Mary) Carol Stearns, Nov. 7, 1946

"September seems like so long ago because so much has
happened since then. As you can probably tell, I'm rather
in a sentimental mood right now. I've just been having
such a great time here (not always fun and easy, but such
a learning experience)."

—Alison Carpenter, May 5, 1976

"I'm really feeling good about things out here now. I know
I was supposed to come back this year and everything will
work out. I belong here."

—M.C., Oct. 7, 1976

Chapter 8

Final Letters Home

"Some say I always seem to have a good time though. Well, I do these days, and I'm really beginning to feel sorry that they will soon be over."

—Lucy Allabach, Mar. 25, 1895

Letter from Lucy Allabach to her mother

May 19, 1895

Dear Mama,

. . . Yesterday afternoon was the last "At Home" of the Jordan's. . . .

Dr. & Mrs. Jordan[6] and the faculty have issued invitations for the reception to the Ninety-five class. It will be given next Friday evening.

Last Tuesday was Memorial Day[63] and therefore a holiday. There were not enough who desired to go to have the excursion to Monterey this year. The celebration consisted in exercises in the Chapel the evening before and in scattered picnics on the day.

The exercises were student productions, music, a duet by Miss Holbrook and Mr. Harris, A History of the Campus by Roy Ballard, reading of a poem by Mr. Neidig by Kate Nash, and a retrospect of the University by Mr. Donald were the numbers. The last was quite caustic in some respects and received some criticism.

Our family, that is the part of it that has no regular appendages, went on a drive back in the mountains.

Friday night Mr. Laushe and Louise and Mr. Pauly and I, all in the one-seated cart . . . went to call at the Smith's. We spent a delightful evening. All the time now I am so impressed with the fact that it is the last time that I feel sad rather than glad. . . .

Well, it will not be long until you have me home to stay, and we'll have lots of time to finish things up as you want them. . . .

With lots of love,
Lucy

Letters from Rose Payne to an older relative

San Jose at Gertrude's
May 31—[18]97

Nonnie dearest—

Well, well, the very first Sunday after the routine was over I missed writing my letter to you—not that I did anything that day—but just luxuriated in my laziness from morning till night. The week has been such a full one and has ended by my finding myself here at Mrs. McMillan's eating my head off at her excellent table. I don't know which end to begin [with] but guess with this morning's happiness—for Gertrude, after she saw Theodora off for Stanford on the 8 o'clock train went with me out to the cemetery. We . . . had such a happy, cool ride and found the dear resting place beautifully kept. . . .

. . . The last commencement days were full of utmost confusion. The most delightful thing was the Promenade Concert[150]—the night was just warm enough—mild & bright with stars—the dear Quad was outlined with Chinese lanterns & San Francisco's best orchestra gave the most beautiful music near the east entrance—the whole reminded me more of the World's Fair than anything else—all of the short arcades were transformed into pretty booths where different sets of girls met their friends & served refreshments. . . . Prof. Allardice gave a little dinner party just before inviting two Miss Risings—daughters of Prof. Rising of Berkeley—who were visiting the University. . . . It was the most charming dinner I was ever at. . . . It certainly takes men to entertain beautifully. I felt very honored to have my first & last promenade with Prof. Allardice and to have him escort me home. . . . I find my most congenial friends among the young professors—though the boys are lovely to me, yet their tastes grow toward freshman girls as mine grow toward the faculty. . . .

Tuesday morning.

. . . Theodora must have told you about Dr. Wakefield's and Miss Wakefield's call—They certainly have been lovely to Theodora & me—indeed everybody is—Thanks to Mama & Papa. It is nearly time for me to go to take my train so I must end this awful scrawl—

Be sure and don't worry about Toodles for everyone exclaims about my healthy appearance. I certainly was never better in my life—I do hope you are the same and have entirely recovered from the grip [grippe]—

Bye-bye
Rose

Letters from Fred (Frederic) Jewell Perry to his mother

[April 1900]

My dear mother:

. . . My name was published in the Chronicle yesterday among the candidates up for graduation at commencement this year. No person whose name is omitted from this final list can graduate. But that does not mean that everyone indicated in the list will positively graduate. The final examinations are yet to come and the theses are to be handed in, and one can never prophesy who will be able to pass muster at the final rally on the 25th of May. We do not know until a few hours before ascending the platform to receive our degrees whether we have passed or not. Oh! It's nerve-wracking anticipation. I expect to graduate, but . . . I can't tell for a certainty until I have my parchment in my hands. . . .

Stanford, May 27, 1900

These closing days of our senior life are crowded with reunions and festivities which will leave pleasant memories of our student life. Friday Dr. Jordan & Mrs. Jordan received the seniors in Roble Hall,[4] Friday evening our class entertained the faculty & undergraduates, Saturday morning the seniors played the annual baseball game with the faculty and alas![151] Dr. Jordan and two or three profs swatted the ball so hard, and caught so perfectly we could not beat them. Saturday night the celebrated farce over which the sensational newspapers have fumed so vigorously was given before a big audience, and carried the house. It was full of local joshes on profs. & students, and replete with farcical situations.

Today Rabbi Voorsauger preached an impressive sermon from the 26th chapter of Isaiah, the second verse, to the graduating class. The burden of his remarks was that the students should form the "righteous nation" which should put into practice the ideals of our college life.

Tomorrow is Class Day and our place in the Quad, the class plate[152] beneath which rests our class roll with the signatures of all of the graduates. Tuesday is Alumni Day[153] and in the evening comes the Promenade. Wed. we receive our degrees and then our college life is at an end. . . .

[Fred]

Letter from J. B. (Jesse Brundage) Sears to his parents

Apr. 14, 1909

Dear Father & Mother:—

You know I have always been looked upon as next to the dumbest one in the family, if not the dumbest. Well now the smart Searses will have to swallow a pretty big dose. What do you think, I (that Jess) have been elected to membership in the greatest national honor society in America . . . the Phi Beta Kappa (pronounced "fi bata kappa") honor society.[142] The society is entered only upon excellent scholarship. Only twenty in the University received the honor; thirteen women and seven men, and I (that Jess) was one of the seven men. Of course I'm proud of it. The fact is I am simply about to bust, I'm so tickled over it.

The badge to be worn is a gold key . . . and it is usually worn as a watch charm by men. The Pres. of Mo. State Univ. wears one, several of the Profs. here have them, so you see it is some distinction to belong to it.

Now don't you think your two Stanford boys have done fairly well? We haven't got the big head very bad, but if we had you couldn't blame us much. . . .

You see I was so pleased over this that I couldn't wait till Sunday to write about it. I don't really know how it all came about. I have worked hard but I didn't suspect that I was making such an impression as that. But you can never tell in a big university who is watching you.

Of course, that doesn't pay my bills but it is something that stands for prestige all the rest of my days so it may mean more indirectly than it does directly. I was congratulated by a good many people today over my election.

The Phi Beta Kappa is the oldest, and most honorable, and most exclusive of the American college fraternities.

School is going along as usual & will soon be out, only a little more than four weeks till I'll have my "sheepskin."[154]

This coming Fri. evening the lady students of education are to entertain at dinner the faculty of the Dept. of Education. Stella and I are invited as part of the faculty. . . .

Well, I must get to my work, so good night.—We are all well & all busy.

With much love from us all, your loving son,

J. B. Sears

Letter from Carol Hodge to her family

12 June 57

Dear Mom, Dad, and Grandma,
My last final exams as an undergraduate are over, and I'm beginning to feel a little nostalgic. Hugh and I can now relax and enjoy our final days on the Farm.[1] I keep thinking how thankful I am to you for my Stanford education. I only hope I live up to your expectations and the Stanford reputation in years to come. . . . My 22nd birthday has come and gone, and, in fact, sort of got lost in the other important things happening this June. It was a fine day. . . .

Love,
Carol

Letter from Elaine Lavis to her family

Tuesday, June 4, 1963

Dear Family,

. . . Last Sunday was also the day of the traditional Senior
Breakfast here. Each house gets together and decorates the
dining room in honor of the graduating seniors, and then the
dorm prepares a special meal. The other girls entertain the
seniors, and we receive corsages. You know—just about like a
repeat of Palladian days. The meal is most noted for the fact
that it is the only time during the quarter when we get steak. It
was very pleasant, and we all felt duly honored. . . .

Love,
Elaine

Letter from Peter King to his father

May 15, 1965

Dear Dad,

This has been a hectic week, and with so little time left in the
quarter, I guess the rest of the weeks will be the same. I have a
paper due Monday, but I figured you'd want the latest news on
graduation plans.

Commencement is at 4:30 on Sunday the 13th. I sent for
and got my allotted four tickets, and also got two for the
baccalaureate ceremony.[155] I really have no desire to attend the

latter, but if you want to, be sure to mention it. Otherwise, I'll give my tickets to someone else. . . .

My last final is on Friday, so I'll be all packed by the time you arrive. From then until Sunday the only thing that I want to attend is the Senior Class Day ceremony, which includes three professors chosen by the class. [Prof.] Pease will be one of the three speakers. . . .

I plan to leave for home on Monday the 14th, spending a night in a motel and getting home on the 15th. That will leave me plenty of time for straightening out my service plans, and for seeing Roger Magnuson over at the Great Northern office for an introduction and an endorsement. He was in the room last night explaining how simple it is to be a brakeman and earn all that fantastic money. . . .

Dad's comment that Stanford was a lot easier in the old days is very true, and in fact the old days for me may extend only four years back! The latest entering class had an application-acceptance ratio of 6 ½ to 1, according to TIME. Since it's tougher to get in, the grades will come harder, also. But Dad shouldn't feel too inferior. After all, intelligence is relative in any group. If he could get A's and B's back in the 30s, he would do the same today if his old class were here. The relativity factor is why I got A's in high school for sometimes not giving an A effort, and it's also why I haven't been able to crack the "A" bracket at Stanford more often. . . .

Well, that's all the news that's pit to frint. Oops, guess I had too much of that gin and lemon!

Your hard-working Stanford senior,
Peter

The Death of Student Drama

Joe Jacobs and Peter King at the
Stanford Daily Offices, 1965

Courtesy of the *Stanford Quad*

Words from Joe: *Stanford Daily*,
May 26, 1965

Courtesy of the *Stanford Daily*

Letter from Joe (Joseph) Lewis Jacobs to his parents

May 29, 1965

This is going to be a long—and no doubt confusing—letter, but
I have to get it done in time to get it out this afternoon so Dad
gets the card.

Speaking of that, since I don't know what you want for your
birthday, Dad, I'll just wait until I get home and come up with
something for your birthday and Father's Day put together.
(Besides, by then maybe I'll have some money—I sure as hell
don't now.)

First of all, about the enclosed clipping. It took me a great deal of time to write (and weeks to think about), but I am very happy with it. After it was set in type it was much too short, so I added the four paragraphs beginning with "In a sense. . ." As you may notice (most people haven't), in that first paragraph I used the word "the latter" when I meant "the former," and the word "source" is spelled wrong at another point, but I am extremely happy with the editorial and have gotten a great many compliments on it from all kinds of people (including a professor in the Speech and Drama Department, but that's a story for a later letter). . . .

I called Charlotte, told her what books Carl and I would like and told her about the toothbrushes. She says that once you did get toothbrushes for her at about 35¢ apiece. If you can't get them for that price, don't bother, as she'll have her dentist get them for her.

About the night of the 12th: Charlotte wants to go to San Francisco for dinner and then go to some place like the Whisky a Go Go.[156] This is all right with me, but I'm worried that if we stay up too late Saturday night you and Dad will be too tired to drive home Sunday night. In any case, I am going to make a dinner reservation for the six of us at a place called Nino's, which is right near Whisky a Go Go. It's on Invitation Dinners—you get a full dinner with no choice of the entree, which is veal cordon bleu, for $5.50. If this doesn't suit you, let me know and I'll make a reservation someplace else. Jack's is less than two blocks from Whisky a Go Go, but of course it isn't on Invitation Dinners. If you don't want to necessarily be confined to Invitation Dinners, let me know and I can make a reservation someplace else. But let me know . . . so we can make some kind of reservation somewhere. . . .

Also, Carl wants to get together with Barbara and family for brunch either Saturday (after his graduation) or Sunday.[157] He prefers Saturday—I gather because that way Barbara can get out of her dorm's senior lunch, which she doesn't want to go to. I prefer Sunday. . . .

I expect a letter from you by next weekend, and if this whole thing isn't at least somewhat cleared up, I will call you next Sunday when Carl is down to pick up my car.[59] That way we'll have two of us together here and the two of you there and maybe we can get it straightened out. . . .

Oh, earlier in the day I had gone with a reporter to cover a press conference by a guy who was speaking at a Junior Chamber of Commerce luncheon at Whisky a Go Go. After the press conference, the reporter said I could stay for lunch if I wished and after I asked him if he was sure it was all right and he reassured me, I stayed for a free steak lunch. I can't complain. It's a wild place just in its decor.

Last night was the DAILY[2] banquet at Rickey's.[158] This one I had to pay for. I had four vodka gimlets there. Two I bought, a third I was treated to (and I treated this guy to a drink also so in effect I paid for it) and the fourth was also treated. They weren't as good as the ones Thursday had been, but they were cheaper (65¢ vs. 90¢), and of course the banquet was fun. There was a party after the banquet, but it was dull and I was tired so I left early (midnight) and came home and, after chasing Clay and his girlfriend out of the room, went to bed and slept for a solid 10 hours. Tomorrow I have a luncheon. It's a rough life. . . .

Incidentally, the six of us who met for cocktails Thursday were five girls and me. Boy, did I get stares!! . . .

That's all. Write.
Love,
Joe

Kona Inn

AN INTER-ISLAND RESORT

KAILUA-KONA, HAWAII

May 29, 1965

Dear Mom and Dad,
        This is going to be a long--and a no doubt confusing--
letter, but I have to get it done in time to get it out this
afternoon so Dad gets the card.
        Speaking of that, since I don't know what you xxxx want for
your birthday, Dad, I'll just wait until I get hom and come
up with something for your birthday and fathers day put together.
(Besides, by then maybe I'll have some money--I sure as hell don't
now.)
        First of all, about the enclosed clipping. It took me a
great deal of time to write (and weeks to think about), but I
am very happy with it. After it was set in type it was much too
short, so I added the four paragraphs beginning with "In a
sense..." As you may notice (most people haven't), in that first
paragraph I used the word "the latter" when I meant "the
former," and the word source is spelled wrong at another point,
but I am extremely happy with the editorial and have gotten a
great many compliments on it from all kinds of people (including
a professor in the Speech and Drama department, but that's a
story for a later letter).
        I will tell Terry, Murray and Clay about the Open House.
You did say 8 p.m. on the 19th, didn't you? I just got a
letter from Allen Delevett, and when I answer I plan on inviting
him. I'd rather not invite Peggy--I'm not sure that having her
at a party with many of the VMT people is an especially wise
idea, since I don't know how strained relations are--and if I
invite Faye there are all sorts of other VMT people I should
invite as well--Bill Holland, Mrs. Gamble and so on. I'm inviting
ayo and Hale because they're my bosses and Dave Holland because
imagine I'll be working more with him than with anyone else
his summer, and since I worked closer with him than with
nyone else last summer. Did you invite Gary Plummer? If so,
lease let me know, so I can tell Les when I write him and
erhaps they can come up together. We may have a lot of people
eeping on the floor that night.
        Let me know what happens with the Schwartz' house.
        The Bauers haven't called me yet, but then I've been out
st of the weekend so far (more on that later).
        I called Charlotte, told her what books Carl and I would
ke and told her about the toothbrushes. She says that once you
d get toothbrushes for her at about 35¢ apiece. If you can't
t them for that price, don't bother, as she'll have her dentist
t them for her.
        About the night of the 12th: Charlotte wants to go to San
ancisco for dinner and then go to some place like the Whisky
o Go. This is all right with me, but I'm worried that if we
ay up too late Saturday night you and Dad will be too tired
drive home Sunday night. In any case, I am going to make a
ner reservation for the six of us at a place called Nino's,
ch is right near Whisky a Go Go. It's on Invitation Dinners--
get a full dinner with no choice of the entree, which is
l cordon bleu, for $5.50. If this doesn't suit you, let me

Letter from M.C. to her parents

18 March 79

Dear Mom and Dad,

. . . Actually, the biggest news is that your youngest daughter is now a graduate of Stanford University (if I passed everything!) . . .

So how do I feel? Everyone keeps asking me & I honestly haven't felt too much yet. On Friday I had to turn in my take-home at the beginning of class, then the prof lectured; it was Jean's and my last class at Stanford. Two of our good friends were also in the class & we talked Nance into going, too. At the end of the lecture, I popped a cork & we had champagne. We gave our prof. some & also had him put a "Stanford University" sticker on our foreheads. (The class was about power elites in the U.S. & he made the comment that when you graduate from "elitist schools" like SU & Harvard, it's like you have a Stanford stamp on your forehead saying you know how things are done. So Jean & I decided we should have the prof put the SU stamp on us when we graduated.) All in all, it was really a fun way to end my classes.

. . . I'm not fully comprehending it yet, but during the past week I have periodically had glimpses of it & it's kind of hard to take. I am ready for the work to be over, but not the experience. It seems as though I have been here forever. Consequently, I usually walk around without being fully conscious of everything around me. But last week I really tried to be aware of the campus. It really is pretty & it holds so many memories. It was nice to just walk around the Quad & think of different classes I've had in the rooms & all that. As I looked around I also realized that it was exactly 5 years ago, to the very week, that I first came to Stanford. . . . I remember being awestruck with the beauty of the campus & being so impressed with how smart all the people seemed to be. I thought then, "I could never go to a place like this." And then I remembered the incredible elation I felt when I found out I'd gotten accepted to Stanford. . . .

It's hard to believe that this is actually me. Five years later, I did make it to Stanford. Four years later I am graduating from Stanford. Things have not been all easy or good for me & Stanford is no ideal place. But oh, I'm glad I came here. It's all been worth it. Even if I never ever did anything at all with my "Stanford education," it would all be worth it. A hundred times over it's worth it.

It will be hard to leave. The hardest thing will be leaving my friends. They have been the main factor in making Stanford what it is to me. While I've been here, I've sort of developed a "philosophy of Stanford" (as opposed to . . . life). It's "you've got to get your priorities straight." For me, that means you've got to take time to party, to give & receive from friends. And that seems to be the feelings of my friends, too. We all do well in our classes & take it seriously, but we also know there's more than just classes & studying here. And that people part is so important, too. This year in particular I've really gotten extremely close to Nance & Jean & also to a group of about 8 other friends. It's going to hurt to leave them. We'll still be friends, but it will never be the same on a day-to-day basis. I know things must change & I wouldn't really want them to stay the same forever, but it still makes me a little sad.

I've thought a lot about you all, too. Our relationship has changed a lot since I've been here & I think it's gotten stronger.

Things haven't always been easy, but I do appreciate your support of my decision to come to Stanford & my decision to stay. I know you all were behind me & that means a lot. I love you both very much.

I guess this is the last letter you will get from me from Stanford. It's been a good four years. Thanks.

Love,
M.C.

Letter from Karen Kinney to her grandmother

1/17/83

Dear Gran,
It is always so much fun to talk to you on the phone! I was happy to hear how strong your voice sounded—not scratchy anymore. Good! I'm doing well at Stanford. This will be a hard, fun, and very important quarter. I am taking some interesting (and difficult) courses on environmental policy, human physiology, coping with illness, and perhaps a German conversation class. I am also writing something like an undergrad thesis for human biology, and I am a teaching assistant for a psychology class with the famous Dr. Philip Zimbardo! . . .[132]

I am going to finish school in March. I'll still graduate in June with my class, but I won't have to pay to go to school in spring. Instead of school I will be auditing courses—Searching for jobs, etc. It will still be three months of school but I will only be paying an auditing fee.

I am also applying to the Stanford Graduate School of Education. It is not a sure bet, though, since they only accept 40 people a year—I'll be competing for a very valuable spot. I am going to take my GRE (exam) in February, I hope. One more thing to study for!! (and be scared about). . . . It is an extremely intense program, so I may be wanting the "year off" option before beginning. I do hope that I am accepted! . . .

I surely do love you!!
Love,
Karen

Texts between Laine Bruzek and her mother

Laine [2016]

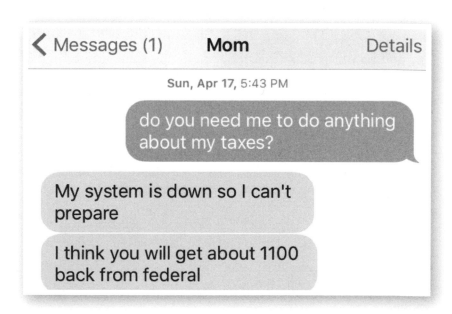

Texts from Kat (Kathleen) Gregory to her mother

6/17/16, 10:41 a.m.

It's been a full end of the quarter. You'd get a kick out of this. I spent 7 hours at a football match between Argentina and Chile - the #1 and #5 ranked teams worldwide, respectively - with the Crothers staff and residents.[159] Walked the mile and a half back from the train under the stars to frantically finish up a final project in my room with my three awesome project partners. The task we chose was: given someone's written description of their trip on a recreational drug, can we guess which drug they were on? Zach and I had spent the impossibly crowded caltrain ride home typing up descriptions of drugs (based [on] the weights our classifier learned about the emotions each elicited) on an iPhone. Lost my debit card on said train too, by the way—but don't worry, I canceled about 2.5 seconds before my phone died. After submitting our final paper at midnight, I headed over to Narnia[160] to pull an all-nighter with my senior project team for our software fair demo today. Biked home via Lake Lag as the sun was rising. Hand wrote notes to each of my residents with end of year messages and "freed" them with crazy socks . . . (fuzzy socks, monster face socks, knee high socks, socks with Starry Night and the Scream. . .) [Ellipses in original.] I heard two girls gasp when they opened their door, and over the course of the morning at different places around campus two other residents showed me that they were wearing their socks :). And then, since I had an hour left before our senior project team reconvened and that's too short for a decent nap, I went for an eight mile run in Matadero[161] - and hit my fastest time on that loop. If everything seems under control, you're just not going fast enough.

6/7/16, 2:00 pm
ARGGG MOM I got my grad gown last week but after I got it I went to lunch with a friend and I just realized that I don't think it ever got back to my room!! My pack was loaded with packages of socks—what if it just fell out?? I waited an HOUR in line just to pick it up. . . . [Ellipses in original.] What do I do?! I'm taking pictures with TWO different groups this afternoon, and I need at least the stole for those! :(:(

6/7/16, 2:24 pm
Haha I actually remember it is in my room.

6/7/16, 2:24 pm
but idk where it is

6/7/16, 3:30 pm
JK FOUND IT

6/7/16 3:30 pm
I'M A FOOL

6/7/16, 3:30 pm
Mom—"So much for thinking things were running too smoothly?"

6/7/16, 3:30 pm
OH I never said smoothly!

Final Letters Home: Further Comments

"We, of the class of ninety-five, of the feminine gender, had a meeting and decided to lay aside the traditional seminary commencement gown and appear as college women in street suits on that memorable day when David Jordan's school grants us our 'Bachelor's Degrees.' I am very glad it is to be so."

—Lucy Allabach, Mar. 25, 1895

"I don't believe there is a thing to write about this week—it is oozing in upon my consciousness that there is not much more than three weeks of college left & that a large amount of work lies between the now & the then."

—Rose Payne, May 2, 1897

"I am sending out free commencement announcement cards to our relatives and close friends. . . . Wish you could be here May 19 at 10:30 a.m. Think of me anyway."

—J. B. (Jesse Brundage) Sears, May 6, 1909

"I dread to think of leaving everything up here forever but such is life. After going to school all one's life it's rather hard when that ends—and you have no other definite plans."

—Julia Hamilton Conkling, [May 10, 1916]

"Well, I feel myself growing up quickly. And with growing pains, too. It would have been so much easier to have gone home and live there with you, but this I feel is good for me, although I feel like a little girl going out to face the cold, hard world for the first time."

—Nancy Christine Smith, Oct. 1, 1947

"Several people . . . said a degree from Stanford will start you at a higher salary than from somewhere else. I hope so. Actually, I just want a job."

—M.C., Nov. 13, 1976

Chapter 9

Snapshots from the Quad

"I always think about how you rode your bike on the same pavement as I do."

—Ben Rosellini, Feb. 24, 2012

Photos courtesy of Erik Hill, Class of 1979

"Your letter is before me, and I'll try to help you to more fully understand the view in the quadrangle. As you stand in the court looking east you see on your left the main arch which leads into and out of the quadrangle. This is the main arch only because the main roadway leads up to it not because it is any finer. On your right is the tall chapel-looking building but as this is unfinished I can't tell what it will be. On the west and east are also high arches leading out beyond the buildings. The rows of smaller regular arches are the supports to the roof of the arcade, whose floor is paved with diamond-shaped stone of dull red and gray. The arcade is nothing more nor less than the porch which runs around in front of and connecting all the various buildings of study. The rooms are numbered according to a regular plan and there are 125 at least including the chapel and library, which each occupy a whole building. . . . If you take the main arch and walk perhaps a block on the asphalt road you reach the cement walk which, going east leads to Encina, . . . [going] west to our hall and north of you is the museum,[162] which will be very fine when finished. . . . I hope so much that you can come see it for yourself."

—*Lucy Allabach, Roble Hall,*[4] *Nov. 1, 1891*

"This is a doubly interesting day to me, because it is your birthday and because it is Presidential Election Day also. I have just come back from the quadrangle where the election returns are being read. Everybody is excited, the band is playing Columbia the Gem of the Ocean, and sleep seems to have taken wings and flown away."

—*Francis J. Batchelder, Nov. 8, 1892*

"Your letter, coming before Friday, was especially welcome. They are always that though, as you would be very sure if you could see me as I walk from the Quad, reading them. I go very slowly, smile broadly, and heave a sigh of regret when the letter is finished."

—*Lucy Allabach, Palo Alto, Nov. 12, 1892*

"Then the night was cold but the moon made up for that as it shone in its loveliness down into the Quad."

—*Lucy, Oakland, California, June 12, 1892*

"The picture I sent you was of Theodora, so Elsie was right after all, those little photos are the craze now, and it is positively unsafe to go on the quadrangle for you are sure of having one of those snapped."

—*Rose Payne, May 4, 1896*

"We have been having peculiar weather here of late. No sunshine & much wind. The mornings are cold & frosty & the air makes a fellow's ears tingle as he rides up to the Quad on the wheel."[87]

—*Fred (Frederic) Jewell Perry, KE House, Stanford, Jan. 28, 1900*

"Then when the show was over everybody went over to the Quad and the Juniors paraded around the inner Quad in their new plugs[8] which the seniors on all sides smashed . . . in. The object of the whole thing was to christen the plugs."

—*Julia Hamilton Conkling, Oct. 27, 1911*

"I had enough troubles yesterday to drive me to an early grave. To begin with it was Friday and I was to have two exes., one at 9:15 in French, & one at 10:15 in algebra. Well at 9:15 I went over to [the] French building with my pen and two ex. blanks, one marked Math 3 and the other El. French. Well before the hour was up I finished my French ex., & handing in my paper I strolled leisurely over to [the] math. building, on the opposite end of Quad, a distance of about ¼ a mile. Well when Prof. Green marched to the board & started to put on problems, I opened my ex. blank to find I had my French ex. and had handed in an empty blank marked Math. 3 to the French prof. Well up I got and fairly tore along the Quad. When almost to [the] French building out came Prof. Allen and down the Quad he went. Well, amid the remarks of "I'll bet that's a freshman" I kept on running till I overtook him. I didn't have the slightest idea that he would take my paper after all that time but he was awfully nice. He hunted up my math. blank for me and asked me what I ran so for. I told him I was afraid he would be gone and I wouldn't get anything in French and he said I needn't have worried about that. . . ."

—*Julia, Nov. 4, 1911*

"I bumped into Stew on Quad yesterday. He got a B in Evidence this summer & was very happy. . . . A couple of photographers from Holiday magazine who are planning to feature campus life in a future issue (a couple of months) asked if they could take our picture walking down Quad. We said 'sure'—& Stew muttered 'Pete wouldn't like this.'"[144]

—*(Mary) Carol Stearns, Sept. 24, 1946*

"Tonight was a funny night! My roommate Marilyn and I were tired of studying and were standing in the lobby of the library when in walked Jack. He is one of the hashers[54] where we eat our meals at [the] Union and a fun person to know. After a bit of conversation, he said, 'Let's go to a show.' We each thought he was asking the other gal, but he saw the confusion and said, 'I mean both of you!' So off we went in his little, blue car which we call The Blue Beetle. The three of us had a great date! The show was good, very colorful, about Napoleon. Afterwards, we went to get a hamburger then started back for campus. It was a full-moon night, and we started kidding around about the moon and Stanford tradition—to be kissed by a senior in center Quad under a full moon.[163] Well, one of us said, 'We should go spy on Inner Quad where there are bound to be couples kissing under this lovely full moon.' No sooner than this idea had been planted, Jack DROVE his little Blue Beetle right into the Quad, much to the surprise of others already there! And, what's more, right in the center of Quad, he kissed each of us IN THE CAR."

—*Carol Hodge, Dec. 10, 1954*

"On Monday, some of the football players came and ate dinner with us, and yesterday was Red and White day, when everyone wore the school colors. Today is 'Lick Cal' day, and lollipops and Beat Cal buttons are being handed out all over Quad."

—*Elaine Lavis, Nov. 16, 1960*

"Monday night was Full Moon night. There is a tradition at Stanford that a Stanford girl does not become a Stanford woman until kissed for one full minute under a full moon at midnight by a senior boy in front of the church on Inner Quad. And the freshmen always descend on Inner Quad loaded with water balloons. This year the freshmen had been informed that there would be plenty of senior fraternity boys out to get them, so a mob of over a hundred freshman boys showed up, and there were only about two dozen seniors with dates. The battle was rather one-sided, and the mob got a bit rowdy. As a matter of fact, an article in this morning's Daily[2] called it an 'appalling act of pure crudeness and stupidity.' Unfortunately, I was hit by a water balloon early in the proceedings, and merely stayed on the sidelines for the rest of the melee."

—*Joe (Joseph) Lewis Jacobs, Oct. 25, [1961]*

"The whole house was awakened at this ungodly hour by a boy yelling at the windows. We were all pretty mad until we realized what all the commotion was about—it was SNOWING outside, and had been doing so for quite a while, judging by the layer of snow on the ground. Everyone got up and started running around screaming and yelling. Some brave souls even went outside in it, but we waited for a little while. About seven-thirty it started snowing again, and so Carol and I decided to get dressed and go out walking in it. We walked all over Quad, and it was amazing to see all the trees and roofs and lawns covered with a blanket of snow. Everyone was throwing snowballs, and making snowmen, and all—there was enough snow for that. It was . . . [all so] amazing to see—[the] campus, which is usually dead on Sunday morning until about noon was jumping with people at eight in the morning. I guess everyone else, like us, had to go out and see it for themselves."

—*Elaine Lavis, Jan. 21, 1962*

"After one math lecture in a plush lecture room, all of us sat down at 9 today expecting a lecture. Turned out that the room was being used for a class in Greek architecture! We traipsed down the Quad to an old classroom with Puritan-type straight-back wooden pew desks. It, unfortunately, will be permanent."

—*Peter King, Sept. 29, 1962*

"P.S. I hope I fully explained the nature of the speaker stunt over at Cal. . . . I emphasize the fact that the Dean of Freshman Men, Dwight Clark, was behind us and pulling for us 100% all the way. Also our stunt was not breaking any laws and was a lot less malicious than the people from Cal who came over to Stanford with spray cans of blue paint and sprayed "C" and "Cal" all over the walls of Quad."

—*Gary, 2:00 p.m., Nov. 23, 1963*

"I think you would find it interesting to see Stanford when it's alive—if for no other reason but to wonder how people keep from getting run over by the multitudes (& I do mean multitudes) of bikes at 10:00 in front of the Engineering Corner of the Quad. (Remember where that is, Mom?)!"

—*M.C., Oct. 7, 1976*

"Next news! There is a Stanford tradition that if a freshman girl is kissed by a senior guy at 12:00 in the center of the Quad under a full moon, she becomes a Stanford woman! Well, Kevin, a friend from SAE, asked me out for the full moon last night, and—Don't worry, Gran! I was too late!! We got there at 12:20. . . . After we watched 'the crazy Stanford women,' we went and snuck onto the roof of Terman Library and the 4 of us disco-danced,[164] without music, for an hour or more."

—*Karen Kinney,, Oct. 6, 1979*

"Tonight after work I am going to . . . [celebrate] Patty's birthday (21)—all of us roommates are going to blindfold her and bring her to the center of the Quad, where we will have a picnic and a cake with candles lit, all at midnight under a full moon!"

—*Anonymous, Thursday, Oct. 20, [Early 1980s]*

On Quad: Hope, the Freds, Joe, Laine— and all of us

Courtesy of the Stanford University Archives

Biographies of the Letter Writers

Unless otherwise noted, biographies were submitted by alums, their descendants or relatives, or current students. Biographies were requested of letter writers with roughly one or more pages of letters and/or emails, or more than one text.

Alice Louise Clark (Harris) attended Ventura Community College
for two years before transferring to Stanford, where she earned a
BA in political science in 1937. Alice spent many years as an
executive secretary—for the medical director of Orthopedic
Hospital in Los Angeles, for private physicians' offices, and for
Orthopedic Audio Synopsis, which provides professional
development for orthopedic surgeons.

Anne Peters (Battle) followed her mother's dream of attending
Stanford. She loved intramurals and dorm life while earning
degrees in psychology ('75) and education ('76). In 1973 she
attended the Beutelsbach campus in Germany, going on field trips
to Rome, Prague, and Berlin. She remembers the joy of
hitchhiking adventures on the long weekends. The letters of her
mother, Carol Stearns, also appear in this book.

"Anonymous 1990" spent one quarter studying abroad in Chile. The
summer after he wrote this letter, he spent two months training
with the navy in Coronado and Long Beach, California. He
graduated from Stanford in 1991 (BA, International Relations and
Economics). After receiving his commission, he served for five
years as a naval officer. He is married, has one son, and works for a
global Fortune 300 company in Minneapolis.

Babe (Mabel) Bartlett (Gould) of Ventura, California, was a
Stanford sophomore when the Great San Francisco Earthquake
hit in 1906. She left Stanford later that year and never returned.
She married her childhood sweetheart, Thomas Gould Jr., a
farmer in Ventura, California, where they raised their family. A
botany major at Stanford, she was an avid gardener and specialist
in native plants and flowers. She was the mother of Dick
(Richard) Bartlett Gould ('34), whose letters also appear in
Letters Home from Stanford.

Bob (Robert) Lowell Swetzer worked on his family's peach orchards in Wheatland, California, before attending Stanford, where he spent freshman year in the Encina Hall[5] bullpen, the small enclave over the Encina auditorium, making lifelong friends. At Stanford he was on the Chappie staff and in the Hammer and Coffin National Honorary Society,[120] graduating in 1952 (BA, Political Science). He went on to serve in the Korean War, as an intelligence analyst for the State Department, an Air Force historian, and a reserve intelligence officer, retiring as a colonel at the end of the Cold War. Since then he has written magazine articles and resumed painting.

Bob (Robert) Richardson Sears received a BA from Stanford in 1929. A prominent psychologist specializing in childhood psychology, he taught at Yale, the University of Iowa, and at Harvard before returning to the Farm,[1] where he headed the psychology department and later was dean of the School of Humanities and Sciences. Bob married Pauline Snedden ('30; sister of Hope Snedden, whose letters appear in this book). Pauline went on to become a prominent psychologist and Stanford professor. Bob's father was J. B. [Jesse Brundage] Sears, whose letters also appear in this book.

Burnham P. Beckwith graduated from Stanford in 1926 (BA, Philosophy). He went on to write books on socialism and economics, including *The Modern Case for Economics* and *The Economic Theory of a Socialist Economy*. At Stanford, per his autobiography, he became "fascinated by the world of the intellect." (Burnham P. Beckwith, "Autobiography of Burnham Putnam Beckwith," typescript, 89033, Hoover Institution Archives)

Carol Hodge (March) was the first person in her family to attend college. She graduated from Stanford in 1957 with a BA in history, earning an MA in education there the next year. She married Hugh March (BA, Geography, '57; MBA, '60), and they raised their two children in the home they built themselves close to campus. Carol played the violin in the Stanford Symphony as a student and remains an avid violinist today.

(Mary) Carol Stearns (Peters) was the youngest by seven years of four children, living most of her childhood alone with her single mom, a high school cafeteria worker in Long Beach, California. She followed her older sister Betty to Stanford, completing one year of law school before marrying fellow law student Colin Peters. She loved Stanford with complete devotion, by both enthusiastically cheering on the Cardinal and dedicating herself to raising her three children in such a way that they too had the chance to attend. One of them was Anne Peters, whose letter from Beutelsbach appears in *Letters Home from Stanford*.

Chrissie Huneke (Kremer) graduated from Stanford in 1984 with a BA in international relations. She went on to pursue a marketing career and raise three boys with her husband, John. Her first time traveling overseas was with Stanford's overseas program, which ignited a passion for travel that has taken her to live overseas and to explore much of the world. The letters of her father, Johnny Huneke, also appear in this book.

Dan Lythcott-Haims hasn't strayed far from the Farm[1] since graduating. He lives in Palo Alto with his wife, Julie, and their two children. He has worked as a designer of museum exhibits, graphics, products, experiences, websites, and apps. Now his eye is turning toward photography as a way to express how he sees the world.

Dick (Richard) Bartlett Gould received his BA in economics from Stanford in 1934. He never made varsity football as he had hoped, but football was an important part of his years on the Farm. After Stanford, he followed in his father's footsteps and became a farmer in Ventura, California, where he was active on many local boards, including the Farm Bureau. He served on the state Republican Central Committee. He was the son of Babe (Mabel) Bartlett, whose letter about the Great San Francisco Earthquake also appears in this book.

Elaine Lavis (Lindheim) graduated from Stanford with a BA in English in 1963, the same year she married Richard Lindheim. After some years of teaching high school English, Elaine received an EdD in research methods and evaluation from UCLA and pursued a career in educational measurement. She has two grown children and one granddaughter, loves to travel, and has hosted many foreign exchange students in their home.

Erica Toews graduated from Stanford in 2010 (BA, English). She worked in the legal department at Google for two years and then spent a year in Malaysia on a Fulbright scholarship. She currently lives in Brooklyn with her boyfriend Bill Loundy (also Class of 2010) and works at an education technology startup called Zearn.

Francis J. Batchelder was the first student of 555 to register at Stanford University in its first year. He attended Stanford from 1891 to 1893 and returned to study from 1903 to 1904, earning a BA in civil engineering. ("About Stanford: University Milestones, Stanford through the Years," Stanford Facts 2016, stanford.edu/about /chron; Letters from Francis J. Batchelder, 1891–1892; bibliographic information, Francis J. Batchelder Correspondence, SC1025, Department of Special Collections and University Archives, Stanford University Libraries, Stanford, California)

Fred (Frederic) Jewell Perry, Class of 1900, went on to work in the
fire insurance industry in the Los Angeles and Palo Alto areas. He
married Adelaide Hazlett of Belfast, Ireland, and had one son,
Robert. Fred remained involved with the Stanford community
throughout his life, participating in class reunions and taking his
family to watch Stanford football games weekly. Throughout his
life, Fred told stories, made jokes, and recited Shakespeare, and was
a skilled leader at the Commonwealth Club, Toastmasters, the
Masons, and the local Methodist Sunday school.

George D. Green graduated from Stanford with a BA in history in
1961 (but is Class of 1960), having attended the Stanford in
Germany campus his senior year. He went on to earn a PhD
(1968) in history and economics from Stanford. He taught at the
University of Minnesota for forty-eight years before retiring in
June 2013. He married Anne Rose ('62), and they have four
children, five grandchildren, and three great-grandchildren. In
more recent years, they have made seven trips back to Europe,
most recently a Danube River cruise. The dormant travel bug has
awakened and is alive and well.

Herbert C. Hoover was a member of the Pioneer Class and by
many accounts the first person to spend the night in Encina Hall.[5]
He reportedly flunked Stanford's entrance test, but the professor
administering it admitted him provisionally—he saw a spark.
During his time at Stanford, he served terms as the student body
treasurer and football team manager, a position he held at the first
Stanford-Cal game. (See Lucy Allabach letter, page 45.) In 1928
Hoover became the thirty-first president of the United States.
(Christopher Klein, "10 Things You May Not Know about
Herbert Hoover," Oct. 20, 2014, History in the Headlines, history.
com/news/10-things-you-may-not-know-about-herbert-hoover;

Susan Wels, *Stanford: Portrait of a University*, Stanford, California: Stanford Alumni Association, 1999, pages 27, 30; Herbert Hoover Presidential Library)

Hope Snedden (Carlsmith) attended Stanford from 1918 to 1920, then went on to graduate from Columbia University and the New York Presbyterian Hospital School of Nursing. She married fellow Stanford student Leonard Carlsmith (BS, '21). Hope taught in a one-room schoolhouse during World War I, as well as a special education class during World War II. More than thirty-five people in the Snedden and Carlsmith families have attended the Farm, including Hope's sons L. Allan Carlsmith ('50) and J. Merrill Carlsmith ('58). Merrill Carlsmith taught in the Stanford Psychology Department, and his son Christopher Carlsmith ('86) returned to Stanford as a visiting scholar for the 2016–2017 academic year.

Jason Seter, born and raised in Milwaukee, Wisconsin, is a junior majoring in history and English. As a *Letters Home from Stanford* editorial intern during winter quarter in 2016, he gained a newfound respect for and interest in Stanford's impressive past. Jason loves to read and write, though he does occasionally find the work at Stanford difficult to accomplish in the beautiful yet distracting California weather. Unless he gets Packers season tickets, he may never return to the Midwest.

J. B. (Jesse Brundage) Sears graduated from Stanford in 1909 with a BA in education, having migrated from the East to California with his wife, Stella. As a student, he earned money cleaning off the bricks that came from the collapsed buildings damaged in the 1906 earthquake. (See Babe Bartlett letter, page 74.) Also earning his PhD at Stanford, he was an avid biker in his younger years, a professor of education at the Farm (1912–1942), and the father of two sons, including Robert Sears, whose letter about becoming the "editor of the Lit" is included in this book. J. B. lived to be ninety-seven years old.

(J.) Fred Weintz Jr. transferred to Stanford after serving in World War II. From the Farm, where he earned a BA in 1948, he went to Harvard Business School (MBA, '51), then to Wall Street. He was a partner at Goldman Sachs in the New Business Department, Investment Banking Services. He has also served on the Stanford Board of Trustees. As of this writing, he had just celebrated his ninetieth birthday. Three of his children graduated from Stanford (Beppie Weintz Cerf ['79], Eric Weintz [BA, '85; MD, '99], Karl Weintz ['88]), as did his grandson (Jake Cerf, '12).

Joe (Joseph) Lewis Jacobs graduated in 1965 with a BA in communications from Stanford, where he was in the band, participated in student drama productions, and was entertainment editor for the *Stanford Daily*.[2] A sergeant in the Army, he was killed in Vietnam on February 21, 1967, at the age of twenty-two. (Also see Peter King biography on page 322.)

Johnny (John) Murray Huneke (BS, Mechanical Engineering, '53; MBA, '55) was a member of the tennis team and Phi Kappa Psi and went on to become a senior executive with Bechtel Investments in San Francisco. He passed away in 2005 and is survived by his wife, Pencie; one son, Murray ('83); two daughters, Christine Kremer ('84) and Lorraine; five stepdaughters; four grandchildren; seven step-grandchildren; one brother; and two sisters. His daughter Chrissie's letter home from overseas can be found in this book.

Julia Hamilton Conkling (Horton) received a BA (1915) and an MA (1916) in math. After her Stanford years, she taught math at

Central Union High School in her hometown of El Centro, California. She married Harry W. Horton (who studied law at Stanford), and they had two daughters, Mary Kathryn Horton Knox ('40) and Barbara Horton Erickson. She lived an active life until her death at the age of ninety-five. She had two granddaughters who attended Stanford, Marvie Knox ('63, '65) and Nancy Knox ('65), as well as a great-grandson, Reggie Norris ('98).

Karen Kinney (Gregory) earned a BA in human biology from Stanford in 1983, followed by an MA in STEP/math–science the next year. She attended Stanford with her siblings John and Katy and later married David Gregory (MS, '85). While at Stanford, Karen was on the equestrian and ski teams, played soccer and horse polo, was a member of Kappa Alpha Theta and an R.A.,[115] and attended Cliveden.[139] She witnessed "The Play."[165] (His knee was down!) Karen is the mother of Kat Gregory, whose email and texts also appear in *Letters Home from Stanford*.

Kat (Kathleen) Gregory graduated from Stanford in June 2016 with a BS in computer science. She currently is a co-term CS student at Stanford. When not training for an Ironman or researching chocolate, Sacha Baron Cohen, or pirates, Kat runs with the Stanford Running Club, skis with the ski team, and loves adventuring. Kat was an R.A.[115] and a member of Chi Omega sorority. She section-led and T.A.-ed seven classes and served as junior class president. She was awarded the Booth Prize for writing and the Terman[164] Award in the Engineering School. Kat is the daughter of Karen Gregory, whose letters appear in this book.

Laine Bruzek graduated from Stanford with a BS in product design engineering in 2016 and expects an MS in management science and engineering in 2017. As an undergrad, she was a Mayfield Fellow, an a cappella choreographer, and an avid writer. She's always looking to use her many interests to discover and tell stories and thus was drawn to *Letters Home from Stanford*, for which she designed the website and marketing materials. She also took the cover photo of the Quad.

Lanny Levin experienced Branner Hall,[77] Stanford's first coed dorm, in 1967, spent two quarters at Stanford in Italy (Florence), and lived through the tumultuous late 1960s at Stanford, graduating in 1971 with a BA in economics. He and his wife, Atara, live in Highland Park, Illinois, and have two adult children. After forty years of running his own financial services business, Lanny divested his management responsibilities in 2011 and has slowed his business pace. He walks while listening to mysteries and historical fiction on his iPod and has traveled extensively in the past few years.

Lucy Allabach (Litchy) was a member of Stanford's Pioneer Class, earning her BA in English in 1895. She came to Stanford from Iowa, where she later married William Gilcrest Litchy. (United States Census: 1900, 1910, 1920, 1930, 1940; "The Class of '95: Who the Pioneers Are and What They Have Done," *Stanford Daily*, May 29, 1895, stanforddailyarchive.com/cgi-bin/stanford?a=d&d=stanford18950529-01.2.2)

Mary Allie Lesnett (Carpenter) graduated from Stanford in 1948 (BA, Political Science). She married John D. Carpenter ('44/'47), having met him at Stanford upon his return from World War II. They raised three children in Los Angeles. Mary's mother saved all the letters she wrote home from Stanford. As of this writing, Mary lives in Santa Barbara, California, and celebrated her ninetieth birthday in August. Her daughter Alison's letters also appear in this book.

M.C. graduated from Stanford in 1979 with a BA in economics and psychology. She found her professional calling, though, as an undergraduate admissions officer and has worked at several universities in the CSU and UC systems since graduating from the very best university, Stanford.

Michitaro Sindo graduated from Stanford with a degree in physiology in 1905. He worked with David Jordan[6] on studying Hawaiian fishes. ("Biographical/Historical note," Michitaro Sindo Letters, 1901–1902, Stanford Student Letters and Memoirs Collection, SC0103, Department of Special Collections and University Archives, Stanford University Libraries, Stanford, California)

Mike (Michael) Clonts graduated from Stanford in 1985 with BS and MS degrees in petroleum engineering. The following year he married Cathy Janus (BA, '84; MA, '85) at Stanford Memorial Church.[19] They now live in Calgary, Alberta, having lived in the UK and Australia for fifteen years. The oldest of their three children currently attends Stanford.

Myron Carlos Burr earned a BA in civil engineering from Stanford in 1907. He worked as a civil engineer and an insurance broker. He lived in Monrovia, California. His letter in this book about Jane Stanford's funeral is presumably to his sister Gladys. (United States Census: 1930, 1940; "Biographical/Historical Sketch," Myron Carlos Burr Papers and Memorabilia, 1902–2006, SC0470, Department of Special Collections and University Archives, Stanford University Libraries, Stanford, California)

Nancy Christine Smith (Creger) drove across country to Stanford from Somerville, Massachusetts, in 1946. After earning her MA in economics in 1947, she worked as an editor for the Federal Reserve Bank of San Francisco and met Dr. William P. Creger (BA, '43; MD, '47; and professor of medicine, '47–'92), who was working at Stanford Hospital. At the time, their salaries were equal. They married shortly thereafter and in 1956 moved to the Stanford campus, raised four children, and opened their home to hundreds of student boarders over the years. Nancy, age ninety-one as of this writing, still lives in the old house, next door to the president's.

Natasha Pratap graduated from Stanford with a BA in English in 1994. After a law degree (second BA, Cambridge, UK) and creative writing degree (MA, Boston University), she moved back to India, where she established Words for Any Occasion (WAO). She conducts workshops in effective business and creative writing and is the author of *Wanna Study in the US? 101 Tips to Get You There!* Her articles and short stories have been published in the United States, the United Kingdom, and India. She also teaches yoga and meditation through the international Art of Living Foundation.

Peter King was a sportswriter for the *Stanford Daily* and spent six months at the overseas campus in Florence before graduating in 1965 (BA, History). One of Joe Jacobs' best friends at Stanford, Peter also developed a friendship with Joe's twin brother and Cal student Carl Jacobs over the course of Carl's many visits from across the bay during college. When Peter got married in 1969, he asked Carl to stand up for him as his best man, where Joe would have stood. Peter served in the Army Reserve, earned an MBA in 1969, and worked for both Mobil Chemical and T-Mobile. He has two children. He loves to travel, spend time with his ten grandchildren, play water volleyball, and watch Stanford football. Peter King and Carl Jacobs still keep in touch. (Peter King and Carl Jacobs; also see biography for Joe [Joseph] Lewis Jacobs on page 318.)

Phil (Philip) B. Laird Jr. came to Stanford from a small farm in the Central Valley, California, graduating from the other Farm in 1970 with a BA in history. He was a walk-on on the freshman football team and worked as a hasher[54] as well as a campus tour guide, which he had dreamed of doing since taking a tour of Stanford as a high school junior. He reports that he is now a lawyer in Visalia, California, in "small-town America." When going through his parents' things after they both died recently, Phil discovered approximately one hundred letters he'd written home from Stanford that his mother had saved. He hadn't known that she'd saved nearly every one of his letters home.

Rose Payne graduated from Stanford with a BA in English in 1898. She was the older sister of Theodora Payne (Class of 1900), whose letter is also included in this book. Both Rose and Theodora addressed their collected correspondence to "Nannie," who was perhaps an aunt. Their parents appear to have died by the time they wrote these letters. ("Christmas Graduates," *Stanford Daily*, Jan. 14, 1898; "Scope and Contents," Payne Family Letters, 1895–1897, Stanford Student Letters and Memoirs Collection, SC0103, Department of Special Collections and University Archives, Stanford University Libraries, Stanford, California; Payne Family Correspondence, 1897, Stanford Student Letters and Memoirs, Stanford Digital Repository, available at purl.stanford.edu/jv222bg0652)

(William) Russell Smith graduated from Stanford in 1941, then went on to medical school at USC and to a surgical practice at the Good Samaritan Hospital in Los Angeles. He married Virginia Hunter in 1947 and they had four children, three of whom went to Stanford and two of whom became doctors. His favorite place to vacation was on the Kona coast of the island of Hawaii, where he and his Stanford fraternity brothers had a reunion in the 1980s. Russell died in 1988 at the age of sixty-nine. He dedicated his life to his work and his family.

Tex Bollman Allen graduated in 1933 from Stanford, where he was a member of Alpha Tau Omicron. He worked as a civil engineer at Boeing Company in Seattle, retiring after twenty-five years there in 1975 and moving to Fernandina Beach, Florida, in 1997. ("Obituaries: 1930s," *Stanford* magazine, July/August 1998, stanford.edu/get/page/magazine/article/?article_id=42070)

Tom is a 1978 graduate of Stanford who received an MBA from the Kellogg School of Management at Northwestern and headed to Madison Avenue. After thirty-five years in advertising, he is now a Distinguished Careers Institute Fellow back on the Farm. In 2013, thirty-six years after Tom served in Leon Panetta's DC office, his son John served as an intern for Congressman Sam Farr in the same office.

Vanessa Hua graduated from Stanford with a BA in English and an MA in media studies in 1997. For nearly two decades, she has written about Asia and diaspora in the *New York Times*, the *Atlantic, Guernica, ZYZZYVA*, and elsewhere. A *San Francisco Chronicle* columnist, she is the author of the recently released short story collection *Deceit and Other Possibilities* and two forthcoming novels. She lives with her husband and twin boys in the San Francisco Bay Area. She wrote for the *Stanford Daily*.[2]

Wendell W. Birkhofer graduated in 1978 with a BA in English. After working with his father, George W. Birkhofer ('55), for six years as a stockbroker in Los Angeles, he received his MBA degree from Stanford in 1987. Wendell has spent the last twenty-nine years at the investment management firm Dodge & Cox in San Francisco, where he is a senior portfolio manager. He is married to Celeste Phaneuf Birkhofer, PhD, and has two children, Wiley ('09, deceased) and Elise ('12).

Wendy majored in English and graduated in December 1975. She has worked with her husband, Roger, at his company, Creative Think, since 1977, to stimulate creativity and innovation through books, seminars, conferences, apps, and other products. They raised two children, Athena ('03) and Alex, and are now grandparents to Athena and David's son Max. In 1994 Wendy found her true vocation and has offered spiritual guidance and energy work for more than twenty years.

Notes

All websites accessed in September and October 2016.

1. Stanford is also known as the Farm because the land on which it was built was the stock farm of university founders Jane and Leland Stanford, who bred and trained many racehorses there. (Eschenbach, Suzanne and Stephen, "What You Don't Know about Leland Stanford's Horses," *Stanford* magazine, September/October 2005, alumni.stanford.edu/get/page/magazine/article/?article_id=34389)

2. The student newspaper was called the *Daily Palo Alto*, nicknamed the Dippy, from its first edition in 1892 until 1926, when it was renamed the *Stanford Daily*. ("Daily Celebrates 75 Years," *Stanford Daily*, Sept. 22, 1967, stanforddailyarchive.com/cgi-bin/stanford?a=d&d=stanford19670922-01.2.21)

3. Green Library, Stanford's main library, is home to the Department of Special Collections and University Archives, which preserves and provides access to most of the correspondence excerpted in this book. The library opened in 1919 in a location east of the main Quad after the 1906 earthquake had demolished its predecessor, one of three earlier renditions of the library in other locations on campus. The East Wing of the library was constructed in 1980, at which time the entire library was renamed the Cecil H. Green Library after Texas Instruments cofounder Green, one of the principal funders of the library renovation and expansion. ("Cecil H. Green, Longtime Stanford Benefactor, Dies at 102," April 16, 2003, news.stanford.edu/news/2003/april16/greenobit-416.html; "Cecil H. Green Library: History of Green Library," library.stanford.edu/green/visitor-information/history-green-library; Stanford University Archives)

4. Originally built as a residence for the more than seventy women who entered as freshmen in 1891, Roble Hall was renamed Sequoia Hall in 1918 when a new Roble was built. Since its construction, the "new" Roble's basic floor plan has remained unchanged: the side rooms in the three-room suites have sinks, while the larger middle room has the only door to the hallway. Stanford's oldest continuously used dorm "went coed" in the late 1960s. Sequoia Hall was torn down in 1996. (Jane Lilly, "If These Walls Could Talk: A History of Roble Hall," *Sandstone & Tile*, Spring/Summer 2006, statistics.stanford.edu/sites/default/files/Sandstone-and-Tile_Old-Roble.pdf; "Sample Floor Plans," rde.stanford.edu/studenthousing/roble-hall#Floor)

5. Encina Hall was built for the university's opening. Modeled after a hotel in Switzerland, Encina features long, wide hallways that invited mischief-making among its all-male residents. At times called the "zoo," Encina became an all-freshman dorm in 1923. The last men moved out in 1956, and Encina now houses the offices of Stanford Global Studies, the Department of Political Science, and the Freeman Spogli Institute for International Studies, as well as the Bechtel Conference Center. (Bartholomew, Karen, and Claude Brinegar, "Encina Hall: Leland Stanford's Grand Hotel," *Sandstone & Tile*, Winter 2000, drive.google.com/file/d/0B_r1zy3kp6x5Y0lIVDZWNDdzdlk/view; John D. Carpenter, Class of 1944/47, former Encina Hall resident)

6. An ichthyologist, naturalist, and educator, David Starr Jordan was the first president of Stanford (1891–1913). Arriving in Palo Alto three months before the university opened, Jordan charted its course through some early challenges. But his legacy is a complicated one given his involvement with the now-discredited field of eugenics, as well as his actions in the wake of Jane Stanford's death. (Theresa Johnston, "Meet President Jordan," *Stanford* magazine, January/

February 2010, alumni.stanford.edu/get/page/magazine/article/?article_id=29584)

7. Joe was Julia Hamilton Conkling's brother. (Marvie Knox, Class of 1963, granddaughter of Julia Conkling)

8. In Julia's era, each class had its own distinct hat. The freshmen wore beanies; the sophomores, pork pies; the juniors, plugs (top hats); and the seniors, sombreros. Juniors and seniors participated in the Plug Ugly, a Stanford tradition from 1898 to 1913, in which the seniors tried to smash the juniors' plugs. The annual event was canceled in 1913 after it devolved into a violent brawl. It was later reinstated, then discontinued for good in 1915. (Sam Scott, "The Mad Hatters of Stanford," *Stanford* magazine, September/October 2015, alumni.stanford.edu/get/page/magazine/article/?article_id=80756; Susan Wels, *Stanford: Portrait of a University*, Stanford, California: Stanford Alumni Association, 1999, page 26)

9. A Jolly-Up was a Stanford term for an informal social gathering, or mixer, that a student attended without a date. "Queening" referred to courting. (J. Ernest Thompson, "Queening at Jolly-Ups," *Stanford Daily*, May 2, 1911, stanforddailyarchive.com/cgi-bin/stanford?a=d&d=stanford19110502-01.2.11)

10. The "elderly" people to whom Hope Snedden refers may be boarders at Alvarado Hall, where Hope lived at the start of the 1918–1919 school year because Roble Hall was full. She moved to Roble several weeks after she wrote this letter. (Hope Snedden letters to Genevra and/or David Snedden, Fall 1918, Snedden Family Papers, SC1207, Department of Special Collections and University Archives, Stanford University Libraries, Stanford, California)

11. At the time Alice Louise Clark wrote this letter, the N.Y.A. (National Youth Administration) existed to help America's young people find employment and educational opportunities. ("National Youth Administration," Eleanor Roosevelt Papers Project, gwu.edu/~erpapers/teachinger/glossary/nya.cfm)

12. The Roble⁴ telephone operator activated a buzzer in a student's room when a phone call came in or a visitor or caller arrived downstairs. Residents often left a bobby pin in their buzzers when they went out; if the bobby pin was on the floor when they returned, that meant their buzzer had rung. (Barbara Cooper Prince, Class of 1949 and former Roble Hall president)

13. "Paly" refers to Palo Alto. The "Bowl" possibly refers to the then Indian⁵⁵ Bowl at 735 Emerson St. in Palo Alto. (Matt Bowling, "Bowling in Palo Alto: The Final Frame?" paloaltohistory.org/bowling-in-palo-alto.php)

14. Synchronous clocks, popular in the 1930s and 1940s, were consistently more accurate than typical quartz clocks. They relied on the utility frequency of the AC electric power grid (what Mary calls the "electric cycle"), so it was important to specify whether the building used 50 or 60 Hz (unit of frequency that refers to one cycle per second). ("History of the Clock," Anderson Institute, andersoninstitute.com/history-of-the-clock.html; Leslie Philip Pook, *British Domestic Synchronous Clocks 1930–1980: The Rise and Fall of a Technology*, New York: Springer, 2015, pages 19, 81, 82, books.google.com)

15. What Mary Allie Lesnett calls the Stanford honor system is the Stanford Honor Code, which Stanford students wrote in 1921 regarding the level of

integrity they expected of themselves and fellow students in their academic work. ("Honor Code and Fundamental Standard," communitystandards.stanford.edu/student-conduct-process/honor-code-and-fundamental-standard)

16. The traditional Western Civ. (Civilization) Program was required of all Stanford freshmen from 1935 to 1969. For the next twenty-eight years the curriculum underwent various iterations and was finally dropped in 1997 amid concern that the course reflected a far too narrow worldview. A resolution to bring back Western Civ. recently was voted down by the student body. (Diane Rogers, "What Freshmen Need to Know," Stanford magazine, March/April 2004, alumni.stanford.edu/get/page/magazine/article/?article_id=36193; Diane Manuel, "On Campus: Reshaping the Humanities: Scholars Debate Anew the Role of Cultures, Ideas, and Values," Stanford Today, May/June 1997, stanford.edu/dept/news/stanfordtoday/ed/9705/9705ncf1.html; Fangzhou Liu, "2016 ASSU Election Results Announced," Stanford Daily, April 11, 2016, stanforddaily.com/2016/04/11/2016-assu-election-results-announced/)

17. The Cellar was "the soda fountain-restaurant on campus." (Joe [Joseph L.] Jacobs letter to his parents, Oct. 11, 1961, Joseph L. Jacobs, Class of 1965, letters home, Stanford Student Letters and Memoirs Collection, SC0103, Department of Special Collections and University Archives, Stanford University Libraries, Stanford, California)

18. Enrollment in the fall of 1946 was 7,051. Bill was Nancy Christine Smith's brother. ("Ratio Climbs to 3.7 as 3,863 Vets Register," Stanford Daily, Sept. 25, 1946, stanforddailyarchive.com/cgi-bin/stanford?a=d&d=stanford 19460925-01.2.28; Russell Barajas, daughter of Nancy Christine Smith)

19. Memorial Church (Mem Chu) is the spiritual and logistical focal point of campus. Dedicated by Jane Stanford to the memory of her husband, Leland, in 1903, the church is visible from a long distance down Palm Drive as one approaches the Farm. ("Stanford Memorial Church," stanford.edu/group/religiouslife/cgi-bin/wordpress/memorial-church/history/)

20. J. E. Wallace Sterling was Stanford's fifth president (1949–1968). A former history professor at Cal Tech, he earned his PhD at the Farm in 1938. During his presidency, the number of graduate students and faculty members at Stanford increased significantly, the Stanford Linear Accelerator was built, and the first five overseas programs were established. (Robin Toner, "Wallace Sterling; Led Sanford U," New York Times, July 3, 1985, nytimes.com/1985/07/03/us/wallace-sterling-led-stanford-u.html)

21. Memorial Auditorium (Mem Aud), dedicated in 1937, is the largest indoor auditorium on campus. The walls of its lobby list the names of the alumni, students, faculty, and staff who have died at war. ("Memorial Auditorium," live.stanford.edu/plan-your-visit/venues/memorial-auditorium; Kathleen Sullivan, "Stanford Community Pays Tribute to Military Veterans," Nov. 11, 2015, news.stanford.edu/thedish/2015/11/11/stanford-community-pays-tribute-to-military-veterans/)

22. A designated student group now runs Flicks, Sunday-night movies that are a long-standing Stanford tradition. In the late 1980s, throwing toilet paper rolls at Flicks was prohibited after one unfurled itself during a dignified visitor's lecture on a Monday, having landed on a ceiling fixture the previous night. (Chaney

Rankin Kourouniotis, "Flicks," *Stanford* magazine, January/February 2011, alumni. stanford.edu/get/page/magazine/article/?article_id=28092)

23. Stanford Village was established as a student residence on the site of Dibble Hospital in Menlo Park when enrollment swelled with returning soldiers post–World War II. The Village provided three hundred apartments for married students and fifteen hundred dorm beds. (Carol Blitzer, "The 1940s: On the Home Front," *Palo Alto Weekly*, April 13, 1994, paloaltoonline.com/news_ features/centennial/1940SA.php)

24. Convocation has been held each fall since 1891 to welcome new students to the Farm. (Clifton B. Parker, "Convocation: What It Means to Be Part of Stanford," Sept. 16, 2015, news.stanford.edu/2015/09/16/opening-convocation-ceremony-091615/)

25. In 1896 Jessie Knight Jordan, wife of then Stanford president David Starr Jordan, founded the Stanford University Women's Club. When Elaine mentions the Faculty Wives Association, she could be referring to this group. ("About SUWC," stanfordsuwc.com/about/)

26. A large coed dorm complex on East Campus, Wilbur Hall is named after alumnus and third Stanford president, Ray Lyman Wilbur.[71] The university built Wilbur Hall after World War II as an all-male residence. ("Wilbur Hall," rde. stanford.edu/studenthousing/wilbur-hall)

27. The building that is now the Barnum Family Center for School and Community Partnerships, part of the School of Education, housed the Western Civ.[16] library from 1960 to 1967. (Lisa Trei, "Alumni Couple Donates $3 Million to Establish New Education, Community Center," Sept. 24, 2004, news.stanford. edu/news/2004/september29/barnum-924.html)

28. President Sterling's answer to the query, as reported in the *Daily*: "Sterling explained that a top faculty is top priority. He confessed that high salaries and 'that prostitution of the soul that Americans call salesmanship' (a long remembered quote) were contributing factors, but felt that the part played by 'good students and good programs' ('Throw in climate and coeds') was undervalued." Earlier in his talk, per the *Daily*, Sterling said: "I would much rather have a first-rate teacher of 100 students than place a second-rate instructor before 10." ("'Better for All'—Says Sterling of SU Future," *Stanford Daily*, Sept. 28, 1961, stanforddailyarchive.com/cgi-bin/ stanford?a=d&d=stanford19610928-01.2.9)

29. In 1975 freshmen took a writing seminar unless they had tested out of it on an AP English test. Today there is a writing requirement through the Program in Writing and Rhetoric (PWR). Students take a PWR-1 elective as freshmen and a PWR-2 elective as sophomores. They cannot test out of PWR. ("Director's Message," undergrad.stanford.edu/programs/pwr/about-pwr/ director%E2%80%99s-message; Alison Carpenter Davis, '79; *Letters Home from Stanford* interns)

30. "OKC" refers to Oklahoma City and "OSU" to Oklahoma State University.

31. "Hanh" is not a spoken word. It's an expressive sound, like some people would say "oooo" or "aahhh." Natasha came to Stanford from India, where she and her circle in the '90s would squirm when people adopted American

expressions or accents to appear cool when, in fact, they may have spent barely any time in the United States, if at all. Here she defends the use of "How's that" as a phrase she commonly used at home and not one she had acquired after just a month's stay on campus. (Natasha Pratap, Class of 1994)

32. "Cat" was slang for "cool" in the 1980s. (Natasha Pratap, Class of 1994)

33. Dandiyas are interactive festive dances in which dancers cross hand-held foot-long sticks in rhythm with the music and their movements. Diwali is a festival celebrating the Hindu New Year. (Natasha Pratap, Class of 1994)

34. Students use electronic i>clickers to indicate attendance and to answer professors' questions. "SLE," or Structured Liberal Education, is an opt-in academic and residence-based program for freshmen sometimes described as "a liberal arts college experience." (1.iclicker.com/; "Structured Liberal Education [SLE]," undergrad.stanford.edu/programs/residential-programs/sle)

35. Gaieties premiered as the "Football Follies" in 1911, and with one eight-year hiatus, has run every year since. The annual student-written and -performed extravaganza pokes fun at Cal and runs during Big Game Week. For those reading Nora Tjossem's September 28, 2011, email on page 39: She went on to participate in the annual student show all of her years at Stanford, including 2013, when she produced Gaieties. (Marnie Berringer, "The History of Big Game Gaieties," ramshead.stanford.edu/history.html; Nora Tjossem, Class of 2015)

36. FaceTime is a built-in trademarked application allowing video and audio calls between many Apple products. "FaceTime" is now often used as a verb to replace "call" or "video chat." (collinsdictionary.com/dictionary/english/facetime)

37. "Approaching Stanford" is the handbook for incoming freshmen and transfer students that contains information about life at the Farm. ("About This Guide," undergrad.stanford.edu/advising/student-guides/app)

38. "RFs" are resident fellows, members of the university faculty or senior administrative staff who live in student residences, where they foster intellectual and interpersonal community. ("What Is a Resident Fellow?" resed.stanford.edu/get-involved/what-resident-fellow)

39. The team from Berkeley won the 1918 game 67-0. In her Dec. 1 letter that year, Hope tells her parents she is glad she didn't go to that other school, score notwithstanding. Stanford's official record books do not list the score because the 1918 Stanford team included both student and nonstudent members of the Student Army Training Corps[72] unit headquartered on campus during World War I. (Gary Migdol, *Stanford: Home of Champions*, Champaign, Illinois: Sagamore Publishing, 1997, page 58; Terry Johnson, Class of 1978)

40. "Code, Downing, or Clemans" refers to Thomas K. Code (1896), Paul M. Downing (1895), and Carl L. Clemans (1893), all members of the 1892 football team. Code was Stanford's first quarterback. (Thomas K. Code Papers, SC0586, Department of Special Collections and University Archives, Stanford University Libraries, Stanford, California)

41. The Lick presumably refers to Lick Observatory near San Jose, California.

42. In this context, "tally-hos" most likely refers to passenger coaches led by a team of four horses.

43. Miss Hill is Nell May Hill of Independence, Oregon. Hoover lived with relatives in Iowa and Oregon after his parents died when he was young. ("Five Letters of Herbert Hoover," *Call Number*, Eugene, Oregon: Library of the University of Oregon, Spring 1966, page 2; Herbert Hoover Presidential Library)

44. Herbert Hoover was elected student body treasurer on April 24, 1894. (Herbert Hoover Presidential Library)

45. J. C. Branner was John Casper Branner, one of Stanford's founding faculty members and later its second president (1913–1915). He was a geologist and a former classmate of David Starr Jordan[6] at Cornell. See also Branner Hall.[7] ("Branner at 100: A New Exhibit on John Casper Branner," library.stanford.edu/blogs/special-collections-unbound/2015/04/branner-100-new-exhibit-john-casper-branner; Theresa Johnston, "Meet President Jordan," *Stanford* magazine, January/February 2010. alumni.stanford.edu/get/page/magazine/article/?article_id=29584)

46. "Walton, Whitehous[e] & MacMillan" refers to Stanford football players Harry Walton (1893), Louis Whitehouse (1894), and George McMillan (1894). After Stanford, all three went on to play for the Reliance Athletic Club in Oakland, California. (Gary Migdol, *Stanford: Home of Champions*, Champaign, Illinois: Sagamore Publishing, 1997, page 58; "Leather and Mud," *San Francisco Call*, Oct. 21, 1894, cdnc.ucr.edu/cgi-bin/cdnc?a=d&d=SFC18941021.2.82; Terry Johnson, Class of 1978)

47. The "nice young lady" is Lou Henry (1898), the first woman to earn a geology degree at Stanford. She married Herbert Hoover on February 10, 1899. ("Five Letters of Herbert Hoover," *Call Number*, Eugene, Oregon: Library of the University of Oregon, Spring 1966, page 8; Herbert Hoover Presidential Library)

48. Arthur Perry was probably Fred (Frederic) Jewell Perry's cousin. (Benjamin Perry, great-grandson of Fred Perry; Elizabeth Perry Ford, granddaughter of Fred Perry)

49. The town of Mayfield dates to the early 1850s, when a stagecoach stop and tavern opened near the corner of what is now California Avenue and El Camino Real in Palo Alto. The city's present-day California Avenue Caltrain Station sits on the Mayfield depot's original site. (Palo Alto Historical Association)

50. Now a neighborhood of San Jose, California, Alviso was an independent city until 1968. (preservation.org/districts/alviso.html)

51. The Axe is awarded annually to the winner of the Big Game between Berkeley and Stanford. Various Axe heists have occurred over the years, notably the Immortal 21 heist of 1930. Stanford leads Cal in number of Big Games won. As of this writing, the Cardinal also leads the Bears 4–3 in Axe thefts. ("Handbook of Stanford University: History, Tradition, and Lore," Stanford Axe Committee, 2015–2016, pages 5, 10, stanford.edu/group/axecomm/cgi-bin/wordpress/wp-content/uploads/2015/08/handbook.final_.pdf)

52. The bonfire was held yearly at Big Game Rally in Lake Lagunita's dry lakebed

from 1898 until 1976, when it was canceled for safety reasons. It returned in 1985, to be canceled again four years later, reinstated, then canceled once and for all in 1993 out of concern for amphibians that breed in and around the lakebed. In 2012 the Stanford Axe Committee reinstated the rally, this time with a fireworks display. (Marisa Cigarroa, "Big Game Bonfire Is a Tradition of the Past," Oct. 1, 1997, news.stanford.edu/pr/97/971001bonfire.html; "Handbook of Stanford University: History, Tradition, and Lore," page 13)

53. "Boola Boola" may refer to the Yale fight song of the same name, written in 1901. "Oski! Wow Wow!" is the first line of the Oski Yell, Oski the Bear being the Cal mascot. ("Yale Fight Songs," bands.yalecollege.yale.edu/yale-precision-marching-band/music/yale-fight-songs; "Oski the Bear," calspirit.berkeley.edu/oski/history.php)

54. A hasher is a student who works in one of the dining halls.

55. The "Indians" was adopted as the official Stanford nickname in 1930. From the early 1950s to 1972, a Yurok Indian named Timm Williams, known as Prince Lightfoot, performed at Stanford football games, basketball games, and rallies. In 1972 the Stanford Student Senate voted to retire the mascot amid criticism and protests by Native American students and others that it was cartoonish, racist, and offensive. The decision was supported by then Stanford president Richard Lyman.[129] Today's Stanford sports teams are called the Cardinal, first adopted as the school color in 1892. (Stanford adopted the color white as an additional school color in the 1940s.) The LSJUMB[57] mascot and unofficial campus mascot is the Tree, a reference to El Palo Alto, the redwood tree that is the namesake of nearby Palo Alto and is more than a thousand years old. ("On Campus: What Is the History of Stanford's Mascot and Nickname?" gostanford.com/sports/2013/4/17/208445366.aspx; Dr. Dean Chavers, "Eliminating the Stanford Indian Mascot," March 7, 2013, indiancountrytodaymedianetwork.com/2013/03/07/eliminating-stanford-indian-mascot-147857; Lisa M. Krieger, "El Palo Alto, a Tree That's the City's Namesake, Undergoes High-Tech Testing," *Mercury News*, Aug. 12, 2016, mercurynews.com/2013/08/12/el-palo-alto-a-tree-thats-the-citys-namesake-undergoes-high-tech-testing/)

56. In 1953 the Axe[51] went missing for five months from its location at Cal. Hours before Big Game that year, the Axe and an anonymous note showed up in the car of Stanford football team captain Norm Manoogian ('53). More than four decades later, two alums admitted to stealing and harboring the Axe, then planting it in Manoogian's car. ("An Old Story Comes into Sharper Focus," *Stanford* magazine, November/December 2001, alumni.stanford.edu/get/page/magazine/article/?article_id=38417)

57. Founded in 1893 and student-run since 1963, the LSJUMB, or Leland Stanford Junior University Marching Band, is known for its quirkiness, irreverence, and "scatter-style" field shows. ("History," lsjumb.stanford.edu/history.html)

58. "Johnny-on-the-Spot" is someone who is ready to complete a task well and on time. (Michael Quinion, "Johnny-on-the-spot," worldwidewords.org/qa/qa-joh3.htm)

59. Their junior and senior years, Joe (Joseph) Lewis Jacobs and his twin brother, Carl, a Cal student, shared a Plymouth, trading the car back and forth between Palo Alto and Berkeley. (Carl Jacobs)

60. "The Lathrops" likely refers to the family of Jane (Lathrop) Stanford, Leland Jr.'s mother and wife of Senator Stanford. Jane's younger brother, Charles Lathrop, served as Stanford's first business manager and treasurer. Charles and his family lived in a large house on a seventeen-acre estate close to what is now the Stanford Golf Course entrance. The Lathrop daughters reportedly hosted social events in its large ballroom. (Theresa Johnston, "These Old Houses," *Stanford* magazine, November/December 2005, alumni.stanford.edu/get/page/magazine/article/?article_id=33831)

61. In 1893 like many well-to-do families in the Bay Area, the Stanfords had employed a number of servants in their home, most of whom were Chinese. Senator Leland Stanford had died on June 21, 1893, with the (financial) Panic of 1893 as a backdrop. (Christopher Lowman, "Our First Chinese: American-Chinese Interaction in 1890s Palo Alto," May 17, 2010, academia.edu/2928662/Our_First_Chinese_American-Chinese_Interaction_in_1890s_Palo_Alto; "About Stanford: Stanford through the Years," facts.stanford.edu/about/chron; David O. Whitten, "The Depression of 1893," Economic History Association, eh.net/?s=Depression+of+1893)

62. Rose Payne wrote this letter the day after the circuit court ruled in favor of Mrs. Stanford. The government lawsuit against Stanford's estate ultimately was settled on March 2, 1896, by decision of the US Supreme Court, and the transfer of the monies bequeathed in Senator Stanford's will to the university was completed thereafter. Financial concerns and the legal battle had threatened the closure of the school. ("Judge Ross Affirmed: A Verdict for Mrs. Stanford by the Court of Appeals," *San Francisco Call*, Oct. 13, 1895, cdnc.ucr.edu/cgi-bin/cdnc?a=d&d=SFC18951013.2.73; Helen Guerrant, "SU Position Precarious in 1896 Suit: Students Cheer When Mrs. Stanford Wins $15 Million Lawsuit," *Stanford Daily*, Apr. 11, 1957, stanforddailyarchive.com/cgi-bin/stanford?a=d&d=stanford19570411-01.2.42; Stanford University Archives)

63. Founders' Day, originally called Memorial Day, was first held on May 14, 1891, to honor the birthday of Leland Stanford Jr., the Stanfords' only child, who died at age fifteen of typhoid fever. Today the event celebrates the founding family. (Lisa Trei, "Annual Founders' Day Celebration Expanded," Apr. 9, 1997, news.stanford.edu/pr/97/970407founders.html; "Stanford Founders' Celebration 2016," founders.stanford.edu/)

64. George Edward Crothers[159] (BA, 1895; MA, 1896) and his brother Thomas G. Crothers (BA, 1892) led a campaign to amend the California state constitution so Stanford would be exempt from taxation based on its status as an educational organization. The exemption would be passed, allowing Jane Stanford to donate her stock holdings to the university and paving the way for future grants and donations. (Bartholomew, Karen, Claude Brinegar, Roxanne Nilan, *A Chronology of Stanford University and Its Founders: 1824–2000*. Stanford, California: Stanford Historical Society, 2001, pages 33, 34; Stanford University Archives)

65. Memorial Arch, which marked the entrance to campus, was completed in 1899 and dedicated to the memory of Leland Stanford Jr. Sculptors completed a frieze at the top of the Arch in mid-1902, but less than four years later the earthquake severely damaged both the Arch and Memorial Church.[19] The university rebuilt the church, but not the arch. Only its surviving columns remain. ("Gallery, Campus Structures, Memorial Arch," quake06.stanford.edu/centennial/gallery/structures/memarch/)

66. A Brownie Kodak was an early Kodak roll-film camera. "Palie" refers to Palo Alto.

67. Madroño Hall was a women's residence at Stanford. ("Madrono to Give Reception." *Stanford Daily*, Feb. 15, 1907, stanforddailyarchive.com/cgi-bin/stanford?a=d&d=stanford19070215-01.2.5)

68. The statue to which Babe (Mabel) Bartlett refers was of Swiss naturalist and geologist Louis Agassiz. David Starr Jordan[6] had been inspired by Agassiz to become an ichthyologist. ("Earthquake Impacts on Prestige: Memorial Arch & Agassiz Statue," quake06.stanford.edu/centennial/tour/stop3.html; "Spencer Baird and Ichthyology at the Smithsonian: Ichthyologists, David Starr Jordan (1851–1931)," vertebrates.si.edu/fishes/ichthyology_history/ichs_colls/jordan_david.html)

69. Although early reports were not favorable, the vote for women in California did in fact go through by a narrow margin in October 1911. (Mae Silver, "Women Claim the Vote in California," 1995, foundsf.org/index.php?title=WOMEN_CLAIM_THE_VOTE_IN_CALIFORNIA)

70. The Armory [Hall] was a large meeting space for community events in Palo Alto. Jolly-Ups[9] sometimes were held there. ("'Biggest and Best' Will Crowd Armory," *Stanford Daily*, Apr. 9, 1912, stanforddailyarchive.com/cgi-bin/stanford?a=d&d=stanford19120409-01.2.4; Palo Alto Historical Association)

71. Ray Lyman Wilbur[26] was Stanford's third and longest-serving president (1916–1943). An alum (BA/MA, Physiology, 1896/1897), he became a physiology professor at Stanford, dean of the School of Medicine, and then president. He also served as secretary of the interior. (Frank Huntress, "Ray Lyman Wilbur . . . President for 27 Years," *Stanford Daily*, Jan. 18, 1956, stanforddailyarchive.com/cgi-bin/stanford?a=d&d=stanford19560118-01.2.22)

72. "S.A.T.C." stood for the Student Army Training Corps. The S.A.T.C. was created to encourage young men to get a college education before serving. ("Student Army Training Corps," sites.google.com/a/mail.ic.edu/icinworldwari/home/student-army-training-corps)

73. William and Francis were friends of Hope Snedden. Ruth is likely a reference to Hope's younger sister Ruth Snedden ('26). (Christopher Carlsmith, Class of 1986, grandson of Hope Snedden)

74. Donald Bertrand Tresidder was Stanford's fourth president (1943–1948). A Stanford alum (BA, Preclinical Medical Science; MD, 1927), he died of a heart attack while president. He is the namesake of Tresidder Memorial Union on campus, dedicated in 1962. ("Tresidder and Old Union Histories, Tresidder History: Who Was Tresidder?" studentaffairs.stanford.edu/tresidder-and-old-union-histories)

75. Rossotti's, as it was known in the 1940s, was a favorite destination spot for Stanford students, who often called it "Zotts." Despite the protestations of David Starr Jordan[6] to the San Mateo County Board of Supervisors about its proximity to campus, the roadhouse remains open today after more than 160 years. In 1933 the lease passed to Enrico Rossotti, who ran the establishment until 1956, when the new owners renamed it the Alpine Inn Beer Garden. (Steve Staiger,

"Echoes of Alpine Inn's Early Days," *Palo Alto Weekly*, Jan. 24, 2001, paloaltoonline.com/weekly/morgue/spectrum/2001_Jan_24.HISTRY24.html)

76. In the four-plus weeks before Phil's letter of May 8, 1968, Dr. Martin Luther King Jr. was assassinated (April 4, 1968), Stanford organized a convocation called the "Colloquium and Plan for Action: Stanford's Response to White Racism" (April 8, 1968), and approximately seventy black students from Stanford's Black Student Union took the microphone away from then provost Richard Lyman[129] as he spoke at the Mem Aud[21] event. The students called on the university to take action on ten demands aimed at giving greater voice, presence, and representation to students and faculty of color on campus. In 1960 there were two black students in the entering freshman class, and in 1965 only one Native American student was enrolled. Today, more than 45 percent of undergraduates at Stanford are students of color. As of 2015, people of color made up 24 percent of the faculty. ("Get to Know Us: History/Background," Black Community Services Center, bcsc.stanford.edu/get-know-us; Neel Thakkar, "Community Centers at Stanford: A History of Activism," *Stanford Daily*, Dec. 5, 2012, stanforddaily.com/2012/12/05/community-center-history-fraught-with-struggle-symbols-of-progress/; "The Student Perspective: Diversity at Stanford," admission.stanford.edu/student/; Kathleen J. Sullivan, "Senate Hears Reports on Diversifying the Faculty and Improving the Leadership Climate on Campus," May 27, 2016, news.stanford.edu/2016/05/27/senate-hears-reports-diversifying-faculty-improving-leadership-climate-campus/)

77. Branner Hall, across from Wilbur Hall,[26] opened in 1924 and is named for John Caspar Branner.[45] Originally all-male, it was later an all-female dorm before becoming coed. Branner was the freshman dorm of Sandra Day O'Connor, the first female justice of the US Supreme Court. Today Branner is an upper-class dorm with a public-service focus. ("About Branner Hall," brannerhall.wordpress.com/about/branner-hall/)

78. Donald Kennedy served as Stanford University president from 1980 to 1992. A biologist, he first came to Stanford in 1960, serving as Biology Department chair (1964–1972). During that period, he helped found Stanford's Human Biology program, for which he served as director from 1973 to 1977. ("Donald Kennedy, PhD: Bio," Freeman Spogli Institute for International Studies, fsi.stanford.edu/people/donald_kennedy; Louise Roche, "The Program in Human Biology: The First 30 Years, 1971–2001," stanford.edu/dept/humbio/alumni/humbiohistory.pdf)

79. Kenneth Sanborn Pitzer was Stanford's sixth president (1968–1970). An influential chemist, he resigned the presidency amid the student protests of that era. (Marisa Cigarroa, "Former Stanford President, Renowned Chemist Ken Pitzer, Dies," Jan. 6, 1998, stanford.edu/dept/news/pr/98/980107pitzer.html)

80. Seven years after Lucy Allabach wrote this letter, Jane Stanford limited the enrollment of women to five hundred. By 1932 women made up only 14 percent of students, and the following year the Board of Trustees lifted the five hundred limit, reinstating the school's original ratio. In 1973 that ratio was thrown out completely. The Women's Collective, which would evolve into the Women's Community Center, first started organizing to advocate for and discuss the role of women on campus in the 1970s. As of September 2016, women made up 47.6 percent of undergraduate students and 38.5 percent of graduate students. ("About Stanford: University Milestones, Stanford through the Years," facts.

stanford.edu/about/chron; "Our History," humsci.stanford.edu/about/history; "History," wcc.stanford.edu/who-we-are/history; "Academics: Undergraduate Student Profile, 2015–2016," facts.stanford.edu/academics/undergraduate-profile; "Academics: Graduate Student Profile 2015–2016," facts.stanford.edu/academics/graduate-profile)

81. "My dear Friend" is Miss Nell May Hill.[43] ("Five Letters of Herbert Hoover," *Call Number*, Eugene, Oregon: Library of the University of Oregon, Spring 1966, page 2; Herbert Hoover Presidential Library)

82. "Snow goes" may refer to William Freeman Snow (1896). ("Five Letters of Herbert Hoover," *Call Number*, Eugene, Oregon: Library of the University of Oregon, Spring 1966, page 4; Herbert Hoover Presidential Library)

83. "Dr. B." refers to John Casper Branner,[45] who would later become president of Stanford. During his student days, Hoover worked as an office assistant for then geology professor Branner, who also helped Hoover get his first job with the US Geological Survey. ("Five Letters of Herbert Hoover," *Call Number*, Eugene, Oregon: Library of the University of Oregon, Spring 1966, page 4; Herbert Hoover Presidential Library)

84. Life vests were made of cork at the time, so Branner may be assuring Hoover that if the $46.23 does not suffice, a cork (funding) may be provided to help Hoover stay afloat. (Herbert Hoover Presidential Library)

85. In 1891 the year Stanford opened, the university employed 150 Chinese workers as cooks, janitors, and housekeepers. Chinese workers were discriminated against and demeaned throughout California, and Stanford students who wanted their jobs at the university often resented them. By 1893 there were far fewer Chinese workers employed by the university, though they were employed by fraternities, and other people of color worked for the university. When Hoover wrote this letter in 1892, the number of Chinese workers on campus may have started to dwindle, which could explain his comment, "No Chinese around anywhere." (Christopher Lowman, "Our First Chinese: American-Chinese Interactions in 1890s Palo Alto," May 17, 2010, academia.edu/2928662/Our_First_Chinese_American-Chinese_Interaction_in_1890s_Palo_Alto)

86. Rose Payne most likely is referring to the village of San Quentin, adjacent to the prison.

87. In the late 1890s, a bicycle was commonly called a wheel. (merriam-webster.com/dictionary/wheel; Meg Dunn, "Bicycling through the 1800s in Fort Collins," Apr. 14, 2015, forgottenfortcollins.com/foco_bicycle_history_1800s/)

88. Dean was J. B. [Jesse Brundage] Sears's brother. (David O. Sears, Class of 1957, son of Bob [Robert] Richardson Sears and grandson of J. B. Sears)

89. Following rules or norms came to be known as doing things "according to Hoyle," most likely a reference to Edmond Hoyle, an eighteenth-century authority on card-game rules. The expression expanded to refer to following rules and regulations in other arenas. ("The meaning and origin of the expression: According to Hoyle," phrases.org.uk/meanings/according-to-hoyle.html)

90. By the time Hope Snedden wrote this letter in 1918, Roble had both a matron and a housekeeper. The matron attended to a dorm's social needs, and the housekeeper to its management and business interests. ("Mrs. D.S. Green Chosen Matron of Roble Hall: Housekeeper to Attend to Business Management. Matron Has Social Responsibilities," *Stanford Daily*, Sept. 4, 1913, stanforddailyarchive.com/cgi-bin/stanford?a=d&d=stanford19130904-01.2.3)

91. Author Hamlin Garland wrote this about his mother's visit to the 1893 Chicago World's Fair: "[My] mother sat in her chair, visioning it all yet comprehending little of its meaning. . . . Her life had been spent among homely small things, and these gorgeous scenes dazzled her. . . ." (Paul S. Boyer et al. *The Enduring Vision: A History of the American People*, 8th ed, Boston, Wadsworth, Cengage Learning, 2014, page 535, books.google.com)

92. Francis was a friend, and Ruthie was Hope Snedden's younger sister, who later attended Stanford (Ruth Snedden, '26). People mentioned later in this letter are Donald Snedden ('23), Hope's younger brother, and Peggy Carlsmith (BA '22, MD '26), a friend of Hope's at Stanford and her future sister-in-law. (Christopher Carlsmith, Class of 1986, grandson of Hope Snedden)

93. "Roughnecks" may refer to "roughs." The Stanford rough was someone who was casual, spontaneous, and relaxed, not constrained by fancy clothing or manners, and who did not come from an affluent background. (Davis, Margo Baumgarten, and Roxanne Nilan, *The Stanford Album: A Photographic History, 1885–1945*, Stanford, California: Stanford University Press, 1989, page 221)

94. Leonard Carlsmith ('21) was the brother of Hope Snedden's friend Peggy. Hope and Leonard later married. (Christopher Carlsmith, Class of 1986, grandson of Hope Snedden)

95. In his handwritten letter, Burnham inserts an "F" on top of an "M" to create this "ambiguous heading." (Burnham P. Beckwith letter to his parents, March 4, 1923, Stanford Student Letters and Memoirs Collection, SC0103, Department of Special Collections and University Archives, Stanford University Libraries, Stanford, California)

96. A lettering course would cover the design and presentation of letters of the alphabet.

97. A goof was someone on a back-up (goof) football squad. (Andrew R. Boone, "The Coaching Staff," *Stanford Illustrated Review*, October 1922, page 39, books. google.com/)

98. Two years after Dick (Richard) Bartlett Gould wrote this letter, Stanford football player Bruce Tarver was one of two Stanford students killed in a car accident en route to campus after a Big Game celebration in San Francisco. Tarver had played substitute right guard for Bill Corbus.[101] (M. Jack Newman, "Tarver, Karr Killed as Bayshore Crash Causes Four Deaths," *Stanford Daily*, Nov. 27, 1933, stanforddailyarchive.com/cgi-bin/ stanford?a=d&d=stanford19331127-01.2.8)

99. David Packard went on to cofound Hewlett-Packard with fellow Stanford alumnus Bill Hewlett. Both graduated in general engineering in 1934, earned master's degrees in electrical engineering in 1939, and were mentored by Frederick Terman.[164] (David Jacobson, "Founding Fathers," *Stanford* magazine,

July/August 1998, alumni.stanford.edu/get/page/magazine/article/?article_id=42103)

100. Stanford football coach Glenn "Pop" Warner (1924–1932) is considered one of the greatest college football coaches of all time. At Pop's first Big Game as coach, Stanford came back from a 20–6 score to tie Cal 20–20, and the team eventually went to the Rose Bowl that year. ("Pop Warner: American Football Coach," Encyclopedia Britannica, britannica.com/biography/Pop-Warner; Scott Allen, "1924 Big Game: An Instant Classic," July 18, 2011, ruleoftree.com/2011/7/18/2282389/1924-big-game-an-instant-classic)

101. All-American Bill Corbus ('33), a guard and at times a placekicker for Stanford, was nicknamed the "Baby-Faced Assassin." (Ginny McCormick, "Big Game at 100—The Athletes and Coaches: Ten Gridiron Greats . . . and the Brains Behind Them," *Stanford* magazine, November/December 1997, alumni.stanford.edu/get/page/magazine/article/?article_id=42928)

102. Claude Earl "Tiny" Thornhill, Stanford offensive line coach when Dick (Richard) Bartlett Gould wrote this letter, was in fact named the head coach (1933–1939) the next year post–Pop Warner. James "Rabbit" Bradshaw had been named the head freshman football coach in 1930. ("Claude Earl 'Tiny' Thornhill," oldestlivingprofootball.com/claudeearlthornhill.htm; "Bradshaw to Coach Frosh Football Here," *Stanford Daily*, Aug. 14, 1930, stanforddailyarchive.com/cgi-bin/stanford?a=d&d=stanford19300814-01.2.42)

103. Ernie Nevers ('26), an all-American fullback, returned to the Farm to coach (1933–1935). Nevers was the first Stanford player to have his jersey retired, followed by Jim Plunkett ('71) and John Elway ('83). (Ginny McCormick, "Big Game at 100—The Athletes and Coaches: Ten Gridiron Greats . . . and the Brains Behind Them;" Kate Chesley, "Stanford Football Will Retire John Elway's No. 7," Aug. 7, 2013, news.stanford.edu/thedish/2013/08/07/stanford-football-will-retire-john-elways-number-7/)

104. Ben Eastman ('33) set six world middle-distance records in outdoor track during his Stanford years; his record for 440 yards stood for forty years. (Tori Babin, "A Legendary Runner; There Was No One Quite Like Blazin' Ben Eastman," *Stanford Daily*, Oct. 25, 2002, stanforddailyarchive.com/cgi-bin/stanford?a=d&d=stanford20021025-01.2.39; Richard Gould)

105. The Oaks, on N. Melville Avenue, was an off-campus residence in Palo Alto that housed a number of transfer students. Alice Louise Clark wrote her mother that "I waste almost an hour waiting for the bus and riding back and forth on it each day." (Letter from Alice Louise Clark to her mother, Sept. 30, 1935, Alice Louise Clark student letters and photographs, SC1202, Department of Special Collections and University Archives, Stanford University Libraries, Stanford, California)

106. Originally built in 1875, the Palace Hotel was gutted by San Francisco's 1906 earthquake and ensuing fire. Architect George W. Kelham designed the post-earthquake Palace, as well as the "new" Roble Hall.[4] Many Big Game and Stanford festivities were held at the hotel. (Alex Bevk, "A History of the Palace, San Francisco's Oldest Surviving Hotel," Mar. 24, 2014, sf.curbed.com/2014/3/24/10127954/a-history-of-the-palace-san-franciscos-oldest-surviving-hotel; "Cardinal to Rally at Palace after Big Game," *Stanford Daily*, Nov.

8, 1915, stanforddailyarchive.com/cgi-bin/stanford?a=d&d=stanford19151108-01.2.8; "George Kelham: 1871–1936," noehill.com/architects/kelham.aspx)

107. Y:W is an abbreviation for young women. In this case, Alice Louise is likely referring to the YWCA. (Jeanne Armstrong, daughter of Alice Louise Clark)

108. Professor Yamato Ichihashi, an alum (BA/MA, Economics, 1907/1908) and professor at Stanford for thirty years, was among the Japanese Americans on campus who left for the Santa Anita, California, assembly center in late May 1942. Ichihashi and his family were in the internment camp system until 1945. (Diane Manuel, "Historian's New Book Traces Internment of Japanese American Professor," Nov. 15, 1996, stanford.edu/dept/news/pr/96/961115ichihashi.html; Susan Wels, *Stanford: Portrait of a University*, Stanford, California: Stanford Alumni Association, 1999, pages 78, 80)

109. Sororities were discontinued the April before Mary arrived on campus. In December 1977, however, the Board of Trustees reinstated them, though sororities would not have housing again until the 1998–1999 academic year. (Alison MacKinnon, "Sororities on the Row: Part Two?" *Stanford Daily*, Jan. 15, 1998, stanforddailyarchive.com/cgi-bin/stanford?a=d&d=stanford19980115-01.2.4)

110. In this era, there were few Jewish students at Stanford and the atmosphere was sometimes less than welcoming. "I understand from others that we were coming out of a period during the 1950s where people didn't really speak about being Jewish," said Ronda Spinak ('80), who arrived at Stanford in 1976. Compared to perhaps 2 percent of undergraduates in 1935, today an estimated 8 to 9 percent of Stanford undergraduates are Jewish, most of whom participate at the Hillel@Stanford Ziff Center for Jewish Life. ("Hillel@Stanford: Celebrating a Half-Century, Community Report," pages 2, 7, stanford.hillel.org/docs/default-source/default-document-library/hillel@stanford-community-report.pdf?sfvrsn=4; Hillel@Stanford)

111. (J.) Fred Weintz Jr.'s brother George Weintz ('55) later attended Stanford. (Beppie Weintz Cerf, Class of 1979, daughter of Fred Weintz)

112. Toyon Hall was built in 1923 as an all-male residence, and is one of the most historic dorms on campus. Renovated in 2001, it is now a coed sophomore dorm. ("Toyon Hall," rde.stanford.edu/studenthousing/toyon-hall)

113. The Pacific Coast Conference, a predecessor of the Pac-12, consisted of ten schools and was officially dismantled in 1959. (Braden Gall, "The History of Pac-12 Conference Realignment," July 2, 2012, athlonsports.com/college-football/history-pac-12-conference-realignment)

114. Dead Week, or pre-finals week, typically involves just a fair bit of studying and not much sleep. Since Fred was on campus, a more recent tradition has evolved: students let out the Primal Scream at midnight on any given night of Dead Week. ("Handbook of Stanford University: History, Tradition, and Lore," Stanford Axe Committee, 2015–2016, pages 21, 32, 34, stanford.edu/group/axecomm/cgi-bin/wordpress/wp-content/uploads/2015/08/handbook.final_.pdf)

115. Resident assistants, or RAs, live in the dorms to help "build strong and healthy residential learning communities which complement as well as extend classroom learning." Typically RAs are juniors or seniors though grad student

Nancy Christine Smith was asked to be one, as she recounts in her letter dated January 9, 1947, letter on page 152. ("Resident Assistants," resed.stanford.edu/ get-involved/student-staff/appointment-types/resident-assistants; Nancy Christine Smith letter to her mother, Jan. 9, 1947, Nancy Christine Smith letters, Stanford Student Letters and Memoirs Collection, SC0103, Department of Special Collections and University Archives, Stanford University Libraries, Stanford, California)

116. Hilltop House was once located at 610 Cabrillo Avenue, having been given to the university in 1941 as a house for female graduate students by Mrs. Elwood P. Cubberley, wife of the longtime dean of education. Renamed Cubberley House in 1951, it was later demolished to make room for the expansive lawn of the Lou Henry Hoover House. (Russell Barajas, daughter of Nancy Christine Smith)

117. Ray Dean ('37) assisted Jack Weiershauser (BA, '38; MA, '42), head track coach at Stanford (1946–1956). Both coaches ran for Stanford while students there. (Dwight Wilbur, "Ray Dean Was Great Farm Sprinter," *Stanford Daily*, Feb. 20, 1948, stanforddailyarchive.com/cgi-bin/stanford?a=d&d=stanford19480220-01.2.54; Bob Mierow, "Weiershauser Retires as Card Cinder Coach," *Stanford Daily*, Jan. 19, 1956, stanforddailyarchive.com/cgi-bin/stanford?a=d&d=stanford19560119-01.2.36; "Obituaries: Faculty, 1930s, Jack Weiershauser," *Stanford* magazine, September/October 2000, alumni.stanford.edu/get/page/magazine/article/?article_id=40608)

118. Bob Mathias ('53) became the first person to compete in both the Rose Bowl and the Olympics in the same year, placing first in the decathlon in July 1952, winning his second gold medal in that event. ("Handbook of Stanford University: History, Tradition, and Lore," page 6)

119. A class in foundry covered casting and working with metals.

120. Founded in 1899, the *Stanford Chaparral*, nicknamed the Chappie, is the world's second-oldest continually published humor magazine. Hours before the Great San Francisco Earthquake of April 1906, Chappie staff members established the Hammer and Coffin National Honorary Society, which developed into a national collegiate humor organization. ("The Info List— Stanford Chaparral," theinfolist.com/php/SummaryGet.php?FindGo=Stanford%20Chaparral; "Chronology," Hammer and Coffin National Honorary Society, Chaparral Chapter, Records, SC0228, Department of Special Collections and University Archives, Stanford University Libraries, Stanford, California)

121. Paloma is one of seven student residences within Florence Moore Hall. ("Florence Moore Hall," rde.stanford.edu/studenthousing/florence-moore-hall)

122. According to Joe (Joseph L.) Jacobs's twin brother, Carl, Joe would later consider being Gaieties[35] producer his biggest accomplishment at Stanford. In this letter, Joe makes plans with his family for Gaieties weekend: Carl would drive over from Berkeley to see the performance on Thursday, November 21, 1963, and spend the night on campus. Their parents would arrive the next day to see Friday's performance. Carl saw the Thursday performance, then heard about JFK's assassination before Joe did the next day. Like so many young people of their generation, Carl and Joe were JFK fans, and Carl broke the news to his brother. The remaining Gaieties performances were canceled, but Joe and Carl's

parents still came to Stanford so the family could be together. After that weekend, Carl reports, his and Joe's relationship began to shift from "competitive and combative," as it had been in high school, to "mutually supportive" during their last years of college and for the remainder of Joe's short life. After he graduated from Stanford, Joe served in Vietnam, and he sensed he might not make it home. Joe knew how hard that would be on their parents, and he asked Carl to exercise his wishes upon his death. Carl carried through on every one. (Carl Jacobs)

123. The all-male Mendicants were the first a cappella group on campus. Hank Adams ('64) founded the group in 1963 when he transferred from Yale to Stanford. The Mendicants are prone to singing in stairwells. ("Stanford's Original a Cappella Group," stanfordmendicants.com/; "The Stanford Mendicants," stanfordmusiccollective.com/stanford-mendicants.html)

124. The LASSU stood for the Legislature of the Associated Students of Stanford University, which ran the legislative branch of the ASSU (Associated Students of Stanford University) until 1968. (Jeremy Quach, "A Look Back at the History of the ASSU," *Stanford Daily*, March 30, 2016, stanforddaily.com/2016/03/30/a-look-back-at-the-history-of-the-assu/)

125. A newcomer compared to Rossotti's,[75] the Oasis is closer to campus. The "O" has served a mean burger and beer since 1958. ("The 'O'—Founded in 1958," theoasisbeergarden.com/aboutus.html)

126. The Circle Star Theatre, a popular music venue in San Carlos, California, closed in 1993. (Peter Hartlaub, "Gone but Not Forgotten: The Circle Star Theatre," Sept. 17, 2010, blog.sfgate.com/parenting/2010/09/17/gone-but-not-forgotten-the-circle-star-theatre/)

127. It did in fact snow on February 5, 1976, in the middle of the night and again that afternoon. Snow last had fallen on campus on January 21, 1962. (Ron Beck, "What State Is This? The State of Confusion!" *Stanford Daily*, Feb. 6, 1976, stanforddailyarchive.com/cgi-bin/stanford?a=d&d=stanford19760206-01.2.2)

128. Over the course of Stanford's history, its well-known fountains often have been turned off during periods of drought. Most recently, the fountains were turned off in 2014 and only switched back on in April 2016. Stanford has eighteen fountains on campus, all of which use recirculated water. When the fountains are on, fountain hopping is a time-honored Stanford tradition. (Kathleen J. Sullivan, "Stanford's Fountains to Begin Flowing Again," April 20, 2016, news.stanford.edu/2016/04/20/stanfords-fountains-begin-flowing/; Anne Marie and Kendrick, "Fountains of Stanford," ccr.stanford.edu/archive/Baxter/FountainsOfStanford.pdf)

129. Richard (Dick) W. Lyman[55, 76] was Stanford's seventh president (1970–1980). At Stanford for twenty-five years in different capacities, Lyman often is remembered for his position against student protests on campus during the late 1960s and early 1970s. (Kathleen J. Sullivan, "Richard W. Lyman, Stanford's Seventh President, Dead at 88," May 27, 2012, news.stanford.edu/news/2012/may/richard-lyman-obit-052712.html)

130. What was called Stanford in Washington when Tom wrote home is now Stanford in Government, which fosters student engagement in public policy. Established in 1988, the Bing Stanford in Washington Program allows students

to pursue academic interests and internships while living in Washington, D.C. ("Stanford in Government: A Nonpartisan, Student-Led Affiliate of the Haas Center for Public Service," sig.stanford.edu/about-us/; "Overview," siw.stanford. edu/bsiw-program/overview)

131. Here, Tom ribs his dad, who attended "the school across the Bay." See the "Beat Cal" chapter. (Tom, Class of 1978)

132. Social psychologist and longtime Stanford professor Philip Zimbardo, now a professor emeritus at Stanford, is famous for his 1971 Stanford Prison Experiment. In this letter, Tom is referring to Zimbardo's Introduction to Psychology class, for which Tom had been head proctor. (Lea Sparkman, "Philip Zimbardo Reflects on 'The Stanford Prison Experiment' Movie," *Stanford Daily*, July 17, 2015, stanforddaily.com/2015/07/17/philip-zimbardo-reflects-on-the-stanford-prison-experiment-movie/; "Philip Zimbardo," psychology.stanford. edu/zimbardo; Tom)

133. KZSU is Stanford's noncommercial, all-volunteer FM radio station, which began broadcasting in 1947. ("About KZSU," kzsu.stanford.edu/about/)

134. The World Wide Web still had relatively few users in 1995. ("World Wide Web Timeline," March 11, 2014, Pew Research Center: Internet, Science, & Tech, pewinternet.org/2014/03/11/world-wide-web-timeline/)

135. In Mandarin, "jian mian" means to meet, or to see one another. ("The Chinese word jianmian," Han Trainer Dictionary, dictionary.hantrainerpro.com/ chinese-english/translation-jianmian_meeteachot.htm)

136. Alice Louise Clark quotes "sojourn in a world so fair" from "The Wanderer" by poet Alan Seeger, who died in World War I. (Alan Seeger, "The Wanderer," mypoeticside.com/show-classic-poem-25822)

137. Between the 1910s and 1960s, college students sometimes sent laundry home in a reusable laundry box to mom, who would mail back the box with clean, pressed clothes inside. Students found this method cheaper than using a cleaners and less time-consuming than washing them themselves. Often metal, the boxes were considered by many to be an essential back-to-school item. With the advent of laundromats and automatic washing machines, laundry box use began to wane, and by the 1970s they had disappeared. Stanford first installed washing machines in residences in 1948. The cost: 10¢ a load. (Lynn Heidelbaugh, "Laundry Box," September 2007, postalmuseum.si.edu/ collections/object-spotlight/laundry-box.html; Jim Thurber, "This Is the Way to Wash Our Clothes—Pretty Soon," *Stanford Daily*, Aug. 13, 1948, stanforddailyarchive.com/cgi-bin/stanford?a=d&d=stanford19480813-01.2.20)

138. George D. Green attended the Stanford campus in Beutelsbach, Germany, which had been established two years before he wrote this letter as the university's inaugural study abroad program. The program moved to Berlin in the mid-1970s. Today, the Bing Overseas Study Program has campuses in more than ten locations worldwide. ("About the Berlin Program," undergrad.stanford. edu/programs/bosp/explore/berlin/about-berlin-program; "Bing Overseas Studies Program," undergrad.stanford.edu/programs/bosp)

139. Cliveden House, the grand former home of Lady Astor, served as the Stanford-in-Britain campus from 1969 to 1984, when the campus was relocated to Oxford. Part of the National Trust, Cliveden House is now a luxury hotel.

(Elizabeth Carr, "Student Voice: To the Manor Borne," *Stanford* magazine, May/June 2011, alumni.stanford.edu/get/page/magazine/article/?article_id=28170; Theresa Johnston, "A Whole New World," *Stanford* magazine, March/April 2008, alumni.stanford.edu/get/page/magazine/article/?article_id=31109; "A Brief History of Cliveden," nationaltrust.org.uk/cliveden/features/a-brief-history-of-cliveden)

140. "SA" in this letter refers to South America. "CORTRAMID" in the next paragraph refers to Career Orientation Training for Midshipmen.

141. "Dhaping" is not exactly bluffing. It's presenting very confidently something you're unsure of and riding on the hope that sheer confidence will convince others of the veracity of what you're saying and your command of the subject. (Natasha Pratap, Class of 1984)

142. Phi Beta Kappa is the oldest honors society for liberal arts and sciences in the United States. Founded in 1776, it has 286 chapters. A gold key identifies someone as a member. ("A Brief History of Phi Beta Kappa," pbk.org/WEB/PBK_Member/About_PBK/PBK_History/PBK_Member/PBK_History.aspx?hkey=44391228-bb7c-4705-bd2e-c785f3c1d876; "About the Phi Beta Kappa Society," dornsife.usc.edu/phi-beta-kappa-about/)

143. "Bones" is slang for dollars. (Mark Nichol, "50 Slang Terms for Money," dailywritingtips.com/50-slang-terms-for-money/)

144. "Pete" was law student Colin Peters (JD, '47), who (Mary) Carol Stearns would marry. (Anne Peters)

145. Manzanita Trailer Park, with 118 mobile homes installed in 1969 as temporary residences, housed students for more than twenty years. "Rinc" is short for Rinconada, the all-freshman dorm that is part of Wilbur Hall and is located at 658 Escondido Road. ("Manzanita Trailers to House Webb Ranch Workers," July 24, 1991, stanford.edu/dept/news/pr/91/910724Arc1246.html; "Rinconada: House Description," resed.stanford.edu/residences/find-house/rinconada)

146. Claude was Fred (Frederic) Jewell Perry's younger brother. Claude Perry went on to become a dentist. (Benjamin Perry, great-grandson of Fred Perry; Elizabeth Perry Ford, granddaughter of Fred Perry)

147. "Miss Cone" refers to Elizabeth Cone, who tutored Michitaro Sindo in English. From 1906 to 1908, she was a graduate student and an assistant in the Stanford English Department. ("Biographical/Historical note," Michitaro Sindo Letters, 1901–1902, Stanford Student Letters and Memoirs Collection, SC0103, Department of Special Collections and University Archives, Stanford University Libraries, Stanford, California)

148. Harry Sears (1911) was a younger brother of J. B. (Jesse Brundage) Sears'. (David O. Sears, Class of 1957, son of Bob [Robert] Richardson Sears and grandson of J. B. Sears)

149. A year-plus after she wrote this letter, "Anonymous 2015" says: "Stanford is the best place I could be for my undergraduate education."

150. The Promenade Concert was "the Seniors' time to say farewell to the Quad before the final exercises of Commencement morning." ("Promenade Concert," *Stanford Daily*, May 26, 1897, stanforddailyarchive.com/cgi-bin/stanford?a=d&d=stanford18970526-01.2.20)

151. The senior–faculty baseball game was played annually before commencement until at least 1912. ("Much Secrecy over the Senior-Faculty Game," *Stanford Daily*, May 8, 1912, stanforddailyarchive.com/cgi-bin/stanford?a=d&d=stanford)

152. The "class plate" is the Senior Class Plaque. Since 1896, a plaque with each senior class's graduating year inscribed on it has been laid in the pavement of the Inner Quad Arcade. The 1892–1895 class plaques were installed later. The class plaque sits on top of a time capsule in which soon-to-be graduates place mementos of their Stanford days. The Class of 2016 became Stanford's 125th class to follow this tradition. (Barbara Wilcox, "125 Sealed Capsules in the Quad Hold Mementos of Student Life," 125.stanford.edu/hidden-snapshots-history/)

153. Alumni Day typically is no longer held as part of graduation ceremonies. Alumni weekend is held every year in the fall. (Barbara Wilcox, "125 Sealed Capsules in the Quad Hold Mementos of Student Life," 125.stanford.edu/hidden-snapshots-history/)

154. A sheepskin refers to a diploma.

155. Baccalaureate is the annual end-of-year multifaith celebration for all graduates. ("Baccalaureate," commencement.stanford.edu/events/baccalaureate)

156. The Whisky a Go Go in San Francisco was a short-lived cousin of the more famous West Hollywood nightclub. ("Whisky A-Go-Go, San Francisco, 1965–67," Aug. 18, 2009, rockprosopography101.blogspot.com/2009/08/whisky-go-go-san-francisco.html)

157. Barbara was Carl Jacobs's girlfriend at the time. (Carl Jacobs, twin brother of Joe Jacobs)

158. For six decades, alums and others visiting Stanford stayed at Hyatt Rickey's hotel. The site of many local events, it closed in 2005. (Jocelyn Dong, "Close of Hyatt Rickey's Sends Groups to New Locations," *Palo Alto Weekly*, June 8, 2005, paloaltoonline.com/weekly/morgue/2005/2005_06_08.rickeys08ja.shtml)

159. Crothers is an upper-class residential community named after alum George Edward Crothers (BA, 1895; MA, 1896). Following a conversation over tea with Jane Stanford in 1898, Crothers set out to review the Founding Grant, ultimately determining it contained flaws that threatened the university's future financial stability. He played a vital role in Stanford achieving tax exemption,[64] assisted Mrs. Stanford with revising the Founding Grant, and is credited with securing Stanford's financial future. ("Crothers Hall: Overview," rde.stanford.edu/studenthousing/crothers-hall; David S. Jacobson, "George E. Crothers: He Was the Third 'Founder' of Stanford," law.stanford.edu/wp-content/uploads/sites/default/files/child-page/292312/doc/slspublic/by_Jacobson_'George-E-Crothers'_from_Stanford-Historical-Society-Newsletter_1979-Spring-Summer_Vol3-No3.pdf; Stanford University Archives)

160. Narnia is a Stanford residence on Campus Drive. ("Narnia: House Description," resed.stanford.edu/houses/narnia)

161. Matadero refers to Matadero Creek Trail, a 1.5-mile hiking, running, and biking trail running along Page Mill Road. (Kate Chesley, "Missing the Dish? Try the Matadero Creek Trail," July 19, 2015, news.stanford.edu/thedish/2015/07/19/missing-the-dish-try-the-matadero-creek-trail/)

162. The museum, originally called the Leland Stanford Jr. Museum, opened to the public in 1894. It was severely damaged by the 1906 earthquake (see Babe Bartlett's letter, page 74), and again by the Loma Prieta earthquake in 1989 (see Dan Lythcott-Haims's letter, page 100), after which it closed, reopening ten years later as the Iris & B. Gerald Cantor Center for Visual Arts. ("Museum History: Museum History Interactive Timeline," Cantor Arts Center at Stanford University, museum.stanford.edu/explore/timeline.html)

163. During Full Moon on the Quad (FMOTQ), first-year students who kiss a senior at midnight in Center Quad under the (usually first) full moon of the academic year become Stanford men and women. ("Handbook of Stanford University: History, Tradition, and Lore," Stanford Axe Committee: 2015–2016, page 33, stanford.edu/group/axecomm/cgi-bin/wordpress/wp-content/uploads/2015/08/handbook.final_.pdf)

164. Frederick E. Terman (BA, '20; EE, '22) was an engineer, inventor, professor, and administrator who mentored William Hewlett and David Packard. His career at Stanford spanned forty years. The Frederick Emmons Terman Engineering Library is located in the Jen-Hsun Huang School of Engineering Center. Until 2010, the library was part of the Terman Building. (Dawn Levy, "Biography Revisits Fred Terman's Roles in Engineering, Stanford, Silicon Valley," Nov. 3, 2004, news.stanford.edu/news/2004/november3/Terman-1103.html; "Terman Engineering Library: History of Terman Library," library.stanford.edu/englib/more-about-terman-library/history-terman-library)

165. "The Play" refers to one of the most notorious moments in college football history. Of course it happened at Big Game. Stanford led 20–19, and the rest is sports history. True to form, the band was involved. (Jackie Krentzman, "And the Band Played On," *Stanford* magazine, November/December 2002, alumni.stanford.edu/get/page/magazine/article/?article_id=37765)

Additional Sources

All websites accessed in September and October 2016.

Additional information: Anne Peters Battle, daughter of (Mary) Carol Stearns; Becky Smith, daughter of (William) Russell Smith; Benjamin Perry, great-grandson of Fred (Frederic) Jewell Perry; Beppie Weintz Cerf, daughter of (J.) Fred Weintz Jr. ; Carl Jacobs, brother of Joe (Joseph) Lewis Jacobs; Chrissie Huneke Kremer, daughter of Johnny (John) Murray Huneke; Christopher Carlsmith, grandson of Hope Snedden; David O. Sears, son of Bob (Robert) Richardson Sears and grandson of J. B. (Jesse Brundage) Sears; Elizabeth Perry Ford, granddaughter of Fred (Frederic) Jewell Perry; Gene Cubbage, classmate of Joe (Joseph) Lewis Jacobs; Jeanne Armstrong, daughter of Alice Louise Clark; Marvie Knox, granddaughter of Julia Hamilton Conkling; Dick (Richard) Gould, son of Dick (Richard) Bartlett Gould and grandson of Babe (Mabel) Bartlett; Kent Hinckley, stepson of Fred (Frederic) Jewell Perry.

Correspondence submitted to Alison Carpenter Davis: letters from "Anonymous 1980"; letters and photos from Carol Hodge, 1953–1957; letter from Dan Lythcott-Haims, 1989; letters from Karen Kinney, 1979 and 1983; email and texts from Katherine Gregory, 2012 and 2016; letters and photo from Natasha Pratap, 1990–1993; letters from Wendy, 1972–1973.

[Letters from Alice Louise Clark, 1935], Alice Louise Clark student letters and photographs (SC1202). Department of Special Collections and University Archives, Stanford University Libraries, Stanford, California.

[Letters from Francis J. Batchelder, 1891–1892], Francis J. Batchelder Correspondence (SC1025). Department of Special Collections and University Archives, Stanford University Libraries, Stanford, California.

[Letter from Gary, 1963], Student letter regarding campus reaction to JFK assassination and Stanford Daily clipping (SCM0448). Department of Special Collections and University Archives, Stanford University Libraries, Stanford, California.

[Letter from Herbert Hoover to Miss Nell May Hill, Aug. 30, 1892], Hill Family Papers, Ax 47, Special Collections and University Archives, University of Oregon Libraries, Eugene, Oregon.

[Letter from Herbert Hoover to Nell May Hill, Nov. 9, 1894], Hill Family Papers, Ax 47, Special Collections and University Archives, University of Oregon Libraries, Eugene, Oregon.

[Letters from Hope Snedden, 1918–1920], Snedden Family Papers (SC1207). Department of Special Collections and University Archives, Stanford University Libraries, Stanford, California.

[Letters from J. B. (Jesse Brundage) Sears, 1907–1909], Sears Family Papers (SC0523). Department of Special Collections and University Archives, Stanford University Libraries, Stanford, California.

[Letter from Robert Sears, 1927], Sears Family Papers (SC0523). Department of Special Collections and University Archives, Stanford University Libraries, Stanford, California.

[Photo of Cliveden House, Robert Sherwood, Stanford Historical Photograph Collection, 1887-circa 1996 (inclusive).] Department of Special Collections and University Archives, Stanford University Libraries, Stanford, California. Available at purl.stanford.edu/yx507hx5103.

[Photo of Herbert Hoover with geology class, 1894], Herbert Hoover Subject Collection, [Envelope D]. Hoover Institution Archives, Stanford University.

[Photo of Hope Snedden letter, page one, November 12, 1918], Snedden Family Papers (SC1207). Department of Special Collections and University Libraries, Stanford, California.

[Photo of image from Big Game program, 1894], Stanford University, Department of Athletics, Football Collection (SC1185). Department of Special Collections and University Archives, Stanford University Libraries, Stanford, California. Available at purl.stanford.edu/yx507hx5103.

[Photo of Jane Stanford], Stanford Family Photograph Collection, 1850-1975. Stanford Digital Repository. Available at purl.stanford.edu/jv222gb0652.

[Photo of Louis Agassiz, 1906] and [Photo of Quad—Arcades, Views Down.] Stanford Historical Photograph Collection (SC1071). Department of Special Collections and University Archives. Stanford University Libraries, Stanford, California.

[Photo of "The Bedroom" from scrapbook of Mabel (Babe) Bartlett, 1906], Stanford University Alumni Collection (SC1278). Department of Special Collections and University Archives, Stanford University Libraries, Stanford, California.

Stanford Daily (Stanford, California): letter from Jim, October 14, 1948, Vol. 14, Issue 14, page 4; photo of Elaine engagement announcement, April 4, 1963, Vol. 143, Issue 27, page 2; photo of front page, Special Edition, November 22, 1963, Vol. 144, Issue 46; photo of Leaning Tower of Pisa, November 1, 1960, Vol. 138, Issue 28, page 1; photo of Joe Jacobs article, "The Death of Student Drama," May 26, 1965, Vol. 147, Issue 64, page 4.

Stanford Quad (Stanford, California: The Associated Students of Stanford University): photo of Joe (Joseph) Lewis Jacobs and Peter King, 1965, Vol. 72, page 206; photo of Fred (Frederic) Jewell Perry, 1894, Vol. 1, page 215; photo of Tex Allen Bollman and fraternity, 1931, Vol. 38, page 347; photos of Storey House and Mary Allie Lesnett, 1947, Vol 54; photo of Johnny (John) Murray Huneke, 1948, Vol. 55, page38; photo of Rinconada dorm, 1976, Vol. 81, page 216.

Stanford Student Letters and Memoirs Collection. Stanford Digital Repository. Available at purl.stanford.edu/jv222bg0652:

[Letters from Lucy Allabach, 1891–1895]

[Letter from Austin Kautz, 1892]

[Letters from Frederic Jewell Perry, 1899 and 1900]

[Letters from Burnham P. Beckwith, 1923]

[Letter from Myron Burr, 1905]

[Letters from Rose and Theodora Payne, Payne Family Letters, 1895–1897]

[Letter from Tex Allen Bollman, 1930]

Stanford Student Letters and Memoirs Collection (SC0103). Department of Special Collections and University Archives, Stanford University Libraries, Stanford, California:

[Email from Anonymous, 2013]

[Emails from Christopher Lowman, 2006 and 2009]

[Email from Darren Franich, 2007]

[Email from David Weber, 2014]

[Email from Erica Toews, 2008]

[Email from Nicole Bennett-Fite, 2014]

[Email from Nora Tjossem, 2011]

[Email from Tamandra Morgan, 2007]

[Emails from Vanessa Hua, 1995]

[Letters from Alison Carpenter, 1975 and 1977]

[Letter from Anne Peters, 1973]

[Letter from Anonymous, Mid-1940s]

[Letters from Anonymous, 1972]

[Letter from Anonymous, Mid-1970s]

[Letter from Anonymous, 1990]

[Letter from Anonymous, 2015]

[Letters from Barbara Armentrout, 1965]

[Letters and photo from Chrissie Kremer, 1983, John Murray Huneke and Chrissie Kremer letters]

[Letters from Elaine Lindheim, 1960–1963]

[Letter from (J.) Fred Weintz, 1946]

[Letters from John Huneke, late 1940s, John Murray Huneke and Chrissie Kremer letters]

[Letter from Chris Seaman, 1973]

[Letters from Joseph L. Jacobs, 1961–1965]

[Letters from George D. Green, 1960]

[Letter and illustration from Grant Glazer, 2013]

[Letters from Julia Hamilton Conkling, 1911–1915]

[Letters from Lanny Levin, 1968, 1970]

[Letter and telegram from Mabel (Babe) Bartlett, 1906]

[Letters from Mary Caballero, 2014]

[Letters from (Mary) Carol Stearns, 1943–1946]

[Letters from Mary Allie Lesnett, 1944, 1946–1948]

[Letters from Theer, Maryeda Hayes, 1954–1955]

[Letters from M.C., 1975–1979]

[Letter from Michael Clonts, 1982]

[Letter from Michitaro Sindo, 1901]

[Letters and photo from Nancy Christine Smith, 1946–1947]

[Letters from Peter King, 1961 and 1965]

[Letters from Philip B. Laird Jr., 1966, 1968 and 1969]

[Letters from Robert Lowell Swetzer, 1947–1949, 1950]

[Letters from Richard Bartlett Gould, 1931–1933]

[Letter from Tom, 1977]

[Letter from Wendell Birkhofer, 1977]

[Letters from Russell Smith, 1938 and 1940]

[Postcard from Ben Rosellini, 2012]

[Texts from Anonymous, 2016]

[Text from Catherine Goetz, 2016]

[Texts from Jason Seter, 2014]

[Texts from Laine Bruzek, 2013 and 2016]

[Text from Sydney Larson, 2015]

"Then, when the guests had all gone and the lights gone out, with a few candles to lighten us, we dance."

—Lucy Allabach, [May 1892]